AF844072

Informal Work and Social Change

Informal Work and Social Change

A Bibliographic Survey

Edited by

Shelley Feldman and Eveline Ferretti

ILR Press

an imprint of

Cornell University Press

Ithaca and London

Copyright © 1998 by Cornell University

Cornell Industrial and Labor Relations
Bibliography Series No. 19

All rights reserved. Except for brief quotations in a review, this book, or parts thereof, must not be reproduced in any form without permission in writing from the publisher. For information, address Cornell University Press, Sage House, 512 East State Street, Ithaca, New York 14850.

First published 1998 by Cornell University Press

Library of Congress Cataloging-in-Publication Data

Informal work and social change : a bibliographic survey / edited by Shelley Feldman and Eveline Ferretti.
p. cm. — (Cornell industrial and labor relations bibliography series ; no. 19) "Containing more than eight hundred citations, the bibliography covers the period from 1970 to the present"—Pref.
Includes index.
ISBN 0-8014-3504-8 (cloth : alk. paper)
1. Labor—Bibliography. 2. Informal sector (Economics)—Bibliography. 3. Social change—Bibliography. I. Feldman, Shelley. II. Ferretti, Eveline. III. Series.
Z7164.L1I44 1998
[HD4841]
016.331—dc21 98-11446

Printed in the United States of America

Cornell University Press strives to utilize environmentally responsible suppliers and materials to the fullest extent possible in the publishing of its books. Such materials include vegetable-based, low-VOC inks and acid-free papers that are also either recycled, totally chlorine-free, or partly composed of nonwood fibers.

Cloth printing 10 9 8 7 6 5 4 3 2 1

Contents

PREFACE

In the early 1970s, a series of what were to become landmark reports by Keith Hart (1973) and the International Labor Office (1972) placed informal work at the center of discussions of postcolonial industrialization. Their focus on informal work broke new ground in prevailing development theory, which considered economic activity outside the incipient modern sectors of Third World countries backward, unproductive, and sure to be undermined by the robust force of modernization. Initially hailed as a promising means to correct the increasingly evident weakness of this theoretical and policy framework, the configuration and expansion of what was defined as the informal sector quickly became the focus of contentious debate concerning its specific meaning, character, and significance in processes of industrialization and economic change.

Frequently, informality itself was challenged as a concept lacking the analytic rigor and precision needed to address problems of poverty and unemployment. As often, the concept was challenged for being too inclusive, characterizing work that was not formal wage employment. Informal work was also questioned because of its persistence, despite the fact that the proletarianization of rural labor, the forward march of industrialization, and the capitalization of productive activity were assumed to lead to its demise. Notwithstanding this uneven trajectory, discussions of informal work and its place in economic change have been repeatedly rekindled over the past twenty-five years, and recognition of informal work as anything but a diminishing aspect of modernity has become entrenched.

Our interest in providing greater access to literature on the informal sector is the theoretical promise the concept of informal work offers for reframing class analytic, dependency, and conventional economic models of development. Labor economists were the first to reconsider the significance of informal work in understanding economic change, and they continue to play a central role in policy and planning discussions. Over time, sociologists, anthropologists, geographers, and historians, as well as urban and regional development theorists, have made important contributions in retheorizing questions of work, employment, firm organization, labor processes and relations, and development processes and practices.

Of particular significance as well have been the contributions of feminist scholars who have provided a rich terrain for discussing the complex and complicit ways in which work and social reproduction in the late twentieth century have come to constitute everyday life. As Collins (1991) notes, early research on the informal sector underestimated or ignored the numbers of women so engaged and failed to appreciate the various spatial locations and unwaged relations that characterize informal work. It was only with studies framed by the women in development and gender and development literatures that women's informal work became a focus of study. This emphasis led, in turn, to an appreciation of the household and home-based production as arenas that linked women's domestic and reproductive responsibilities to their wage or unpaid labor. Interestingly, the theoretical moment in discussions of informalization occurred before the mid-1990s. Today, the discourse around changing forms of work and employment, particularly in policy circles, is grounded in the language of micro-enterprise development, a perspective quite different in intent and theoretical orientation from that of those who explored debates on informalization.

The broad range of venues for discussions of informal work and labor deployment, social survival, and social reproduction have generated a diverse body of literature embracing varied disciplinary traditions and regional foci. This bibliography is our effort to highlight the diversity and multidisciplinarity of this literature, the range of journals, books, and edited collections[1] that frame distinctive debates on informality, and the broad array of theoretical, historical and community specific analyses that characterize processes of informalization, patterns of "off-the-books," illegal, black-market, unaccounted, untaxed, unregulated, nonmonetary exchanges, and subcontracted and unpaid work. We anticipate that this bibliography will assist students concerned with these issues and the broader questions they raise concerning economic development to optimize their use of varied resources in the course of their work. It is also intended to be of use to those engaged in policy analysis or program development and implementation by clearly identifying the rich resources available on particular substantive issues or regions of the world.

Containing more than eight hundred citations, the bibliography covers the period from 1970 to the present in which studies of informal work have

[1] It would be impossible to include a complete account of the articles included in edited volumes. We have selected to include in our review notable articles from edited collections which address issues such as changing labor processes, effects of structural adjustment and economic reform programs, development practice in the context of poverty alleviation, and analyses of women and work.

become an explicit focus in a wide range of disciplines. Key words describe major themes of each citation, and annotations summarize the argument and approach of substantive works. We have annotated the major sources that have shaped the primary debates in the literature and defined new sites for empirical investigation. Citations noted only with key words indicate additional research that is descriptive in content and well summarized through key terms. With this format, the bibliography's specific objectives are threefold: to provide a broad and up-to-date overview of available literature on the informal activities; to identify salient literature for more detailed study of specific aspects of the informal sector in specific countries and geographical regions; and to indicate key debates and theoretical orientations that have emerged over the past several decades.

To provide an organizing guide in the use of the bibliography as a reference tool, we have prepared an introductory essay that highlights major strands of thought characterizing the broad body of research on informal work of the past quarter-century. Over the years, discussion of informal work has engaged very different assumptions about the relations embodied in such activity: as vestiges of past forms of production, as new relations of work and employment possible only under conditions of contemporary capitalism, as creative manipulations by those marginalized or dispossessed of access to the labor market, or as new mechanisms for and relations of accumulation generated by the interests of firms and entrepreneurs seeking to secure production in a technologically diverse global environment. The purpose of our broad overview is to offer a framework that illuminates key assumptions and highlights key sources in our annotated bibliography.

A second objective of the literature review is to emphasize the valuable insights for the general study of work and labor processes that have emerged from research on informality. A closer look at both the contributions and shortcomings of past work draws particular attention to the importance of assuming a historical and comparative perspective for explaining changing labor processes and relations, locations of production and patterns of growth, as well as new mechanisms of class, gender, and regional inequality. Although informalization is generally conceived as a result of economic duality, labor market segmentation, capitalism's labor needs, or the fragmentation of production in a globalizing capitalist economy, the most promising of past studies highlight how analyses of informal work may contribute to retheorizing processes of economic and social reorganization in the contemporary global economy.

As with all works of this type, a large debt is due many who have assisted the project along the way. Graduate students from the Cornell University Department of Rural Sociology, Julie Zimmerman, Jun Aguilar, and Amita Baviskar, as well as Sharon Brisolara from the Department of Human Service Studies contributed to the list of citations noted in the text. Financial support from the U.S. Department of Agriculture enabled two complementary studies to direct their attention to questions of economic reorganization, informalization, and women's work: *Conceptual and Empirical Analyses of the Rural Nonformal Employment Sector* (USDAHatch) and *Survival Strategies of Low Income Rural Families* (USDA-ERS-ARED). These research initiatives were instrumental in shaping the scope and depth of this bibliographic project. Fran Benson, Editor in Chief of Cornell University Press, had the patience of a saint in working with us toward a final manuscript. Finally, we thank Linda Shaw and Ben Abel for their intellectual and moral support in bringing this project to closure.

SHELLEY FELDMAN and EVELINE FERRETTI
Ithaca, New York

INFORMAL WORK: A CRITICAL READING OF PREVAILING VIEWS

Almost a quarter-century has passed since the first discussions of the informal sector[1] gained international attention (ILO 1972; Hart 1973). Since that time, numerous critical reviews have framed discussions of informal work and sectoral analyses (Breman 1985; Bromley 1985; Connolly 1985; Moser and Young 1978; 1994; Peattie 1987; Rakowski 1994b). As a cursory browse through these discussions quickly reveals, this literature is characterized by two key features. On the one hand, it is defined by a common focus of study–the experience and performance of economic activity beyond established factories, firms, and agencies. On the other, it is marked by almost constant divergence on questions about the identity, role, and future prospects of this activity for industrial development and for processes of economic change. Contestations and tensions about the place of informal relations in the context of economic change give research the striking appearance of a highly disjointed body of work. As one recent review (Rakowski 1994b) emphasizes, differing analyses of the informal sector have even given rise to decidedly different vocabularies, as terms and issues that achieved currency in early research "have fallen from favor" in the course of more recent discussions, only to be replaced by words that presumably more precisely highlight and signify key concepts now needed. Placed in this light, it appears that with each disjuncture, discussion has turned not only to new debates and new assumptions about the place and meaning of informal activity in social life but to very different socioeconomic phenomena.

Understanding the particular distinctions that define key positions on the question of informal work is critical for explaining what is meant by informal economic activities, social processes, and relations of production. As we hope to show, appreciating the contributions that these positions make to

---

[1]Throughout this document the terms *informal work*, *sector*, or *employmentt* will be used interchangeably although we indicate the different meanings embodied in these terms when they represent distinctive theoretical discourses and assumptions. The terms *informal sector* or *employment*, for example, reflect the institutional perspective of the state and its bureaucratic relations which emphasize labor markets and forms of regulation. *Informal work*, in contrast, often is used in analyses of the household and individual survival strategies to describe creative responses to under- and unemployment. *Informal work* thus highlights relations and responses to labor force constraints or to positions of difference and social or economic marginality. In these latter cases, the interests represented are usually, although not always, those of producers who may engage in informal work or exchange relations as creative venues for securing income, as opportunities of last resort or for access to lucrative income, or as a form of resistance.

understanding informality in industrial development requires embedding questions about informalization in parallel theoretical movements in the social sciences. The predominance of different theoretical frameworks over time helps to situate the fluid terrain of debate on processes of informalization. For instance, a recent view of informality focuses on the connections between expanding informal economic activity and processes of economic restructuring in the global capitalist economy. Though these discussions often appear to ascribe a sense of newness and immediacy to informal work and economic restructuring, earlier analyses similarly sought to interpret the expansion of informal economic activities in the context of fundamental changes characterizing postcolonial economies. Our point is that the value of a review of past literature derives from historicizing these discussions as a framework for interpreting the emergence of new forms of production and processes of accumulation in the context of the economic and social reorganization of everyday life.

Providing a broad overview of the key themes and positions explored by past and current researchers on the informal sector will highlight how different conceptions of informality build on and reframe current understandings of processes of global economic restructuring, whether in terms of a critique of modernization theory as a linear process of economic reorganization or in terms of the mobility of capital, labor, and financial exchange in restructuring work and employment in a world economy. Although assumptions framing past discussions of informalization may no longer be fashionable in the current milieu of social scientific inquiry, they provide important insights on the place of informal work in the complex of global production today. As we explore themes in the global reorganization of production, we need also to examine how forms of employment are linked to new political relations, patterns of consumption, local and international realignments and state practices, and the forms of conflict and struggle that characterize contemporary life. Such an embedded approach appreciates both the construction of theories and interpretations of social change and the conditions that give rise to their predominance at a given point in time.

Views of Informality in the Dual Economy

In 1972, the authors of the seminal ILO study on the Kenyan economy (ILO 1972:503) argued that the main problem with conventional economic development theory was that it simply "[did] not correspond with reality in Kenya." To begin, despite industrial progress made during the 1960s and

1970s, income inequality, unemployment, and poverty among the working poor in Kenya had continued to grow, as in much of the rest of the developing world. Second, by dichotomizing the modern and traditional sectors, modernization theory led to a mischaracterization of the latter, homogenizing complex and diverse sets of production relations. Interestingly, findings from emergent fieldwork were making it increasingly apparent that workers involved in the nonmodern sector of urban spaces were not only

> petty traders, street hawkers, shoeshine boys and other groups "underemployed" on the streets of the big towns, . . . [but also included] carpenters, masons, tailors, and other tradesmen, as well as cooks and taxi-drivers, offering virtually the full range of basic skills needed to provide goods and services for a large though often poor section of the population. (ILO 1972:5)

Identifying the range of activities engaged in by informal workers led to recognizing that sector's economic vitality; the informal sector was far from "stagnant" and "undynamic" as it was characterized in the modernization view. There was growing "evidence of technical change in the urban informal sector, as well as of regular employment at incomes above the average level attainable in smallholder agriculture." Contrary to conventional wisdom, the sector should be seen as one of "thriving economic activity and a source of Kenya's future wealth" (ILO 1972:5).

This recognition also led to the replacement of the modern-traditional duality of conventional economic development theory with a view of the Kenyan economy as comprised of formal and informal sectors, each equally "modern" and each critical for the country's economic future (ILO 1972:504). The term *informal*, emphasized the report, was not defined on the basis of particular occupations, locations, or economic activities. Rather, it denoted a particular "way of doing things," characterized by seven specific features: ease of entry, use of indigenous resources, family ownership, small scale of operation, labor-intensive and adapted technology, the acquisition of skills through nonformal means, and participation in unregulated and competitive markets (ILO 1972:6).[2]

---

[2]As will become clear in the following discussion, this definition shifts from a focus on illegality and tax evasion to new relations between the mobilization of state revenues and state responsibility in generating employment.

Sharing a similar approach, other studies offered somewhat different definitions of the informal sector. Hart (1973), for instance, in the other major work recognized for "discovering" the informal sector, distinguishes between wage earning and self-employment based on the extent to which economic activities performed in an enterprise are differentiated and rationalized. Seeking a more analytic definition, Sethuraman (1981:17) argued that the key distinguishing criterion of informal activity is its basic organizing principle: while formal enterprises, even small ones, are oriented to profit maximization, and hence likely to direct resources toward achieving growth and efficiency, informal enterprises remain geared to the goal of employment generation.

Despite shifts in the specific criteria for defining informality during this early period, most studies echoed the ILO's reconceptualization of underdeveloped economies as characterized by a formal-informal rather than a modern-traditional dichotomy. These efforts thus departed from modernization theory while retaining one of its most basic features, economic dualism. Policy prescriptions that followed from this view, however, differed in an important way from earlier dualistic frameworks, reflecting a populist recasting of the role of government in economic development. Where early modernization theory emphasized supporting the promotion of modern industry to the exclusion of traditional or "backward" industries, the newer dual sector framework emphasized coupling growth-promoting measures in the economy at large with explicit support for informal enterprises through measures including government support for the development of appropriate technologies, vocational training programs, and licensing reform, as well as government-promoted linkages to formal industries through subcontracting, subsidies, and credit (ILO 1972:3, 21-22). Embodied in these policy prescriptions was the idea that sufficient government attention to the informal sector would strengthen linkages to the modern sector and break the technological, skill, and market constraints inhibiting its growth. Government support also was based on the dynamism of informal relations and its assumed potential for enabling more equitable and balanced economic growth over the long term.

A Critique of Dualism

Although the promotion of informal sector activities quickly became popular among planners and analysts, debate about the place, meaning, and significance of these activities for understanding economic change continued.

By the late 1970s, critical reviews identified the failure of dual sector models to recognize the heterogeneity of informal sector enterprises. These reviews highlighted as well the fallacy of making global generalizations about the sector and of promoting uniform policy initiatives across national contexts (Bromley 1978a; 1978c; Mosley 1978; Peattie 1980). Critics also observed that informal sector earnings were often higher than those in the formal sector, calling into question basic assumptions about the dual sector framework (Kannappan 1977; Teilhet-Waldorf and Waldorf 1983).

New interpretations of the role of informal activity in processes of capitalist change emphasized linkages between informal and formal sector work. Such studies highlighted the exploitative character of these linkages and the unfavorable position occupied by informal workers. Birkbeck's (1979) groundbreaking study, for instance, demonstrated the significant role played by garbage pickers in Cali, Colombia's thriving materials recuperation industry, who provide raw material for the industrial sector. He also identified the key factors behind the pickers' poor earnings: the downward pressure of low international prices of raw materials and the indirect connection between pickers and factories. These factors discourage collective bargaining among pickers and allow factories to keep the price of collected materials low while maintaining an advantageous flexibility in their procurement system. Already well integrated into the overall materials recuperation flow sustaining industrial growth in Colombia, the country's garbage collectors do not suffer from a lack of adequate linkage to the formal sector, as dual sector models would hold, but from a weak structural position within the industry and economy at large.

The relationship between informal work and economic development also was conceived as one in which informal work subsidizes economic growth by providing low-cost services and goods for those employed in formal enterprises. It was also argued that low-wage informal workers diffuse demands for higher wages. As Portes and Walton (1981), Armstrong and McGee (1985), and Safa (1986) each argue, these subsidies underwrite processes of capitalist development in the economy at large.

The critique of economic dualism also challenged the informal sector concept for its lack of theoretical coherence. Breman (1985) notes, for example, that distinguishing among the various attributes associated with informal work, or between wage labor and self-employment, or protected and unprotected, organized and unorganized, secure and insecure, high and lower paid work exemplifies characteristics that are not always coincidental. This finding led Breman to conclude that dividing developing economies into two separate spheres obscures rather than illuminates basic relations in processes of economic development. And, as he continued, the distinction between formal and informal sectors elevated a hodgepodge of perceived features associated with different kinds of employment to the status of theory when, in fact, such distinctions do not lend themselves to clear analytic comparison. Convinced of the fundamental weakness of economic dualism, critics of the ILO-derived informal sector concept developed alternative theoretical frameworks that emphasized an integrated and totalizing notion of the economy. For example, Breman (1985) proposed replacing notions of a bifurcated economic system with an emphasis on labor market fragmentation. From this perspective, socially constructed divisions between labor markets, rather than the distinctive attributes of different economic subsectors, confine large numbers of people to poorly remunerated work. Exploring these dynamics offers a way to understand employment activities in a variety of settings.

During this period, Bromley and Gerry (1979b) also advanced the notion of economies as consisting of a continuum of activities ranging from stable wage work to true self-employment. From their perspective, work categorized as informal in dual sector theories corresponds to those forms of casual work marked by the lack of income and employment security. Factors explaining the emergence of these forms cannot be traced to structural limitations of the informal sector, such as low levels of technology and the lack of resources, but to changes in the use of technology, the structure of rural economic relations, economic instability, and employer strategies. The work of Birkbeck (1978; 1979) and Bromley and Gerry (1979b) thus implicates the analytic potential of a focus on labor processes and relations of production characterizing different forms of work in capitalist development. This emphasis on processes as distinct from the characteristics and attributes of particular kinds of work marks a significant departure from the economic dualism dominant at the time.

Shaping this emergent perspective on labor processes was the renewed theoretical interest in petty commodity production,[3] most notably reflected in the early work of Lebrun and Gerry (1975), Kahn (1982) and Moser and

---

[3]Work analyzed within the framework of petty commodity production is included among these citations only when they are part of the debate on informalization. A broad literature on petty commodity production in the sociology of agriculture, agrarian transitions, and economic reorganization is excluded from this bibliography.

Young (1978). As highlighted in an important overview by Scott (1986a), although studies of petty commodity production (PCP) emerged from the specific interests of Marxist scholars, others also advanced this perspective for understanding the changing patterns of informal work (Bienefeld 1975; Gerry 1978a, 1978b). Among the most important contributions of studies of PCP were those focused on the concept of "form of production." As defined by Scott (1986b:94), the term draws attention to the "precise combination of technical and social relations of production that result in the production and appropriation of surplus labor." Viewing petty commodity production as a particular form of production makes it possible to distinguish it from capitalist production, while also providing a framework for understanding the persistent though changing existence of noncapitalist production in societies undergoing capitalist transformation. Summarizes Scott (1986a:4)

> Potentially at least, this framework provided the basis for: (a) an analysis of subordinate forms of production that did not presume transition, evolution or passivity in the face of encroaching capitalism, (b) an analysis of the different structures that underlay their relative autonomy on the one hand and their relative dependence on the other, (c) an uncovering of the mechanism of articulation that conditioned general processes of change such as commoditization and proletarianization, and (d) a consideration of the role of political and ideological factors in the articulation process, as well as the economic ones.

Although promising a framework for the rigorous analysis of informal patterns of production and work, studies of petty commodity production were subject to serious weakness that, in some respects, echoed those of dualist development models (Scott 1986b). For instance, analyses generally overlooked historical specificities shaping the distinctive role of petty producers in different contexts, choosing instead to describe the development of petty production as the inevitable process of differentiation between a small number of successful entrepreneurs and a large mass of proletarianized workers. The assumption that petty commodity production was subordinate to capitalist relations also promoted an interpretation of these activities as necessarily derivative of a dominant capitalist mode clearly revealing the functionalist premises of this view. Contemporary critiques of economism and structural determinism have since undermined the heralded status of this approach to analyses of informalization.

Recognition of the weakness of the PCP framework stimulated a rethinking of contemporary forms of work. A noteworthy critique, for example, was Cook's (1984a, 1984b) analysis of the growth and variety of handicraft production in Mexico in which he identified artisanal or workshop-based production as well as subcontracted home-based production under conditions of market exports. The proliferation and diversification of handicraft production, argues Cook, indicates the fallacy of viewing petty production as a "precapitalist" form. Current trends in Mexican handicraft production, he continues, do not simply reflect a process of differentiation between producers but underscore the persistent role petty production plays in capitalist development. Similarly, in her analysis of the complex interplay of social and political factors in shaping petty production, Collins (1990) argues for a new framework to examine the development of waged and unwaged work that avoids privileging the role of economic forces and the logic of capital in their development. As the next two sections will reveal, work like that of Cook and Collins shares strikingly similar themes with current discussions of the meaning and process of economic restructuring in contemporary capitalism, linking these concerns not only to Third World contexts but also to processes of economic reorganization in industrialized countries.

Informal Work in the Age of Economic Restructuring

By the mid-1980s, critical assessments of the informal sector concept proposed by the ILO and labor economists more than a decade earlier appeared to amount to a general dismissal of the sector approach as an effective framework for explaining issues of poverty and unemployment. Yet, despite often sweeping critique, the concept of informal work and income generation not only remains the focus of policy analysis and prescription but continues as a major focus in discussions of capitalist processes of accumulation, development, and economic change. Differerent premises are offered to explain informality. One explanation links the concept's popularity to the political expediency of creating work opportunities while avoiding addressing more fundamental questions of social and economic inequality (Bromley 1985; Harding and Jenkins 1989). Others, including Peattie (1987), note that while problematic, research on informal work has identified a variety of productive activities critical to processes of capitalist development. From this perspective, providing a framework that makes informal activities substantively and analytically visible ensures its currency in contemporary development studies. This view has proven prescient of the place research on informality has assumed in current reinterpretations of capitalist industrialization in the global economy as the twenty-first century approaches.

Research during the 1980s was marked by growing interest in the dramatic changes in global financial and production relations. Developments heralded as hallmarks of this global realignment include the organizational integration of production across national boundaries and a technological transformation that both expedites the global movement of capital and engages electronic micro-technologies to organize production on a world scale. Contributing factors to this interest were the economic rise of the East Asian newly industrializing countries, uneven industrial growth in most other postcolonial settings, rising indebtedness in Third World countries, and recurrent recession in the advanced capitalist economies of North America and Europe.

Over the past decade, growing numbers of analysts have examined the relationship between these global processes and changing local configurations of work and employment. The theoretical approaches shaping these efforts vary widely, and the conclusions drawn about the causes and implications of current trends in the role, capacity, and place of informal work contrast sharply with each other. One approach, best exemplified by the seminal, if much criticized, work of Fröbel, Heinrichs, and Kreye (1980), explains changes in late twentieth century capitalism through an analysis of the new international division of labor (NIDL). Theories of the NIDL focus on the crisis of accumulation faced by industrial capital during the 1970s and highlight the relocation of industrial production from Europe and North America to lower-cost countries of the South in order to regain profitability. Briefly summarized, the NIDL involves the massive loss of industrial jobs in industrialized countries and an increasing role for poorly paid Third World laborers, particularly female factory workers recruited to export-processing zones, to produce for a global marketplace. This framework recognizes the shift from models of import substitution and self-sufficiency to export production, self-employment, and micro-enterprise development to focus their attention on those once considered marginal to the formal labor market, the growing numbers of women engaged in production for export.

A related line of inquiry, shaped by heightened gender sensitivity in development studies, pointed to the feminization of Third World labor forces as an important consequence of recent economic restructuring (Standing 1989b). Studies of export-oriented plants established as joint ventures or through direct foreign investment, for instance, showed a marked preference for hiring female workers. These firms, it was argued, depended on a flexible, pliant, and low-cost female labor force to compete in the global marketplace. Though many of these women continue to be unrecognized, underpaid, and unprotected as workers, they now constitute the main channel along which the new regime of export-oriented industrialization has proceeded (Elson and Pearson 1980; Nash and Fernández-Kelly 1983; Mies 1986). In addition to women being exposed to unsafe working conditions and denied wage levels paid to their male counterparts, they confront contradictions between their new economic roles and local gender ideologies which have contradictory consequences for their social status (Fuentes and Ehrenreich 1984; Elson and Pearson 1980). The NIDL approach has since been challenged for its exclusive focus on labor exploitation as capital's only means for recapturing accumulation.[4] It also has been challenged for ignoring crucial differences across national contexts[5] and for focusing solely on the negative impact of factory employment on women workers.[6]

Despite these shortcomings, theories of the NIDL and the feminization of the labor force have made a lasting contribution to the study of capitalist development. More specifically, the NIDL school has drawn attention to processes of structural change in late twentieth century capitalism, including

---

[4] Jenkins (1984), among others, has identified serious weaknesses of the NIDL approach, particularly its emphasis on cost-cutting as capital's main strategy to extend profits. As a consequence, NIDL theorists have neglected other developments, such as the introduction of new technologies, likely to play an equally important role in reestablishing economic dominance and involving different implications for the emerging structure of production.

[5] As Berik and Çagatay (1992) argue, although in some cases export-led growth may have been accomplished by the growing use of female labor, in other cases a similar industrial restructuring was achieved through the imposition of a new labor management regime among male workers with no significant increase in the female labor force. In such cases, a more accurate description of current trends would be the feminization of the working environment rather than the workforce as male laborers face the same diminished incomes, job insecurity, and lack of protection associated with female employment.

[6] A growing number of studies do acknowledge the contradictory implications of women's factory employment. For example, Foo and Lim (1989) recognize the exploitative relationship between capital and labor but argue that women's growing participation in factory-based manufacturing has opened new possibilities for a reconceptualization of women's gender identity and a more publicly active role of women than afforded by traditionally defined gender roles. Thus women's employment in the export sector actually creates new possibilities for women's gender identity and forms of social engagement.

the implications of these changes for patterns of production and labor force participation. This effort has contributed to a large body of research that has documented processes of industrial restructuring across different geographical spaces. Likewise, studies of the feminization of the labor force have identified the central role of gender and gender ideology in shaping the organization of global production across national landscapes. These efforts are important for recognizing the character of home-based production as a prominent feature of industrial development. Studies by Mies (1982b; 1986), Pineda-Ofreneo (1982), and Hossain (1987), for example, document the rapid growth of export-oriented handicraft production in Asia and Latin America and the increasing numbers of women home-based producers. As Mies (1982a, 1982b) argues, squeezed out of agricultural production by the commercialization of Indian agriculture, women of rural Andra Pradesh were drawn into home-based production, including that of handmade lace for a booming export market. As home-based export producers, lacemakers occupy a highly subordinated position vis-à-vis subcontractors and urban merchants who control both access to markets, credit, and supplies of raw material. Though essential for household survival in India and elsewhere (Berik 1989; Hossain 1987), home-based manufacture maintains patterns of gender segregation, reduces women's control over their own labor, and sustains women's continued impoverishment.

Reflecting on the situation of urban women, Benería and Roldán (1987) document the role of home-based workers in Mexico's export and domestic market-oriented plastics and battery industries. Like Mies (1982a, 1982b), Berik (1989), and Hossain (1987), they cite the interplay between the intra-household division of labor and ideology and changes in the wider economy as key forces drawing women into poorly paid and dependent informal labor in Mexico's expanding export sector. While such employment helps women sustain their households in the face of growing male unemployment, it offers little hope of significant long-term improvements in their standard of living or of their empowerment as workers. As each of these studies shows, the meaning and role of informal labor is now understood as part of complex processes of economic reorganization constituted by new relations of production, control, and finance.

Like earlier work on the informal sector, analyses now assume that informal work is an enduring feature of postcolonial economies. But key characteristics distinguish earlier and more contemporary research. First, unlike dual sector theories popular in the past, research in the framework of economic restructuring conceives informal work not as a distinctive "problem" faced by underdeveloped countries but as an integral component of the industrialization process itself. Second, contemporary literature generally views informal workers as embodied in relationships that are consistent with complex processes of late twentieth-century capitalism. Such studies are distinct from earlier interpretations of petty commodity production, which was viewed as an unfolding process of proletarianization. An important aspect of these latter studies is the unprecedented attention directed at the increasing incidence of informal work in North America and Europe (Guttman 1979; New York State Department of Labor 1982a, 1982b). Of particular interest in these studies is the expanding role played by home-based and sweatshop production in the livelihood strategies of growing numbers of people in industrialized countries, as well as in the general industrial strategy of an increasing number of firms (Mattera 1985; Mitter 1986; Boris 1989b; Fernández Kelly and Garcia 1989b; Sassen Koob 1989). By the mid-1980s, chronic and increasing unemployment in these countries and a growing reliance on part-time, temporary, and nonformal income among more and more people prompted some scholars to claim the advent of a new era in advanced capitalism, marked by the virtual disappearance of the traditional working class (Gorz 1982; von Werlhof 1988).

More recent literature focuses on the specific factors behind the growing trend toward informalization. As Portes and Sassen Koob (1987) show, a review of available evidence reveals a great deal of variability in the timing and specific circumstances of the emergence of an informal economy across different national contexts. Capitalist attempts to evade labor union militancy, the availability of large immigrant or chronically unemployed populations, and the pressures of economic stagnation assume different degrees of importance in the trend toward informalization across various regions. Binding these different national contexts, however, are changes in the world economy marked by recurrent recessions, increased international competition, and the growth of Third World exports. These changes prompt capitalist firms to "increase flexibility and decrease labor costs." The increasing demand for flexibility and cost-cutting assumed by these firms thus sustains the informalization of significant portions of both industrialized and industrializing economies (Portes and Sassen Koob 1987).

Back to the Future: Contending Views on Informalization

As recognition of the global expansion of informal employment has grown, a central concern shaping current research and writing has been the need for appropriate action. Much contention surrounds questions of how informalization affects workers' rights, social welfare, and the ability of the government to stimulate and manage economic growth. Markedly different arguments regarding appropriate policy and patterns of public and private forms of interventions have followed.

With the initial "discovery" of the growing role of informal activity in industrialized economies in the early 1980s, the negative implications of this trend were usually emphasized. Labor advocates and activists identified an alarming "reversal from established rights back to precariousness" for workers with the growth of informality (Mattera, 1985:122), while labor economists and government officials identified a serious new constraint on the ability to maintain appropriate wage and employment levels (Abels, Schwartz, Hackel, and Silverblatt 1983; New York State Department of Labor 1982a, 1982b). Highlighted by Mitter (1986), based on research in the United Kingdom, the proliferation of homework and small sweatshops among female informal workers involved in clothing manufacture spelled growing health hazards, low pay, and vulnerability to abuse and thievery by unscrupulous agents and shop owners. Boris (1989a; 1989b) identified the contradictory interests and needs of women in the United States who seek and secure home-based work.[7]

Echoing the pessimism of these assessments, scholars examining the experience of women's informal work in the Third World also note that such work places women in the role of both sustaining households and contributing to global production, although their position as home-based producers continues to be concretely shaped by their identity in the domestic sphere (Hossain 1987; Mies 1982b; Mitter 1986). That is, while women increasingly come to assume the position of principal household income earners, they continue to be defined as wives and mothers responsible for day-to-day household services. Moreover, as home-based producers confined to the domestic sphere, they occupy a subordinate position to both male kin as well as to subcontracting agents and urban exporters. Low wages and limited possibilities for organizing, given that production occurs in isolated household

---

[7]Research focussed on home-based production and household labor similarly emphasizes the vulnerability of household workers. For some, such as Berik (1989), household relations operate similarly to those of bonded labor where husbands are paid for the labor of their wives and daughters, sometimes in advance. For others, such as Collins and Giminez (1990), household labor marks the complex work of women in sustaining households and local economies. This type of research, however, has a distinct intellectual trajectory, one framed by a discourse that only occasionally intersects with processes and patterns of informalization (Smith, Wallerstein, and Evers 1984).

units, prevent women from achieving independent improvements in income and productivity. This, in turn, hinders women from achieving a more autonomous status as viable small business entrepreneurs. From this perspective, even though informal work provides much needed possibilities for income earning, it affords little prospect for improving the status and economic well-being of a majority of direct producers.

Unfavorable assessments of the implications of informal work for workers and national economic welfare during the early 1980s incorporated arguments for greater government resolve in controlling the growth of unregulated economic activity. But by the late 1980s, a widely heralded analysis by Hernando de Soto (1989) posed a stark challenge to this view. De Soto's study, *The Other Path*, embraced the persistence of informal activity in the Peruvian economy and linked its steady expansion to the constraints placed on urban migrants by a mercantilist regulatory system geared toward protecting the interests of national urban elites in a competitive global marketplace. Argues de Soto, the obstacles posed by this system make a viable livelihood by fully legal means virtually impossible for most petty producers and lead to forms of income earning outside the parameters of state regulation. Escape into informality is "the other path"–the silent and unarmed revolution–chosen by the majority of Peru's population in their struggle to wrest prospects of a better life from a changing economy controlled by national elites.

In the context of advanced capitalist countries, assessments paralleling the optimism of de Soto's view on informal businesses derive from analyses exploring the "economic miracle" of northern Italy. In a widely influential work, Piore and Sabel (1984) highlighted the remarkable success of Italy's regional economies since the 1970s and identified as its key factor the benefits of the craft-based production structure commonly called "flexible specialization." A key component of this structure is the loosely connected yet closely coordinated networks of artisanal producers, often working off-the-books in informal units engaging family labor or hiring neighbors (Brusco 1982; Piore and Sabel 1984). While governed by mutual kin and neighborhood-based social obligations, such networks have been able to escape the rigidities imposed by large firm hierarchies as well as by government tax and labor legislation. In this view, network-based production arrangements characterizing northern Italy point to new possibilities for prosperity as global economic changes increasingly expose the weakness of Fordist, mass production systems.

By the late 1980s, both the de Soto and flexible specialization frameworks were hailed by development scholars and policy analysts as groundbreaking new paradigms for understanding processes of economic growth and for generating new measures ensuring the success of increased informalization. In de Soto's argument, optimal policy alternatives for easing the burdens faced by Peru's working poor are offered by the logic of the informal sector itself: just as petty producers have found the secret to survival in the evasion of burdensome regulations imposed by their government, Peru's development planners would do well to scale down the existing regulatory structure in order to unleash the latent entrepreneurial potential of the country's small businesses. Framed as a specific study of Peruvian development history, de Soto's analysis rests on deregulationist assumptions which are increasingly at the center of analyses of the dynamics and implications of global economic restructuring for employment generation.

Similarly, the flexible specialization framework attribtues a critical dynamism to the activity of small, informal firms, which are assumed to be in a far better position than are large, formal companies to respond to sudden market changes because of their casualized labor pool and flexible forms of production (Piore and Sabel 1984; Benton 1989b, 1990). Analysts working from this perspective argue against forging strong relationships between centralized governments, nationally organized industries, and national labor unions because of their obsolete character. Instead, they recommend a system of "political decentralization" (Benton 1988, 1989b) to provide regional and municipal governments with greater resources to support local networks of small producers, which are assumed to ensure steady innovation and income growth. Recent work also ascribes a central importance to the role of nongovernmental organizations (NGOs) in strengthening micro-enterprise performance; while governments are viewed as having a "mandate to formulate policy and affect the regulatory environment," NGOs are hailed as possessing the flexibility, immediacy, and local accountability needed for successful on-the-ground implementation of direct intervention strategies related to credit, training, and other services (Otero 1994:182-195; see also McKean 1994).

Reflecting the influence of both de Soto's deregulationist critique and the flexibilization school's focus on emergent industrial structures, recent discussions highlight the benefits to be garnered from reforming regulatory structures, particularly given the pressures of globalization and increasingly volatile markets. Though concerned about distinguishing between his own and the "antistatist" thrust of de Soto's argument, Portes (1994:129) suggests replacing "unrealistic laws" and their "erratic enforcement" with a less bureaucratic, "flexible implementation of labor rules" assumed to protect "basic rights" yet allow for the "development of a dynamic small-scale sector." Notes Bromley (1994:148), de Soto's discussion of the "sociolegal obstacles to entrepreneurship and economic growth" point out that "every country in the world could benefit from in-depth research on 'the costs and importance of the law,' and de Soto's . . . simulations of the costs of formality and informality should be replicated in many different contexts." Accordingly, recent work identifies regulatory reforms that ensure minimal standards of worker and consumer protection while relieving small enterprises of what are assumed to be less essential regulations which, poorly enforced, serve little purpose but to constrain competitiveness in changing national and global markets (Tokman 1992b).

A decided alternative to frameworks privileging the role of regulatory reform in strengthening the informal sector are discussions of the promise of effective organizing among the most vulnerable and underprivileged segment of the informal workforce, namely women. Studies like those of Bhatt (1989), Rose (1992), and Mitter (1994) provide rich documentation of new women's movements that focus not on increasing women's entry into formal factory employment but on securing better pay, healthier work environments, and easier access to resources that improve women's returns from informal work. Suggesting the limitations of a legalistic focus to improve the position of self-employed and hired workers in informal enterprises, this research directs attention to the deeply rooted sources of exploitation shaping the terms of informal work, as well as to the factors that make employment outside the factory a necessary, and, in some cases, more promising form of work for growing numbers of people.

Informalization as Process: Dynamics of Work and Social Change

Although views of informal work have shifted over the years, they continue to challenge notions of economic dualism and the marginality and transience of informal activity. Researchers agree that informal work includes work performed in ephemeral workshops or at home, sometimes in addition to formal wage employment and after "normal" working hours. More frequently, however, informal work is carried out on a full-time, highly insecure basis without contract or documented wages. Ongoing discussions also highlight the incongruous relationship between informal activity and classic modernization theory or Marxist inspired analyses of the dynamic and direction of capitalist change. As scholars account for this incongruity, informality itself provides a window for reformulating the diverse perspectives used to analyze work, class, and development. Three recent analyses that illustrate the attention given to rethinking theories of capitalist development are those of Benton (1990), Scott (1994), and Mitter (1994). While all three studies highlight problems that informality poses for policy and political organizing, they also represent insightful attempts to grapple with the fundamental problem that informal work poses for interpreting processes of change in contemporary capitalism.

In her study of the recent industrial change in Spain, Benton (1990) emphasizes the need for a nondeterministic and nonlinear interpretation of capitalist development which would incorporate an understanding of the social and political embeddedness of economic reorganization. Her argument rests on an analysis of processes of "productive decentralization" characterizing the industrial development of Spain since the 1970s. In her detailed study of the electronic and shoe industries, Benton shows how downsized formal firms have become the norm in both industries, paralleled by the subcontracting of production to smaller and often informal operations. With this change, informal production assumes a central place in industrial development and undermines the idea that workshop and home-based production are mere "vestiges of artisan production from an earlier era" (Benton 1990:1).

As Benton also emphasizes, to understand the role played by informal production in Spain's capitalist development, it is critical to recognize the variability of processes of informalization. In the shoe industry, for example, restructuring has resulted in "a two-tiered industrial structure with an informal sector characterized mainly by poor labor conditions and the simple reproduction of tasks formerly carried out by formal firms" (Benton 1990:98). Poorly paid industrial homeworkers form a large part of the labor force, and possibilities for upward mobility are extremely limited. Within this structure, moreover, subcontracting firms remain "highly dependent on larger producers for orders and design specification" and are thus poorly poised to anticipate or constructively negotiate market instabilities (Benton 1990:98). As factory owners hedge their risk by minimizing investments in technology development and sweat their informal labor force to ensure short-term gains, the burden of future industry slumps are likely to be borne by an already vulnerable workforce.

Electronics manufacture, by contrast, highlights the shift from the use of casual labor and the self-exploitation of worker-entrepreneur households toward relative job security, opportunities for skill acquisition, and payment of equal or better wages for labor than in larger factories. As Benton shows, the small electronics subcontractor not only assumes a prominent role in production but is able to achieve a "transition from semi-informal, struggling enterprise to a well-respected small firm" (Benton 1990:72). The development of the electronics industry as a whole suggests an underlying possibility for the emergence of "a system of multiple, interconnected layers of independent producers of high-quality goods" able to anticipate future market changes.

Benton explains the marked differences between these industries on the basis of socially constituted gender relations. Industrial outwork in the shoe industry, she argues, is facilitated by socially prescribed gender roles that discourage employment outside the home for married women and ascribe highly unequal positions of authority to women and men. These relations match and reproduce the hierarchical and autocratic systems of control characteristic of sweatshop production. Moreover, women's subordinated and isolated position as homeworkers limits their contributions to innovative changes in the production process, as well as hampers possibilities for sustained improvement in their position as subcontracted producers. The electronics industry, however, is dominated by male factory employees able to establish semiformal subcontracting firms based on previous work experience, skills, and bonds of friendship. These worker-entrepreneurs form alliances that "improve their position within the industrial structure and contribute directly to product design" (Benton 1990:72). Such alliances promote investment in the development of innovative technology because they are governed less by principles of autocratic control than by cooperation. This, in turn, helps to establish and maintain market footholds and generally better working conditions for labor.

A final emphasis in Benton's work is on the political dimensions of industrial change where productive decentralization and informalization break with past structures of power. At a loss about how to induce desired developments in a rapidly growing decentralized industrial sector, national policy-making authority has increasingly been called into question. Additionally, the failure of national unions to accommodate local worker activism coupled with growing wage differentials among segments of the industrial workforce has undermined union effectiveness in speaking for a nationally organized industrial workforce. According to Benton, realizing the potential for growth in the more dynamic sectors, such as the electronics industry, will depend on a political "realignment of the alliances underlying the broad regulatory context for industrial growth" (Benton 1990:3).

The strength of Benton's work lies in its recognition of industrialization as a contradictory and open-ended process. Yet, although she acknowledges critical differences in the experience of informal work between male electronics and female shoe producers, she fails to consider the implications of heterogeneity for processes of collective resistance. The heterogeneity of informal workers, constituted by gender, generation, and class, suggests an important direction for retheorizing capitalist development. Perhaps most important, recognizing the heterogeneity of informal workers demands moving beyond an understanding of workers as mere respondents to processes of economic reorganization to an analysis sensitive to the ways in which such relations are constituted by everyday experiences. How, for example, do possibilities for resistance emerge alongside the dramatic reorganization of economic relations and across different experiences of work? How can we theorize capitalist development as a contested process that avoids the determinism generated by much of the research on the global character of capitalism or on the role of elites in shaping the reorganization of capitalist society? How, in other words, can we develop a framework that accounts for the agentic capacities and practices of social actors creating history rather than merely responding to their given circumstances?

Answering these questions requires moving beyond a call for local autonomy toward a theorization of emergent relations between social action and social context. It also requires moving beyond the call for political decentralization, a statist-based interpretation of economic change, to questioning how identities, other than those defined by relations of industrial production, provide an important basis for political mobilization. Constructing an analytic framework that avoids determinism and economism, in other words, requires rethinking political mobilization as it is embodied in the social construction of daily life, where identities are multivalent and complex and social action is not solely determined by relations of exploitation on the shop floor.

Mitter (1994) takes as her starting point the agentic capacities of workers to highlight processes of casualization and worker resistance in contemporary capitalism. This focus offers a way conceptually to integrate the predominance of women among informal workers in the Third World and their growing representation among casualized industrial workers in both advanced and industrializing economies. The main factors shaping women's work, she argues, include basic survival needs (particularly in the face of wrenching structural adjustment policies), the incompatibility of women's caregiving responsibilities with the requirements of formal employment, employers' growing preference for a flexible labor force, and new technological developments that make "decentralisation of work commercially viable and efficient" (Mitter 1994:14-15). Together, these factors ensure not only that informal activities, such as petty trade or domestic service, continue to be the main source of income for many Third World women but that growing numbers of women working in advanced industrialized countries and in industries that are the mainstay of growth in developing economies are hired as unprotected casual laborers rather than protected formal employees.

In acknowledging the convergence of experience of all working women, Mitter offers a view of capitalism which recognizes informal economic activity as an integral component rather than as a residual or anomalous phenomenon in processes of economic change. As she observes:

> The informal sector is not a peculiarity of the Third World; neither is it a sector totally dissociated from the formal one. The growing casualisation in the developed countries in the shape of part-time and temporary work has also given rise to a dramatic increase in the types of employment that represent enclaves of informality in the midst of the formal sector. There are degrees of informality, depending on the extent of casualisation in the conditions of work. (Mitter 1994:16)

Like Benton, Mitter argues that processes of informalization provide a window for rethinking theories of modernization and processes of industrialization. In contrast to Benton, however, she emphasizes the forms of organization and social movement which accompany informalization to highlight varying instances of organized resistance among casualized workers. As Mitter demonstrates, although women's need to secure their livelihood through informal work may fragment their experience of the labor process, this experience of struggle forms the basis for a new solidarity that "permeates" women's informal initiatives and forms the "seed of a new type of grassroots mobilisation" (Mitter 1994:25).

The perspective suggested by Mitter is more fully elaborated by Scott (1994) in a detailed study of economic development in Peru which places processes of consciousness and political mobilization at the center of analysis. Like Benton, Scott notes the inability of formal unions to serve as an effective force for class action against the oppressive conditions of work and life imposed by the country's ruling elite. Scott departs from Benton, however, by challenging "productionist" frameworks as the sole ingredient of consciousness through a critical examination of the internal differentiation of the Peruvian working class. As she shows, formally employed factory workers, self-employed entrepreneurs, and informal laborers represent divergent and fragmented experiences and interests. While exploring these divergences, Scott challenges the predominant conception that differentiation stifles a shared working-class consciousness. Instead she highlights possibilities for effective collective action by engaging evidence about collective interests and latent solidarity among workers.

Counter to popular assessments of economic change in Peru, Scott argues that economic growth in the 1960s and 1970s offered large numbers of working-class households tangible, if modest, increases in their standard of living. A major factor enabling this group of recent urban migrants to experience upward mobility was the participation of family members in informal work. For most male workers, this involved frequent shifts both within and between formal and informal employment. Echoing Mitter, Scott concludes that migration and mobility–the survival strategies of Peru's poor–occurred on a mass scale during this period and provided members of this otherwise heterogeneous segment of the population a shared experience that forms the basis for a common identity as members of a broad *clase trabajadora*, or "laboring class."

One striking aspect of this development, however, is the divergent experiences of women and men as workers[8] which limited women's opportunities almost exclusively to low-paying, labor-intensive assembly activities. Also striking about the differences between women's and men's opportunities were that "the crucial conditions for successful self-employment–access to apprenticeships, capital, clients and information–made possible through kinship networks which discriminated against women," limited women's opportunities to domestic and other service work (Scott 1994:215). Thus women's interests differed from, and at times directly conflicted with, those of their male counterparts, a situation both reflected in and reinforced by women's subordinate position in the family.

Important questions emerge from the marked differences between the experiences of women and men. How do the divergent experiences of women and men shape "laboring" class consciousness? How do these gender-specific differences and interests reconstitute what were once defined, in a more narrow, productionist sense, as class-based solidarities? How do social solidarities emerge from experiences that build on, rather than force a choice among, the historically specific circumstances of our daily lives? Given the

---

[8]She also notes the importance of other social identities, particularly ethnicity, as the basis of experience.

striking lack of a self-conscious women's movement in Peru, how are contrasting gender interests mediated to fashion "laboring class" consciousness?

For Scott, a key factor shaping conscious social action is the organization of the household as a unit of consumption. Although prospects for economic gain in Peru are generally realized by male workers, higher standards of living enabled by rising incomes are a socially constituted process that is realized through the institution of the family. In this context, though excluded from direct income from their own employment, women experience upward mobility through household membership in which further gains are secured largely through the future work of children. Under these circumstances, women find themselves "better off sustaining the common class interest of the family than pursuing their sectional interests of gender" (Scott 1994:217).

In this view, the institutions of family and community organize consumption, including services such as education and health care, and are critical for realizing the promise of upward mobility. While all household members have a vested interest in defending family consumption levels, Scott argues that "women's primary responsibility for household consumption extends to wider roles as "community managers" which provide a space for political mobilization" (Scott 1994:32). Contradicting women's subordination to men at home and at work, these spaces enable women to organize around shared interests to improve family standards of living. This occurs by mobilizing institutional resources for the redistribution of material goods, the organization of consumption, and the construction of social status. For Scott, it is through this social economy that class identities are modified and political action is effected. As she concludes: "Scattered evidence of solidarity between unions and community organizations is a manifestation of the structural link between production and consumption and between social and economic class" (Scott 1994:221).

In this analysis, Scott furthers our understanding of processes of informalization by highlighting how diverse work experiences, including those constituting social reproduction, shape patterns of mobilization and constructions of consciousness. As she argues, these differences and contestations need to be placed at the center of analysis of capitalist processes of reorganization, where class must be understood as constituted as well as differentiated by particular social, political, and cultural experiences. This requires analyzing the social construction of labor practices which ruptures the bounded categories of mobilization—as has been done for our notion of employment and work— to enable a better theorization and interpretation of social activity and social consciousness. Said another way, the reproduction of everyday life depends on a better appreciation of how different and divergent interests merge and, at times contest, normative practices.

Conclusion

As we have emphasized throughout this discussion, although many analyses of informality promote a sense of contemporaneousness to interpretations of current socioeconomic patterns, others situate their interpretations within broad structural realignments in the world economy. These broad changes are partially anchored in the accelerated shift from agriculturally based to industrially oriented economies that marked the early twentieth century for some countries and the more proximate postWar period for others. The rapid and widespread impact of the Green Revolution, for instance, set in motion by the technological developments of the 1950s and 1960s, led to fundamental changes in agrarian relations. In the countryside, changing patterns of land ownership and agrarian relations reconstituted rural production and increased the numbers of households dependent on multiple sources of income.[9] This led to expanding nonfarm artisan and craft production, petty trade, and service provisioning and provided the context for a burgeoning number of workers and semiproletarianized peasants to engage in a wide range of unregulated economic activities.

These dramatic shifts in forms of work and employment, clearly underway by the 1960s, have been documented in a spate of studies on the Green Revolution and patterns of Third World industrialization. But by the 1970s, mounting fieldwork revealed a range of unanticipated forms of work, places of production, and new relations of subordination and control. This work offered an implicit critique of the "natural" transition from a modernizing agricultural economy to an expanding industrial sector and, though lacking the language of restructuring in vogue today, identified complex pressures leading to social and economic configurations not accounted for by modernization theory.

---

[9]When agriculture was the mainstay of subsistence and a household depended on additional income to secure subsistence, secondary employment was generally seasonal and involved a single family member employed as a temporary, casual or part-time wage earner. Increasingly, however, households have become dependent on more than a single income earner to sustain daily life, and multiple incomes, including those secured through urban migration and remittances, have helped to transform household employment patterns.

As this latter work highlighted, modernization theory and its assertion of a linear pattern of industrialization and proletarianization–mirrored in the image of North America and Europe–ignored the historically specific ways in which forms of production unfold. This theory also ignored how populations experience and respond to crises and forge new opportunities. Development theories premised on the assumptions of economic liberalism ignore as well the capacities of people to construct and create forms of organization and social life that do not merely respond to conditions given them, but actually constitute the processes by which economic reorganization is realized and promoted.

A new social economy identified by hierarchical as well as horizontal networks of production and exchange made the study of processes of informalization a new arena for theorizing social, political, and economic change. These processes demanded the retheorization of productionist paradigms and attention to the question of whether trends toward informalization should be interpreted as long-lasting transformations of global production or temporary responses to economic and social crises (Mingione 1991). The conclusion that informal relations and a refashioned social economy were lasting aspects of social and economic reorganization opened up for review new questions about work, labor markets, the workplace and the "naturalness" of the division between productive and reproductive work. Debates on processes of informalization also opened to scrutiny the internationalization of labor, capital, and finance in ways that invited renewed interest in commonly accepted assumptions about the state system of the world economy. These questions, in turn, reintroduced the salience of the market, in addition to the shop floor, as a focus of attention; the significance of household work, both paid and unpaid, in establishing wages and value; and a new appreciation of forms of identity not tied to class or work relations in organizing for change. In short, work on the informal economy generated a host of new questions and invited renewed interest in nondeterminist analyses of economic reorganization and social regulation. These new questions suggest important opportunities for reinterpreting patterns of global restructuring, the reorganization of labor and social movements, and a new politics of action as people generate new constituencies for mobilization and create new ways to meet their needs for sustenance and survival.

THEMES IN THE LITERATURE: A GUIDE TO KEY WORDS

Research on the informal sector is diverse, complex, and framed by theoretical and methodological approaches from a wide variety of disciplines. The purpose of this guide to key words is to help users identify the broad scope of this literature. In addition to annotating a select portion of the bibliography, each citation includes key words that describe the main issues addressed and, in most cases, the geographic area of study. Extending beyond this descriptive function, our key word schema aims at broad analytical goals through the use of concepts that help to identify the theoretical approach of individual studies. In many cases the key words also identify the type of study undertaken: whether, for example, the research represents an analysis of policy reforms, explores the underlying class processes or gender relations informing the structure and conditions of informal work, or simply describes the broad characteristics of informal activities in a given time and place.

Consistent classification of a diverse body of literature, however, is never a clear-cut or easy task. While some studies can be readily identified by a specific key word, others are more ambiguous and address numerous aspects of their particular subject at once. In some cases such studies straddle divergent theoretical frameworks or attempt to accomplish different and sometimes seemingly incongruous projects simultaneously. For instance, a number of studies provide an analysis of the long-term structural features of a specific aspect of informal work while also formulating policy recommendations aimed at the immediate reform of how access to resources among informal workers may be increased. Despite such complexity, major themes concerning informal work clearly emerge, along with key trends linking these themes to important debates in social science theory and research. The key terms we have developed to characterize the issues raised in the literature are intended to highlight these patterns, while also informing the reader about the specific content of each citation.

The order of key words chosen for each citation indicates our assessment of the relative degree to which the given term constitutes an organizing focus or framework for the analysis. Many of the key terms used are self-explanatory and require little additional clarification. Where works cited explore informal activity taking place in specific countries or regions, this is indicated by the country or region name at the end of the key word string, for example, *India* and *Peru* or *Asia* and *Latin America*. The terms *Third World, industrialized economies*, and *centrally planned economies*–also placed at the end of the key word string–denote contributions that focus on these particular economic contexts. Studies that examine particular industries or activities are indicated by the appropriate key term–*carpet manufacture, clerical work, construction, domestic service, export production, farmer's markets, garment manufacture, electronics manufacture, flea markets, garage sales, garbage picking, handicrafts, moonlighting, pilfering, prostitution, shoe manufacture, or trading*. Analyses of specific characteristics of informal work, such as the use of *child labor*, production of goods on a *piecework* basis, or the pattern of multiple job-holding among workers, are highlighted accordingly. Also identified in the key word set are a relatively small number of existing *bibliographies* that can direct the reader to further research relevant to the study of informalization.

To ensure the usefulness of the bibliography as a guide to the literature, detailed explanation remains necessary for terms with either greater analytic significance or ambiguity than those identified above. We have prepared the list below to clarify the specific meaning associated with our use of particular terms. Where appropriate, we have identified key terms in the context of the central debates and theoretical frameworks that shape analyses of informal work.

NOTES ON SELECT KEY WORDS

Apprenticeship The problem of access to adequate training is noted as a major constraint to the viability of small and nonformal enterprises. Various sources of training opportunities are sometimes explicitly addressed in the literature, including apprenticeship arrangements offered through formal and informal channels and social networks.

Appropriate technology Technology has featured as an important element shaping or constraining the viability of informal enterprises. Analyses of this theme have sometimes been directed at identifying possible forms of assistance, such as credit, to small firms or individual producers to ensure their access to appropriate technologies.

Artisanal production A number of studies in the literature examine patterns associated with manufacturing by skilled craftspersons who are well integrated into a market economy yet participate in a production process over which they command a large degree of control, often as self-employed entrepreneurs. Artisanal production also is a distinctive category in studies of petty commodity production. In analyses of late twentieth century capitalism, a focus on artisanal producers has framed discussions of flexibilized workshop-based production.

Class formation One concern in the class analytic literature is the role and significance of petty economic activities as they constitute and shape emergent class relations in processes of economic change. The uneven formation of class relations is seen as an integral process in capitalist development.

Class processes This term denotes those studies that examine processes of changing and increasingly complex class relations that develop from emergent informal livelihood patterns. Typically highlighted in research on class processes is a view of the political as well as economic dynamics shaping labor relations and the organization of production.

Comparative Most studies of informal activities focus on particular localities, countries, or regions. A small but important number of citations, however, engage a comparative perspective to identify key distinctions and parallels in the development of informal activities across different contexts. While some studies offer comparative inquiries of processes of Third World development, research also explores informal activities as embedded in processes of globalization which embrace industrialized as well as industrializing economies.

Consciousness Involvement in various labor processes and struggles represents experiences that shape people's perceptions of their identity and interests. While changing consciousness is frequently a process emphasized in class analytic studies, recent foci on crosscutting identities shaped by gender and ethnicity also have emerged as important themes in the literature.

Constraints to accumulation Informal enterprises are often characterized as unable to transform themselves into successful capitalist firms. Highlighted as a key factor in this transformation process are specific constraints to accumulation, including the lack of credit and appropriate skills, which structure a perpetually peripheral status for informal firms within developing capitalist economies.

Continuum debate In the mid-1980s, mounting criticism concerning the arbitrariness of the boundary drawn between formal and informal work led to an alternative framework that placed informal work along a linear sequence of activities ranging from formal wage employment with fixed, long-term security to informal exchanges characterized by varied forms of commodity and service production with limited income and employment security. This debate helped to highlight the heterogeneous relations characterizing informal work and the complex processes that constitute its activities.

Credit Access to credit is a frequent theme in studies examining problems faced by informal entrepreneurs. Such studies generally analyze government policies that shape extant credit institutions and evaluate existing or explore potential forms of intervention through project assistance. Recent literature features case studies of grass-roots efforts to organize informal entrepreneurs into cooperative groups which are assumed to enhance user demand, increase access to formal credit services, or develop viable self-help credit institutions.

Critique of dualism By the early 1980s, the concept of the informal sector as a separate economy was increasingly contested as an arbitrary and theoretically bankrupt assumption. These challenges led to an emphasis on the essential if contradictory relationship between informal and formal economic activities. Writers employing this critique argued that the failure to recognize intersectoral linkages among activities risked misinforming policy-makers since policy measures and forms of program development and implementation were being prescribed by government authorities, often with vague or unfounded notions about their probable effect on the economy as a whole.

Decentralization The term decentralization signifies the process by which industrial production is spatially and organizationally disaggregated in late twentieth-century capitalism. Decentralized production, closely associated with processes of industrial and economic restructuring, involves subcontracting relationships between small firms that produce intermediate parts or final consumer goods and large firms that control market access. While production may take place in various locations, control over the production process may continue to rest with large firms. Some analysts note that this production hierarchy can be challenged and renegotiated if small firms develop the ability to accommodate market changes, develop a broad clientele, and thus lessen their dependence on a limited number of larger firms for market access.

Definition A dominant preoccupation in the informal sector literature, particularly during the 1970s and early 1980s, was the need to establish a general definition for the sector. Early studies tended to construct a comprehensive definition based on the specific characteristics of urban informal workers or enterprises. Challenged by various critiques, such as that framing the continuum debate, subsequent studies offered a more theoretically grounded understanding of informality based on relations both shaping and themselves shaped by processes of socioeconomic change.

Differentiation Discussions of petty commodity producers focus on processes that enable some producers to accumulate capital, increase their size and efficiency, and gain access to formal credit, training, and other opportunities to enhance production and commodity exchange. But this potential for mobility is unrealized by producers who are unable to gain control of resources needed for growth and expansion. This uneven process of success and decline or stagnation is a marked characteristic of informal production.

Disguised wage labor Wage workers who do not control access to their income or are employed as bonded labor equivalents are identified as disguised wage laborers. These disguised wage workers, often women and female and male children, are usually employed in home-based activities such as in carpet manufacturing and handicraft production.

Double-day Pressures faced by women as major, often sole, livelihood earners for the family as well as caretakers of the domestic sphere are the focus of several decades of gender analytic research. The significance, complexity and embeddedness of this double burden for the income-seeking strategies engaged in by women and the mobility prospects they face are frequently emphasized in the literature on informalization.

Dual sector or economy Early research first identifying the informal economy emphasized informal employment as a distinct sphere of activity, separate from the formal economy, neglected by development planners and practitioners, yet potentially central to economic change or "modernization." The informal sector, in short, was envisioned as an autonomous and distinctive arena of production that required policy reform different from that designed for the formal sector.

Economic restructuring Since the early 1980s, studies of economic restructuring have highlighted the intersections among social, economic, and political processes characterizing the reorganization of capitalist economies. This literature went beyond identifying emergent firm types and enterprise relations as part of processes of industrial restructuring to examine the global reorganization of capital, labor, and financial markets. An important theme in these analyses is the convergence of experiences among low-income and unprotected workers from Third World and advanced industrialized economies.

Education An important policy concern in early dual sector analyses as well as in more recent discussions of small business growth is the need to facilitate access to technical and business education for small entrepreneurs. Because entrepreneurial know-how is assumed to be a key means to promote the viability of small industries, strategies for improving educational access and developing appropriate educational programs are key themes in informal labor market analyses.

Empowerment Following struggles for representation and voice are analyses of the consequences of organizing efforts among informal workers and their meaning for the empowerment of dispossessed and marginalized peoples. Drawing on feminist and new social movements literature, researchers have analyzed empowerment as both a process and an outcome among those seeking access to needed resources and more equitable terms of economic and social engagement.

Entrepreneurship A frequent emphasis in analyses of informal work is identifying successful entrepreneurial activity. This interest, often framed in terms of individual characteristics or technological constraints, complements research on small firms and micro-enterprises as the likely source of new employment growth within restructured national economies.

Ethnicity Studies of ethnicity, ethnic identity, and ethnically linked networks and relations identify the opportunities and constraints offered by such collective identities and groups. Such analyses also explore ethnicity as a factor shaping relations of trust and reciprocity that facilitate the success of household survival strategies as well as small-scale, informal entrepreneurial activities. In contrast, literature on labor market segmentation demonstrates the systematic exclusion of ethnically defined segments of the labor force from lucrative forms of employment.

Export processing zones The emergence of export processing zones as a major feature of export-oriented industrialization is perceived to embody new institutional contexts for industrial production, new policy approaches to industrialization, and new arenas for class domination and struggle between international capital and locally constituted labor forces. Often highlighted in this literature is the growing proportion of women among export workers as both a product of women's increased demand for employment and a strategy employed by capital to reduce labor costs and worker unionization.

Female-headed households While the involvement of women in informal work is frequently highlighted in the literature, the particular needs and constraints faced by women who assume the role of female household head is given specific recognition. Female-headed households are a particularly vulnerable group because women's opportunities for balancing household survival with caregiving responsibilities, particularly among single parents, are undermined by the discrimination and structural inequalities they face in securing work and accessing resources especially when dealing with male-dominated institutions.

Flexibilization Researchers from a variety of disciplines have identified a major trend in industrial development: the increased use of casual, unprotected labor and the continuing disaggregation of production structures. The search for greater competitiveness under volatile market conditions is argued to be the key determinant of this trend, which has generated changing structures of particular industries and new forms of state regulation. Research has identified these changes and their implications for labor-management relations, particularly as they reconstitute women's industrial employment.

Flexible specialization Since the mid-1980s, the merits of industrial structures that offer flexible alternatives to the rigidities of mass production have been critical aspects of the literature on informalization. Flexible specialization is defined as an industrial orientation whereby workshops staffed by skilled craftspersons produce specialized goods for niche markets while retaining an ability to shift quickly to new products and production processes in response to changes in market conditions. The role of interdependent small-scale enterprises, both formal and informal, within these new production structures has been particularly salient in discussions of informalization.

Gender division of labor Drawing on feminist critiques of social science theory, gender analysis has become a major framework of inquiry into problems of development, work, and social change. This emphasis highlights gender differential forms of work and exchange and their importance for understanding labor relations and processes of economic change as well as development. As a key term in this bibliography, gender division of labor marks those citations which describe or analyze gender-defined patterns of occupation and employment.

Gender ideology In many of the groundbreaking contributions that theorize labor and capitalist production, authors have highlighted the critical role played by gender ideology in people's experience of labor processes and exchanges within and beyond the home. Frequently highlighted are the contradictory community responses to women's employment that emerge in the context of new patterns of women's labor market participation.

Gender inequality While women face specific problems as informal workers, a relationship of institutionalized inequality between genders structures this experience. The term gender inequality is used to signify those works that explore this relationship and its ramifications as an explicit focus of study.

Gender relations A critical accomplishment of feminist analysis has been its ability to make visible and place in theoretical perspective the work of unpaid female as well male family members, including children, in the household. This has been done by documenting the importance of nonwage and informal activities in processes of social reproduction, exploring the ideological foundations of gender divisions of labor, and linking unremunerated and informal activities to processes of social and economic change. Citations that explore these themes as critical for understanding current socioeconomic trends are indicated by this key term.

Globalization An important theme in literature on the new international division of labor and on economic and industrial restructuring is the trend toward globalized forms of production characterizing the world economy. The key word *globalization* identifies studies that extend discussions of transnationalization and examine how emergent global relations and networks shape economic change, labor processes, and state involvement in particular localities.

Home-based production Informal work frequently takes the form of income-earning activities performed in the home, often by women and children, and is generally associated with the most exploitative aspects of informality; low pay, long hours, and the lack of social security or protection against unemployment and work-related injury. Nevertheless, home-based production also provides women income-earning opportunities that do not conflict with domestic responsibilities or prevailing gender ideology. Studies that explore these often contradictory experiences are identified by the key term home-based production.

Household This key term highlights studies based on data collection and analysis conducted at the household level. More analytically, this key word also indicates bibliographic contributions that explore relations of production in the household and their relation to other economic activities, processes, and trends.

Household division of labor Feminist analyses have shown how gender and age-based divisions of responsibilities and tasks within the household assume a central role in the organization of economic production. A relationship between the household division of labor and women's employment outside the home, and between women's household relations and the changing organization of work and employment, are highlighted by this key term. These relationships are frequently explored for their role in drawing women into particular kinds of work, as well as in shaping the development of informal economies in different sociocultural contexts.

Housing Problems of adequate housing have been an increasingly important theme in discussions of rapid urbanization, where informal construction activities have resulted from self-help initiatives by recent migrants. The literature highlights the need for more appropriate government policy and illuminates the link between housing patterns and patterns of change in other informal livelihood strategies.

Illegal activity The informal sector is often broadly defined by the evasion of formal laws regarding employment and production standards. The distinction is usually drawn between activities that produce legal goods or services and those producing illegal ones including prostitution, drugs, gambling,and smuggling. We use the term illegal economy to denote a focus on the latter.

Industrial restructuring Building on discussions of globalizing production trends, researchers have explored processes of industrial restructuring in advanced capitalist countries. These processes involve less the wholesale transfer of production to the "developing world" and lower wage economies than the adoption of new production processes and technologies everywhere, enabling firms to wrest a leading market edge under conditions of intense competition.

Labor market dynamics This key term identifies literature that highlights the presence of distinct though often linked labor markets by exploring the dynamics of each, examining possibilities for mobility between markets, or highlighting market constraints to both short and long-term mobility.

Labor market segmentation A major concern in studies of informal work are processes of labor market fragmentation and their implications for employment. Frequently emphasized is the process by which the labor market in both industrialized and Third World economies excludes large portions of the population--often distinguished along racial, ethnic, and gender lines--from formal employment, while establishing conditions conducive to low-wage remuneration and job insecurity for informal and other casual employees.

Labor movements Organized struggles by labor against capitalist exploitation have been well documented in the history of capitalist development in both industrialized and Third World countries. We use this key term to indicate studies that address labor movement practices, including those that highlight struggles against the informalization of the labor process and the often uneasy relationship between organized labor and casual workers.

Labor processes This key term identifies literature that places the informal sector in the context of the changing organization of capitalist production. Similar to research on labor market segmentation, studies of labor processes explore the underlying structural relations in the development of the informal sector. But, these studies are most commonly associated with literature on petty commodity production, state practice, and the theorization of the economic restructuring in the late twentieth century.

Labor relations The use of informal labor by both small and large firms is embedded in the historically shaped relations between business and labor as these relations constitute the policy and production environments in specific national and regional contexts. The term labor relations identifies analyses that explore the history of labor and conflicts between laborers and owners of capital drawing particular attention to the institutional arrangements that these struggles have engendered.

Marginalization Critical assessments of government policy that promote the growth of informal activities generally address processes of marginalization as an inherent outcome of the peripheral and subordinated position of informal enterprises vis-à-vis their formal counterparts. From this perspective, informal enterprises are blocked by structural constraints that limit their capacity for growth. Regardless of supportive policy initiatives, informal entrepreneurs and workers alike remain locked into dead-end livelihoods that lack the potential for upward mobility.

Migration The growth of the informal sector has been closely associated with the migration of landless rural residents in search of urban employment. Frequently, the subject of migration occupies a central place in interpretations of the development of the informal sector, its problems, and prospects. A similar emphasis has recently been accorded to migration flows between developing and developed countries in analyzing the growth of underground economies in advanced industrialized contexts.

New international division of labor During the 1980s, researchers used data from major North American and Western European industries to explore the emergence of a new international division of labor driven by the global sourcing tendencies of transnational corporations. While processes of economic decentralization and the fragmentation of industrial manufacturing were seen as a way to transfer the risk and lower the costs of production for large firms, this process also drew large numbers of

Third World female, unorganized and informal laborers directly into the orbit of capitalist production.

Nonmonetary exchange Barter and the reciprocal provision of goods and services within social networks are examined in the literature as common features of informal economic activity. Some analysts give particular attention to the potential these exchange relations hold for providing more equitable and liberating alternatives to the social and economic organization of everyday life and draw a distinction between these relationships and those offered by capitalist principles of free wage labor and nonobligatory wage relations.

Pattern or magnitude Reflecting a dominant preoccupation with "discovering" the informal economy during the early 1970s, a significant number of the early studies of the informal sector described its characteristics and size in different geographical contexts. Contemporary studies continue to include descriptive accounts of informal work, but these accounts more frequently provide background for analytic case studies.

Petty commodity production Literature on petty commodity production, like critiques of economic dualism, stresses the structural relationships between petty producers and producers in the wider economy rather than their classification as independent economic actors. While there is a large body of research on petty commodity production in the sociology of agriculture, agrarian transitions and economic reorganization, selections in this bibliography refer only to citations that address debates on informalization.

Polarization The growth of informal economic activities and the casualization of work have frequently been associated with growing disparities in the livelihood prospects of different social constituencies. The development of the underground economy is seen as both a manifestation of and a contributing factor to this pattern of economic and social polarization.

Policy analysis Early research on the informal sector aimed to develop policies to guide Third World industrial development. The term policy analysis indicates references that explicitly examine existing policy frameworks, such as capital-intensive import substitution or particular national policies such as protective labor legislation to assess their implications for or impact on the informal sector.

Policy prescriptions Though not framed as policy analysis per se, a variety of informal sector research includes policy recommendations, often as a lesson to be drawn from case material. Typically, these recommendations outline measures to improve the conditions for sustaining or increasing informal work opportunities. Frequent policy recommendations include augmenting existing credit and training opportunities and expanding informal sector opportunities to generate employment or encourage new participants, such as women, to engage in remunerative activity.

Political mobilization This key term identifies constraints to building an effective movement for improving the terms of trade or conditions of work among informal workers, including the efforts of small-scale vendors, home-based pieceworkers, prostitutes, or sweatshop employees. The term also identifies studies that highlight the particular relationship between informal workers and the state.

Processes of accumulation The focus of numerous studies is the ability of informal enterprises to accumulate capital and reinvest in their own growth and development so tat they can move from a state of informality to greater security and higher wages for workers. Unlike our key concepts, *constraints to accumulation* and *unequal exchange* or *petty commodity production*, this term draws attention to the processes of change within enterprises and the conditions that potentially could enable their transformation.

Production process Studies that identify and theorize patterns of production, including but not limited to labor relations, are identified by the term *production process*. This key word acknowledges studies that recognize broad historical changes in forms of production, such as the transition from artisan and craft production to mass production or shifts from mass production to decentralized niche market production and new forms of informal subcontracting and putting-out arrangements. The term also highlights studies that recognize the inseparability of economic, social, political, and ideological aspects of production, drawing attention to the complex dynamics of changing forms of work and employment.

Project assistance In addition to the formulation of appropriate policy, studies of the informal sector identify or assess forms of direct assistance to informal workers and enterprises. Development projects organized by government and nongovernmental agencies to provide credit, training in particular crafts, entrepreneurial skills, and linkages to larger firms to facilitate market access to informal workers and small entrepreneurs is the focus of a growing body of literature on the informal sector. Research also examines the formation of cooperatives among informal traders and producers as a strategy to optimize the impact of project assistance and to develop enduring institutions that support the development of small enterprises. The tendency for cooperatives to be dominated by the more powerful of local small businesses and to neglect the interests of informal workers, particularly the more vulnerable entrepreneurs such as female street vendors, also is noted in this literature.

Racial inequality Alongside ethnic and gender inequality, racism is an important constraint defining households' and workers' livelihood prospects. Racial inequality is sometimes featured in the informal sector literature as a key factor impeding the availability of lucrative options for informal workers and limiting large numbers of workers to low-paying, insecure, and poorly protected employment.

Regulation Evasion of government regulation has been identified as a key feature distinguishing nonformal from formal economic activity. In recent years, the literature has included an explicit focus on legislation concerning business activity and labor protection to examine ways in which regulation can promote informal employment. Such analyses often outline possibilities for legislative reform to promote small business growth given shifts in the organization of primary industry and manufacturing.

Relation to capital Beginning in the early 1980s, studies employing class analytic, Marxist, or poststructuralist interpretations of informalization argued that the informal sector had a particular relation to capital. Frequently, this line of analysis was framed by an assumed functionalist relationship between informal sector activities and processes of capitalist development.

Relation to formal economy A major theme in dual sector analyses is the relationship between informal activity and the formal economy. A frequent focus is the connection between formal and informal labor markets and the processes by which workers experience or, alternatively, are blocked from mobility from one type of employment to another. Another focus centers on the impact the different economic sectors have on each other, often with the aim of assisting appropriate policy formulation.

Research methods Questions of research methodology continue to be important in the study of the informal sector given the limited information available on informal work and workers, firms, organizations, or activities in official employment and production statistics. The term *research methods* identifies for the reader citations that include detailed discussions about specific methodological problems and strategies.

Reserve army of labor In class analytic research, the availability of a labor pool easily incorporated into capitalist firms during processes of expansion is viewed as a frequent attribute of the informal sector. Framed either as a consequence of capitalist penetration into local economies that forces traditional artisans out of business, or as a response to the growing numbers of people dependent on wage income but traditionally excluded from participation in paid employment, such as women, this reserve army feeds capitalist growth by keeping wages low. It is also assumed that the reserve army enables capitalists to hire temporary laborers in response to short-term needs or respond to demands for specialized skills while retaining the ability to discharge workers made redundant either during periods of economic stagnation or in response to technological innovation.

Resistance While political mobilization involves organizing collective efforts among workers in pursuit of a common goal, everyday forms of individual and group resistance against exploitation also characterize relations in the workplace. Noting the gender, ethnic, and race-based inequalities that often limit possibilities for unified mobilization, recent literature emphasizes resistance as an enduring if diffuse strategy employed by workers in the face of unequal relations of power in the labor market and the workplace.

Review Over the decades, the subject of the informal sector has involved considerable debate over its appropriate foci, salient terms and features, fundamental analytical value, and theoretical implications. Many of these debates have been summarized in key reviews. Describing major concepts, theories, and contentions in the study of informal activities, these references frequently propose specific theoretical alternatives that mitigate the weakness of past approaches.

Rural Research on informal activities most frequently addresses their characteristics and role in large urban centers and largely ignores processes and relations of informalization in rural settings. The term *rural* has been included to highlight those relatively few but important entries that focus specifically on informal activities and relations occurring in nonurban contexts.

Self-employment Frequently, informal enterprises consist of individuals engaged in income generating activity on their own behalf as petty vendors, craftpersons, and others with specific technical skills. While the particular constraints faced by the self-employed in securing livelihoods are discussed in the literature, the potential for self-employment to help alleviate problems of under- and unemployment and poverty is a particular focus in the literature on informalization.

Self-provisioning Self-provisioning identifies the process by which household members personally secure the goods and services needed for their day-to-day reproduction. Self-provisioning strategies include assuming responsibility for house repair, home gardening, home manufacture of consumer goods, do-it-yourself construction, and providing household services. A steady increase in self-provisioning activities, particularly by women, is noted as a key feature of changes in late twentieth-century capitalism, structured by the effects of contradictory trends such as declining worker incomes, changing consumer demands, and the expansion of time spent outside of formal employment because of growing underemployment and expanding leisure time.

Small or micro-enterprises While radical formulations of the concept of work in capitalist production continue to be an important theme in the literature, a review of recent trends also reveals a resurgent celebration of the merits of small or micro-enterprises for economic development. This theme harkens back to those characteristic of the 1970s literature but differs from previous writings in at least two important respects: First, current policy recommendations focus less on channeling resources into the development of the formal sector and more on reformulating the presumed burdensome regulatory structures that are assumed to informalize small enterprises in the first place. Second, whereas earlier studies argued that informal enterprises should provide employment that parallels work in established firms, the current literature stresses the intersections among small businesses and large firms. These studies conclude that small enterprises constitute components of flexible national production complexes linked to the global marketplace, and that play a key role in the success of export-oriented industrialization.

Social mobility With the growing recognition of the heterogeneity of informal activity, research has identified a differential ability among workers to move from poorly remunerated forms of work, such as domestic service or street vending, to more lucrative forms of income generation, either as successful entrepreneurs or as protected formal workers. These analyses explore the different conditions that contribute to or constrain mobility. Depending on the framework used, patterns of upward mobility are seen to be rooted either in the structural relations shaping capitalist development or a function of specific worker characteristics.

Social networks In the context of informal activity, social networks, including those characterizing kin and neighborhood groups, are identified as an important resource used to organize the production and distribution of informally produced goods and services. While some analyses highlight the unequal relations of power between different family and community members or examine social networks as a resource for expanding and stabilizing production and exchange, others argue that social networks offer a liberating alternative to the presumed rational relations that characterize capitalist relations of production and exchange.

Social reproduction The centrality of different forms of labor–formal employment, household activities, and informal work–to the reproduction of households, communities, and wider social networks is frequently highlighted in the literature. The key concept *social reproduction* identifies the complex institutional and social relations and processes that sustain and reconstitute everyday life.

Social restructuring Processes of industrial restructuring are embedded in complex social and institutional relationships that structure economic change. While there is a wealth of literature on the restructuring of industrial and economic relations, recent attention has included an appreciation of these changes as social phenomena and has highlighted the implications of social and institutional relations for the transformation of communities and society.

Spatial patterns The field of geography has introduced into the study of informal activities the salience of spatial patterns associated with particular industries and trends in capitalist production. This focus assumes special importance in the study of industrial restructuring by highlighting processes of industrial disaggregation and its consequences for the uneven development of local and regional economies.

State practice The significance of state intervention has emerged as a unifying motif among the divergent frameworks used to analyze the informal sector and informal work. Approaches to analyses of state activities differ, however, according to the theoretical orientations of their authors. Policy analysts, for example, tend to emphasize the creative growth potential of the informal sector and to stress the negative impact of government regulation on small business development. Analyses of the structural relations and conditions that shape work in the informal sector, in contrast, generally examine how the state mediates tensions, contradictions, and conflicts in economic development on behalf of dominant class interests, usually with negative consequences for the welfare of informal workers.

Structural adjustment Economic crises plaguing Third World economies have set the stage for basic changes in national policy choices, leading to structural adjustment programs that emphasize the development of export-oriented industries, diminishing state involvement in economic activities, and reductions in state support for social welfare. The salience of informal work has figured prominently in interpreting both the ways household members respond to the challenges posed by processes of structural adjustment and how national governments envision and organize employment generation schemes in the context of tied aid agreements and structural adjustment lending.

Subcontracting Since the late 1970s, research on industrial restructuring has highlighted the expanded role of subcontracting networks in the industrial structure of advanced industrialized economies and newly industrializing economies. An important feature of this trend is the expansion of informal activities in the form of unregulated small-scale, home-based, or sweatshop production of intermediate industrial and labor-intensive consumer goods for large formal enterprises. Subcontracting has been examined from contrasting perspectives in the literature. Sometimes it is hailed for the advantages it offers to restructured corporate entities facing increasingly volatile national and international markets and as a means for sustaining low labor costs and low supply inventories. Other research explores the structural constraints to production faced by subcontracted firms in achieving more autonomous status in the production hierarchy.

Subsidy to capital Early critiques of dual sector economic analyses challenged the notion of informal labor's marginal relationship to capitalist development. Emphasized instead was the role played by informal work in subsidizing capitalist development through the provision of low-cost goods and services to the households whose members were employed by formal firms.

Subsistence production Studies of informal work sometimes explore the activities and relationships associated with ensuring household subsistence. Household subsistence includes forms of income-generating activity that help to ensure household survival but do not provide the means for the accumulation of wealth and entrepreneurial expansion. Critical for understanding these activities is their contradictory relation to capitalist production. While sometimes appearing to be unrelated to the market economy they are often linked through participation in circuits of cash exchange.

Survival strategies Development studies have given considerable attention to the role of household strategies in ensuring family survival against conditions of poverty and exploitation, and feminist analysis has been instrumental in highlighting the central role of women in securing household income and making ends meet. The particular conditions that help to fashion these survival strategies is an important theme in recent research on informal work.

Tax evasion The informal sector literature cites tax evasion as a characteristic feature of informal economic activity. As this literature suggests, lax enforcement and unorthodox accounting strategies not easily detected by standard auditing procedures provide firms with ample opportunity to evade government licensing fees and tax obligations. Frequently cited in this literature is the problem that tax evasion poses for lost state revenues.

Technological change According to conventional economic theory, the ability to develop or use technology is a key factor determining the ability of small enterprises to improve productivity and secure and expand their foothold in competitive markets. Studies of informal enterprises that are identified by the key term technological change highlight the specific conditions that support growth-promoting technological innovations, particularly among small entrepreneurs and firms.

Technological constraints While the use of improved technologies is seen as a key factor in small business growth, constraints to innovation are often highlighted as a key reason for the stagnation of informal firms and their inability to provide more than subsistence-level income for workers. Some analyses highlight the need for government or nongovernmental programs to help overcome these constraints, often based on the need for policy reform. Other studies, highlight the structural conditions that maintain technological stagnation or act as insurmountable obstacles to the expansion of informal firms.

Trade unions Studies undertaken in the 1990s, particularly those in industrialized contexts, have begun to focus greater attention on the role of trade unions, labor conditions, and the need for new forms of social security and protection for informal workers. These studies identify a tension between conventional trade union strategies, which generally exclude informal workers, and the potential power of informal workers either as participants of emergent grass-roots labor movements or as a growing mass of impoverished workers demanding resources from the state.

Un- and underemployment Analyses of the informal sector are frequently framed as an inquiry into problems associated with Third World urban un- and underemployment, where appropriate government support for the sector is hailed as a means to reduce chronic unemployment. More recently, growing job insecurity has been identified as a feature of industrialized economies facing increased global competition. The growth of informal activities is described as one consequence of this trend.

Unequal exchange A frequent theme in class analytic, Marxist and poststructuralist studies of informal activity is the unequal exchange between informal and formal sector firms. Typically emphasized is the advantaged position of formal sector firms characterized by their ready access to credit, markets and advanced technology that enable them to capture most of the profit derived from informal production. The lack of access to state and private resources blocks informal firms from retaining the profit they generate keeping them in a subordinate position in relation to formal sector enterprises.

Unpaid labor An important theme in the literature on informal activities has been a critical exploration of the meaning and use of the concept of work in capitalist society. A significant proportion of these studies focus on the unremunerated tasks performed by individual household members. Now more widely assumed to be essential to the maintenance of households and communities, such tasks include family care, do-it-yourself repairs, volunteer work, or exchanges of assistance offered to neighbors or friends which may involve patterns of obligation and various forms of in-kind or nonmonetary exchange. In some instances, this labor is analyzed primarily for its contribution to paid productive work or to measures of the gross national product. In other cases, unpaid labor directly contributes to production for exchange (as disguised wage labor), but the income earned is paid to others, often male kin.

Urbanization Massive rural-urban migration since the 1960s has shaped the growth of sprawling metropolitan centers in much of the developing world. This pattern has been closely associated with the rapid growth of informal activities as recent migrants find little opportunity for work in formal urban firms. Informal sector research highlights the role that unequal rural-urban resources play in the sector's development. These studies also explore how informal work supports the growth of new urban centers.

Welfare In both advanced industrialized and Third World economies, economic restructuring is associated with a marked decrease in welfare services offered by the state. The informal sector is sometimes seen as a means to help ensure household survival despite these dramatic changes in the social obligations of the state. At the same time, the growth of informal work is seen as a manifestation of the decline in welfare security, as workers are increasingly forced to eke out subsistence from poorly paid, unprotected work with little assurance of government assistance in times of crisis.

Women The framework offered by feminist analysis since the 1970s has emphasized the central role women play in economic development and has highlighted the particular impact of socioeconomic changes on women's lives. Our use of this key term identifies only those citations that assume a focus on women rather than on changing gender relations.

Worker characteristics In addition to the features that distinguish informal firms, the specific characteristics of informal workers are also studied to offer a different interpretation of the social organization of informal activities. Analyses highlight those worker characteristics that define the likelihood of being relegated to informal livelihoods. These characteristics include those which contribute to the ability of some workers to become successful entrepreneurs, as well as those personal attributes that limit others to employment as unprotected laborers in sweatshop or home-based production. Gender, race, ethnicity, and skill base are the attributes of individual workers most often cited.

Annotated Bibliography

ANNOTATED BIBLIOGRAPHY

1. **Abels, Schwartz, Hackel, and Silverblatt, Inc. 1983.** The Chinatown Garment Industry Study. Report to the ILGWU Locals 23-25 and the New York Sportswear Association.

   Pattern or magnitude/ Garment manufacture/ U.S.A.

2. **Acharya, S. 1983a.** The Informal Sector in Developing Countries: A Macro Viewpoint. *Journal of Contemporary Asia* 13: 432-445.

   Acharya defines the informal sector as the working poor who fall outside Government regulations of employment and wages, operate in low-order techno-economic formations, and acquire skills outside formal training systems. Using data from India, he identifies the linkages between informal and formal sector production and marketing to show how the informal sector provides an important source of cheap labor. Acharya also argues that no continuous technological change has occurred to raise productivity among informal workers and that surplus accrues to those in the formal sector. Thus, the informal sector is likely to remain at its low level equilibrium with little prospect for development.

   Pattern or magnitude/ Relation to formal economy/ Small or micro-enterprises/ Unequal exchange/ Technological constraints/ India

3. —— **. 1983b.** Unaccounted Economy in India: A Critical Review of Some Recent Estimates. *Economic and Political Weekly* 18: 2057.

   Pattern or magnitude/ India

4. —— **. 1984.** The Underground Economy in the United States: Comment on Tanzi. *IMF Staff Papers* 31 (4): 742-746.

   Definition/ Pattern or magnitude/ U.S.A.

5. **Adler, H. J., and O. Hawrylyshyn. 1978.** Estimates of the Value of Household Work, Canada 1961 and 1971. *The Review of Income and Wealth* 24: 333-355.

   The authors enumerate household labor costs where housework includes food preparation, cleaning, care of clothing, household repairs and maintenance, marketing and household management, and physical and tutorial child care to show that the imputed monetary value of these activities is 40 percent of the GNP.

Unpaid labor/ Nonmonetary exchange/ Research methods/ Canada

6. **Afshar, H., and M. Maynard, eds. 1994.** *The Dynamics of "Race" and Gender: Some Feminist Interventions*. London: Taylor & Francis.

Early feminist assumptions of the homogeneity of women's experience in the context of patriarchy have been effectively challenged by recent discussions of the interplay of age, class, disability, "race" and sexuality. Twelve essays place analysis of race and gender issues at the center of discussions of social science theory and method, constructions of identity, and experiences of work in different national and occupational contexts. The essays demonstrate the relationship between race and women's position in the labor market, analyzing how race and gender jointly construct a subordinated material position for women in different ethnic groups. They also highlight strategies for resistance.

Gender inequality/ Ethnicity/ Racial inequality/ Labor market segmentation/ Class processes/ Domestic service/ Resistance/ Worker characteristics/ England/ Netherlands/ South Africa

7. **Aftab, K., and E. Rahim. 1986.** The Emergence of a Small-Scale Engineering Sector: The Case of Tubewell Production in the Pakistan Punjab. *Journal of Development Studies* 23: 60-76.

The authors examine the emergence of small producers in tubewell production under conditions dominated by large firms with special government privileges. Though policies did not assign the engineering sector an important development role, its emergence can be explained by a tradition in metal working and skilled artisans in the Punjab; an expanded demand for centrifugal water pumps and slow-speed diesel engines with the Government's focus on agriculture in 1959/60; and the expansion in large-scale government-protected industries. Forming a vertically specialized network of technologically complementary activities, these independent units provide low-quality, low-technology, low-price goods for the market.

State practice/ Small or micro-enterprises/ Rural/ Pakistan

8. **Albrecht, S. L., and P. Goldman. 1985.** Men, Women and Informal Organization in Manufacturing. *Sociological Focus* 18: 279-288.

Production process/ Gender division of labor

9. **Alden, J. 1981.** Holding Two Jobs: An Examination of "Moonlighting". In *Can I Have It in Cash?: A Study of Informal Institutions and Unorthodox Ways of Doing Things*. Ed. S. Henry, pp. 43-57. New York: St. Martin's Press.

Multiple jobs/ Moonlighting/ Britain/ U.S.A.

10. **Alessandrini, S., and B. Dallago, eds. 1987.** *The Unofficial Economy: Consequences and Perspectives in Different Economic Systems*. Aldershot, Hants, U.K.: Gower Publishing.

Included in this monograph are 21 conference papers comparing western and eastern European views of the unofficial economy. In Italy, the availability of estimates of the unofficial economy and its incorporation into official statistics created an interest in developing comparative indices for measuring the contribution of informal work to the GNP. The volume concludes that the shadow economy is the result of the inability of both capitalist and socialist countries to provide sufficient employment to meet current demand. Thus, the underground economy serves to absorb the shock of rising unemployment.

Pattern or magnitude/ Research methods/ Comparative/ Centrally planned economies/ Industrialized economies

11. **Allen, S. 1981.** Invisible Threads. *IDS Bulletin* 12 (3): 41-47.

Allen explores the widespread, though largely invisible labor of female home-based wage workers and argues that these workers comprise an essential part of capitalist production, providing a flexible and cheap form of labor for a wide range of manufacturing industries. The continuance of this form of informal employment cannot be explained by the characteristics of the workers, even though some of these characteristics help to explain the low wages imposed on a fragmented and completely unprotected labor force.

Gender division of labor/ Home-based production/ Worker characteristics/ Relation to capital/ Britain

12. —— . **1989.** Locating Homework in an Analysis of the Ideological and Material Constraints on Women's Paid Work. In *Homework: Historical and Contemporary Perspectives on Paid Labor at Home*. Ed. E. Boris and C. R. Daniels, pp. 272-291. Chicago, Ill.: University of Illinois.

Allen examines homework and the ideological and material constraints which lead to its invisibility. She also illustrates various attempts to organize homeworkers in Britain.

Home-based production/ Gender ideology/ Household division of labor/ Political mobilization/ Household/ Britain

13. **Amin, A. T. M. N. 1981.** Marginalisation vs. Dynamism: A Study of the Informal Sector in Dhaka City. *Bangladesh Development Studies* 9 (4): 77-112.

Amin characterizes the informal sector as a favorable environment for individual entrepreneurs to escape from poverty through ingenuity and hard work. The informal sector includes all unregulated enterprises operating outside the incentive system offered by state institutions. Surveying 437 owners and 353 workers employed in the Dhaka informal sector, he identifies two opposing trends characterizing their work: one toward upward mobility and another toward increasing poverty. Findings confirm that the majority of those engaged in informal work make a substantial or new investment in their enterprises in order to expand production. The author also argues that income earned from informal enterprises compares favorably with both rural and urban wage employment.

Dual sector or economy/ State practice/ Social mobility/ Processes of accumulation/ Differentiation/ Bangladesh

14. —— . **1996a.** The Asian Setting of the Informal Sector's Growth Dynamics. *Regional Development Dialogue* 17 (1): 70-69.

Pattern or magnitude/ Migration/ Comparative/ Asia

15. —— . **1996b.** Two Decades of Informal Sector Studies: Lessons Learned. *Regional Development Dialogue* 17 (1): vi-xxii.

In an editorial introduction to an entire journal issue devoted to lessons learned from informal sector studies, Amin reviews contributions of major streams of thought on development, underdevelopment, and informal work to the analysis of the informal sector. Major policy prescriptions emerging from the research literature are summarized.

Review/ Policy prescriptions/ Third World

16. **Anant, S., S. V. R. Rao, and K. Kapoor. 1986.** *Women at Work in India: A Bibliography*. New Delhi, India; Beverly Hills, Calif.: Sage Publications.

Bibliography/ Women/ India

17. **Andorka, R. 1987.** Time Budgets and Their Uses. *Annual Review of Sociology* 13: 149-164.

Household division of labor/ Unpaid labor/ Research methods

18. **Anheier, H. K. 1992.** Economic Environments and Differentiation: A Comparative Study of Informal Sector Economies in Nigeria. *World Development* 20: 1573-1585.

Anheier examines the relative importance and sources of differentiation in the informal sector in terms of firm characteristics and business behavior. He argues that locational factors are better able to account for differences in firm characteristics and business behavior than are the specific characteristics of an industry.

Differentiation/ Spatial patterns/ Firm characteristics/ Nigeria

19. **Anti-Slavery Society. 1985.** Child Labour in Morocco's Carpet Industry. In *Planning for Small Enterprises in Third World Cities*. Ed. R. Bromley, pp. 171-180. Oxford, U.K.: Pergamon Press.

Field investigations conducted in 1975 and 1977 by the Anti- Slavery Society reveal the widespread employment of children, usually female, for up to 12 hours a day. In Morocco, children's employment has expanded with the increased European demand for carpets. Children work for intermediaries, the "maalema" or supervisor who, like the child laborer, receives wages as a pieceworker. This form of payment and labor control allows factory owners to avoid contact with and responsibility for their workforce. Parents support the employment of their daughters in these arrangements as their wages, however paltry, provide an important supplement to family income.

Subcontracting/ Child labor/ Piecework/ Survival strategies/ Carpet manufacture/ Morocco

20. **Antrobus, P. 1992.** Women and the Informal Sector: Priorities for Socially Sustainable Development. *Development* 3: 54-56.

Women/ Gender division of labor/ Gender ideology/ Policy prescriptions/ Third World

21. **Arias, P., and B. Roberts. 1985.** The City in Permanent Transition: The Consequences of a National System of Industrial Specialization. In *Capital and Labour in the Urbanized World*. Ed. J. Walton, pp. 149-175. Beverly Hills, Calif.: Sage.

Arias and Roberts argue for a heterogeneous view of processes of urbanization and industrialization based on economic specialization and local cultural traditions. They examine the role of gender and Catholic ideologies in shaping home-based work in Guadalajara, Mexico, a commercial center specializing in small and medium size enterprises producing for domestic consumption. The city is characterized by labor mobility in the context of household stability which, the authors argue, reinforces an ideology of female subordination and domesticity and legitimates a particular household division of labor.

Urbanization/ Small or micro-enterprises/ Home-based production/ Subcontracting/ Piecework/ Gender ideology/ Household division of labor/ Mexico

22. **Arizpe, L. 1977.** Women in the Informal Sector: The Case of Mexico City. In *Women and National Development: The Complexities of Change*. Ed. Wellesley Editorial Committee, pp. 27-37. Chicago, Ill.: University of Chicago Press.

Arizpe contrasts the limited participation of women in formal occupations with their concentration in informal work. While Mexican women are under-represented in both the formal and informal economies, they are disproportionately represented in the low-paid service sector which typically includes unpaid work routinely done by housewives for family or friends. Moreover, a highly stratified system characterizes work options for middle-class, working-class, marginal, and recent female rural immigrants where the latter are often limited to work as domestic servants or street vendors. Work patterns are also shaped by age, as older women face both ideological and structural barriers to manufacturing or office work where the employment of young, unmarried women may be common.

Labor market segmentation/ Pattern or magnitude/ Gender division of labor/ Migration/ Domestic service/ Trading/ Female-headed households/ Worker characteristics/ Mexico

23. **Arlacchi, P. 1987.** Effects of the New Anti-Mafia Law on the Proceeds of Crime and on the Italian Economy. In *The Unofficial Economy: Consequences and Perspectives in Different Economic Systems*. Ed. S. Alessandrini and B. Dallago, pp. 247-255. Aldershot, Hants, U.K.; Brookfield, Vt.: Gower Publishing.

Two economic phenomena have emerged in the Italian economy since the early 1970s: the establishment of a vast illegal sector controlled by the Mafia, and an increase in the number of Mafia firms and entrepreneurs in Southern Italy. The crucial element in the expansion of the Mafia's role has been the close relationship between legal and the illegal forms of production where Mafia firms have an advantage over other firms because of their access to financial resources. The "La Torre law" has increased the risk of illegal activities which may force Mafia groups to transfer resources from the illegal to the legal sector.

Illegal activity/ Regulation/ State practice/ Italy

24. **Armstrong, W., and T. G. McGee. 1985.** *Theatres of Accumulation: Studies in Asian and Latin American Urbanization*. London: Methuen.

Armstrong and McGee, drawing on data from Ecuador and parts of Asia, highlight a shift in the process of urbanization with the globalization of production and financial activities since the 1970s. The study examines the extractive relationship exerted by urban institutions and ruling classes on rural hinterlands. They also examine intra-urban relationships between large-scale capitalists, petty capitalist producers and the emerging urban proletariat drawing from case studies of hawkers in Hong Kong and female workers in Free Trade Zones of Malaysia. They argue that national urban systems are a reflection of the incorporation of developing countries into the international economic system where the Third World city is recast from one of peripheral backwater to that of a "theatre of accumulation" and "diffuser" of new patterns of consumption.

Urbanization/ Globalization/ Export processing zones/ Relation to formal economy/ Relation to capital/ Processes of accumulation/ Trading/ Asia/ Latin America/ Ecuador/ Hong Kong/ Malaysia

25. **Aryee, G. A. 1977.** *Small-Scale Manufacturing Activities: A Study of the Interrelationships between the Formal and Informal Sectors in Kumasi, Ghana*. Geneva, Switzerland: International Labour Office.

Dual sector or economy/ Ghana

26. —— **. 1978.** Education and Training and Informal Sector Employment in Kumasi, Ghana. In *Human Resources and African Development*. Ed. U. G. Damachi and V. P. Diejomaoh, pp. 288-317. New York: Praeger.

Aryee reviews manufacturing enterprises in Kumasi to assess the relationship between formal education and other sources of training. The apprenticeship system is examined to show that the informal sector encourages workers to be school leavers.

Dual sector or economy/ Education/ Research methods/ Small or micro-enterprises/ Apprenticeship/ Worker characteristics/ Ghana

27. —— **. 1984.** Some Notes on Intensive Growth and Labour Productivity in Informal Sector Firms in Kumasi: A Case Study. *Regional Development Dialogue* 5 (2): 204-212.

Pattern or magnitude/ Ghana

28. **Assad, R. 1993.** Formal and Informal Institutions in the Labor Market, with Applications to the Construction Sector in Egypt. *World Development* 21: 925-939.

Growing awareness of the ineffectiveness of formal regulation has drawn attention to the role of local social networks, customary norms, and kinship in shaping labor markets. Drawing from theories in new institutional economics, Assad examines formal and informal institutions deployed by Egyptian construction workers. Because of an incompatibility between formal institutions and local conditions, most workers in the industry are hired informally. Informal labor markets are not, however, completely unstructured or governed by principles of pure competition. Information constraints force employers to rely on local networks and social ties to procure and maintain skilled craftspersons. The market for common laborers, by contrast, is much more open and fiercely competititive.

Labor market dynamics/ Social networks/ Artisanal production/ Construction industry/ Egypt

29. **Averitt, R. T. 1968.** *The Dual Economy: The Dynamics of American Industry Structure*. New York; London: W. W. Norton and Company.

An early study of the "dual economy," Averitt divides the U.S. economy into two distinct sectors: the center characterized by the presence of concentrated markets supplied by large firms tending towards vertical integration, geographic dispersion, product diversification, managerial decentralization and increasing expertise at all levels of management; and the periphery characterized by highly competitive markets supplied by small firms with limited financial resources, product lines, geographic dispersion, and centralized management. Though often censured by microeconomists for their oligopolistic tendences, center firms are critical to growth and prosperity in advanced industrial economies because of their leading role in those industries most important to the country's industrial development, their command over resources, and their suitability for accomodating the interests of labor. Given these considerations, argues the author, government policy should be geared to greater support of the economic center than is usually advocated in short-term-oriented microeconomic policy analysis.

Dual sector or economy/ Small or micro-enterprises/ Policy analysis/ U.S.A.

30. **Ayata, S. 1986.** Economic Growth and Petty Commodity Production in Turkey. *Social Analysis* 20 (December): 79-92.

Petty commodity production/ Artisanal production/ Labor processes/ Differentiation/ Relation to capital/ Turkey

31. **Aziz, Q., and Z. Zar, eds. 1992.** *The Urban Informal Sector: Role of Small-Scale Enterprises in the National Economy*. Karachi, Pakistan: Pakistan Media Corp.

Pattern or magnitude/ Policy analysis/ Small or micro- enterprises/ Pakistan/ Third World/ Indonesia

32. **Babb, F. E. 1988.** "From the Field to the Cooking Pot:" Economic Crisis and the Threat to Marketers in Peru. In *Traders Versus the State: Anthropological Approaches to Unofficial Economies*. Ed. G. Clark, pp. 17-40. Boulder: Westview Press.

Trading/ Economic restructuring/ State practice/ Differentiation/ Child labor/ Peru

33. —— **. 1990.** Women's Work: Engendering Economic Anthropology. *Urban Anthropology* 19: 277-302.

Mainstream economic anthropology has lagged behind the wider social sciences in recognizing the role and significance of women's economic activities. Babb proposes a gender-conscious approach to economic anthropology to reconceptualize the role of domestic tasks in economic life, to better understand fundamental changes taking place with changing modes of production, and to address unresolved problems in economic anthropological theory. Neglecting the many informal sector activities performed by women, conventional studies are overly optimistic about the possibilities for upward mobility through informal enterprises. Gender-sensitive studies challenge this view and highlight the role women's informal activities play in the household and regional economy, their restricted range of opportunities for paid work, processes of marked differentiation between successful enterprise owners and poorly paid workers, and the progressive loss of small enterprise autonomy in face of large male controlled commercial interests.

Gender division of labor/ Differentiation/ Research methods/ Peru

34. **Bagachwa, M. S. D., and A. Naho. 1995.** Estimating the Second Economy in Tanzania. *World Development* 23: 1387-1398.

Noting the failure of official national accounts statistics to record informal economic activity in Tanzania, the authors estimate the size of the country's second economy using an econometric method based on a demand for currency equation. Particular attention is paid to the 1986-1990 period of economic change during which the full impact of economic liberalization policies could be accurately gauged. The second economy is found to have grown from less than 10 percent of official GDP during the late 1960s to over 20 percent after 1985 constituting a major source of income for a majority of Tanzanian households. Policy implications of this trend are noted.

Pattern or magnitude/ Policy prescriptions/ Survival strategies/ Economic restructuring/ Tanzania

35. **Bagnasco, A. 1990.** The Informal Economy. *Current Sociology* 38 (2-3): 157-174.

Critical of distinctions between economic and noneconomic aspects of society, Bagnasco highlights their interrelation and the constraints this poses for developing a general theory of the informal economy. Interest in the informal economy emerged with the growing instability of the global economy, new firm production strategies, state deregulation, and important cultural shifts occuring since the 1970s. A key question for Bagnasco concerns the relationship between informal activity and current notions of economic development. New conditions of production and forms of labor relations prompt a rethinking of development as a complex, variable combination of the new and old or differentiated and undifferentiated forms of production. Bagnasco concludes that although a general theory of the informal economy is impossible, work on informality has reinvigorated discussions of a general theory of development.

Globalization/ Relation to capital/ Industrialized economies

36. **Banerjee, B. 1983.** The Role of the Informal Sector in the Migration Process: A Test of Probabilistic Migration Models and Labour Market Segmentation for India. *Oxford Economic Papers* 35: 399-422.

Migration/ Labor market segmentation/ Research methods/ India

37. **Banerjee, N. 1981.** The Weakest Link. *IDS Bulletin* 12 (3): 36-40.

Banerjee argues that the formal/informal sector dichotomy is not based on a classification of economic activities but on differences in labor contracts where modern technology can transfer economic activities to those who provide a source of cheap labor. Moreover, informal workers are among those with little opportunity to gain new skills and with limited political clout to struggle for more remunerative employment. Thus, in a labor-surplus economy where the marketplace responds to those groups who have political visibility, informal workers undermine the strength of the working class movement as a whole, including those currently employed in the formal sector.

Relation to formal economy/ Gender division of labor/ Class processes/ Political mobilization/ India

38. —— **. 1982.** Survival of the Poor. In *Towards a Political Economy of Urbanization in Third World Countries*. Ed. H. Safa, pp. 175-187. Delhi: Oxford University Press.

Banerjee estimates that over 1.2 million or about 40 percent of the labor force of the Calcutta metropolitan area work in the unorganized sector. "Adjustments" made to accommodate these numbers include declining wage rates and generally lower incomes, expanding consumer and employer choice, and the poor's acceptance of a lower quality of life. Viewed synchronically, the unorganized sector has added to the net welfare of society by utilizing available idle and underemployed labor. It is argued, however, that informal sector workers are unable to accumulate human or money capital, work efficiently or learn new skills because of these constraints.

Pattern or magnitude/ Constraints to accumulation/ Under- and unemployment/ India

39. **Barker, G. 1991.** *The Handcraft Revival in Southern Appalachia, 1930-1990*. Knoxville: University of Tennessee Press.

Barker traces the development of handicraft production in the Appalachian region of the southeastern United States, noting the role of local craft organizations, regional guilds, and craft schools in building the industry. An expanding market for handicrafts has encouraged the industry's recent growth with craftspersons becoming increasingly professionalized as individual entrepreneurs. In this context, the significance of craft organizations has declined.

Handicrafts/ Social networks/ Apprenticeship/ Small or micro-enterprises/ Rural/ U.S.A.

40. **Barron, R. D., and G. M. Morris. 1976.** Sexual Divisions and the Dual Labour Market. In *Dependence and Exploitation in Work and Marriage*. Ed. D. L. Barker and S. Allen, pp. 47-67. London: Longman.

Dual sector or economy/ Gender division of labor/ Gender inequality/ Industrialized economies

41. **Barthelemy, P. 1988.** The Macroeconomic Estimates of the Hidden Economy: A Critical Analysis. *Review of Income and Wealth* 34: 183-208.

Pattern or magnitude/ Research methods/ Industrialized economies

42. **Barthelemy, P. et al. 1990.** *Underground Economy and Irregular Forms of Employment (Travail au Noir): Final Synthesis Report of the Program for Research and Actions on the Development of the Labour Market*. Brussels, Belgium: Commission of the European Communities (CECA).

Labor market dynamics/ Pattern or magnitude/ Subcontracting/ Child labor/ Home-based production/ Gender division of labor/ Ethnicity/ Rural/ Policy analysis/ Greece/ France/ Britain/ Italy/ Ireland/ Germany/ Denmark/ Netherlands/ Spain/ Portugal

43. **Basgall, S. 1988.** The Issues of Credit for Women. *Social Development Issues* 12 (1): 21-32.

Women/ Social networks/ Credit/ Rural/ Policy prescriptions/ Third World

44. **Basok, T. 1989.** How Useful Is the "Petty Commodity Production" Approach? Explaining the Survival and Success of Small Salvadorean Urban Enterprises in Costa Rica. *Labour, Capital and Society / Travail, Capital et Societé* 22: 42-64.

Petty commodity production/ Small or micro-enterprises/ Refugees/ Survival strategies/ Costa Rica

45. **Batley, R. 1985.** The Allocation of Public Construction Contracts in Lima and Caracas. In *Planning for Small Enterprises in Third World Cities*. Ed. R. Bromley, pp. 309-318. Oxford, U.K.: Pergamon Press.

Batley questions the feasibility of implementing policies designed to favor or withdraw discrimination against small traders and producers in public sector contracting so as to maximize labor absorption. In his examination of contracting practices in public utility and housing works in Lima and Caracas, he shows that despite formal rules of selection, informal procedures limit the allocation of contracts to a circle of relatively few large firms and notes that one effect of intervention in informal activity would be the elimination of small enterprises and a dramatic decline in employment.

Small or micro-enterprises/ Housing/ State practice/ Trading/ Relation to formal economy/ Social networks/ Peru/ Venezuela

46. **Bawly, D. 1982.** *The Subterranean Economy*. New York: McGraw-Hill.

Definition/ Illegal activity/ State practice/ U.S.A./ Britain/ U.S.S.R./ Latin America/ India/ Europe

47. **Beach, B. A. 1989.** The Family Context of Home Shoe Work. In *Homework: Historical and Contemporary Perspectives on Paid Labor at Home*. Ed. E. Boris, and C. R. Daniels, pp. 130-146. Chicago, Ill.: University of Illinois Press.

Home-based production/ Household division of labor/ Shoe production/ U.S.A.

48. **Bechhofer, F., and B. Elliott. 1981.** Petty Property: The Survival of a Moral Economy. In *The Petite Bourgeoisie: Comparative Studies of the Uneasy Stratum*. Ed. F. Bechhofer and B. Elliott, pp. 182-200. New York: St. Martin's Press.

The authors describe the position of the petite bourgeoisie to argue that they do not represent a class but a dependent stratum characterized chiefly by petty property owners engaging primarily family labor. While hired labor may be utilized and exploited it is more as an extension of rather than a substitute for family labor. Survival of the petite bourgeoisie depends on continuous adaptation, generational reproduction, and the incorporation of new members drawn particularly from among the working class. Politically, petty bourgeois persistence depends on government manipulation and on economic sponsorship from big business, especially those who employ this stratum in the ideological service of capitalism, i.e., to defend a moral economy based on competition. Petty bourgeois discontent is traced to both the growth of monopoly capitalism and organized labor. Protest among this population has helped to bring a number of right wing governments to power.

Class processes/ Political mobilization/ Unpaid labor/ Britain

49. **Beechey, V. 1977.** Some Notes on Female Wage Labour in Capitalist Production. *Capital and Class* 3 (Autumn): 45-66.

Gender division of labor/ Gender ideology/ Class processes/ Labor processes/ Industrialized economies

50. **Bekkers, H., and W. Stoffers. 1995.** Measuring Informal Sector Employment in Pakistan: Testing a New Methodology. *International Labour Review* 134 (1): 17-36.

Research methods/ Pattern or magnitude/ Pakistan

51. **Benería, L. 1989.** Subcontracting and Employment Dynamics in Mexico City. In *The Informal Economy: Studies in Advanced and Less Developed Countries*. Ed. A. Portes, M. Castells and L. A. Benton, pp. 173-188. Baltimore, Md.; London: Johns Hopkins University Press.

This article extracts from the coauthored work of Benería and Roldan to focus on subcontracting as the link between female homeworkers and multinational firms. Subcontracting responds to the labor strategy of lowering costs to take advantage of the existing fragmentation in the labor market, the benefits of lower fixed costs, the transfer of risk, and the avoidance of unionization. Thus, work in the underground economy is characterized by low wages, the absence of fringe benefits, and deteriorating working conditions. The author describes subcontracting linkages as a pyramidical hierarchy of firms where those at the apex enjoy monopsonistic powers which allow them greater flexibility than the smaller firms which are dependent on them.

Subcontracting/ Industrial restructuring/ Home-based production/ Women/ Mexico

52. **Benería, L., and M. Roldán. 1987.** *The Crossroads of Class and Gender: Industrial Homework, Subcontracting, and Household Dynamics in Mexico City*. Chicago, Ill.: University of Chicago Press.

Drawing from detailed statistical, survey, and interview data gathered in Mexico City in the early 1980s, Benería and Roldán explore the growing concentration of women in informal economic activities. Focusing on industrial homework which represents a growing share of export-oriented manufacturing in Mexico City, the authors identify connections between processes of capital accumulation, national and international divisions of labor, and the subordination of women. The research findings challenge the divisions frequently drawn in conventional socioeconomic literature between ideology and economic reality, the privacy of the household and public spheres of production, and the informal and formal sectors of the economy.

Home-based production/ Subcontracting/ Survival strategies/ Household division of labor/ Globalization/ Export production/ Gender relations/ Household/ Mexico

53. **Bennholdt-Thomsen, V. 1984.** Towards a Theory of the Sexual Division of Labor. In *Households and the World Economy*. Ed. J. Smith, I. Wallerstein and H. Evers, pp. 252-271. Beverly Hills, Calif.: Sage Publications.

This paper contributes to the development of a theory of the sexual division of labor by refuting the essentialist argument that women's occupations are predetermined by their role as mothers. Bennholdt-Thomsen examines the connection between gender inequality and occupational difference to show that advanced industrial capitalism is constituted by women's structural separation from each other and by their marginalization from male society. In this context, women are not defined primarily as bearers of labor, but as a "natural resource" for biological and social reproduction where women's capacity for reproduction forms the basis for all capitalist relations of production.

Gender inequality/ Gender division of labor/ Unpaid labor/ Relation to capital

54. **Benson, S. P. 1989.** Women, Work, and the Family: Industrial Homework in Rhode Island in 1934. In *Homework: Historical and Contemporary Perspectives on Paid Labor at Home*. Ed. E. Boris and C. R. Daniels, pp. 53-74. Chicago, Ill.: University of Illinois Press.

Home-based production/ Household division of labor/ U.S.A.

55. **Bental, B., U. Ben-zion, and A. Wenig. 1985.** Macroeconomic Policy and the Shadow Economy. In *The Economics of the Shadow Economy: Proceedings of the International Conference on the Economics of the Shadow Economy*. Ed. W. Gaertner and A. Wenig, pp. 179-193. Berlin, F.R.G.: Springer-Verlag.

While previous studies of the underground economy have almost exclusively focused on conceptual questions and empirical research, this paper offers a theoretical analysis of an economy with a shadow sector. Within the framework of a two-sector general equilibrium model, the authors discuss the impact of government expenditure and unemployment compensation on employment in each sector, on real wages, and on relative commodity prices. A welfare analysis of different policy options is also offered.

Policy analysis/ Dual sector or economy/ Welfare

56. **Benton, L. A. 1988.** Decentralized Industry and the Limits to State Planning: National Pacts and Local Alliances in Spain. *Urban Anthropology* 17: 279-298.

Industrial restructuring/ Pattern or magnitude/ State practice/ Social networks/ Spain

57. **——. 1989a.** Homework and Industrial Development: Gender Roles and Restructuring in the Spanish Shoe Industry. *World Development* 17: 255-266.

Examining women's changing roles in the Spanish shoe industry, Benton shows how women's work has shaped the decentralization of global production. She also argues that contrary to the assumption that low pay and poor working conditions are beneficial to capital, Benton argues that, in the long run, these conditions damage international competitiveness and industrial development.

Subcontracting/ Economic restructuring/ Home-based production/ Gender division of labor/ Gender ideology/ Decentralization/ Shoe production/ Spain

58. —— . **1989b.** Industrial Subcontracting and the Informal Sector: The Politics of Restructuring in the Madrid Electronics Industry. In *The Informal Economy: Studies in Advanced and Less Developed Countries*. Ed. A. Portes, M. Castells and L. A. Benton, pp. 228-246. Baltimore, Md.; London: Johns Hopkins University Press.

Benton examines two contrasting views of subcontracting: one, as a mechanism for siphoning cheap, unprotected labor into modern production processes; and the other, as a mode of decentralization which allows workers a more active role in reorganizing production and devising new technologies. These views are not contradictory but vary according to three factors: the timing of such trends in relation to world economic shifts, the location of a country in the world economy, and the nature of internal political alliances. These factors are analyzed in the restructuring of the Madrid electronics industry where political alliances have limited the ability of industrial outworkers to overcome their dependence on established producers.

Subcontracting/ Decentralization/ Electronics manufacture/ State practice/ Spain

59. —— . **1990.** *Invisible Factories: The Informal Economy and Industrial Development in Spain*. Albany, N.Y.: State University of New York.

Benton examines the divergent roles played by different informal sector industries by comparing shoe manufacturing in rural Alicante and electronics production in Madrid to reveal the marked differences in the position of informal workers. Predominantly female workers in home-based shoe production are highly dependent on producers manufacturing for one or two large firms which control design and product specifications. By contrast, informal small electronics enteprises are linked to an array of other enterprises which provide workers with greater control over both product design and the ability to anticipate consumer trends. Thus, the benefits of decentralization are limited to the electronics industry since shoe manufacture contributes little to long-term industrial vigor and worker welfare. Factors that shape these divergent industrial paths include the dynamic of extant gender relations, local social networks, and tensions between central government control, local government autonomy and institutional support necessary for business innovation. As Benton concludes, while the informal sector harbors some potential as an alternative to mass production, its potential for industrial dynamism depends on the convergence of various social and political conditions.

Home-based production/ Labor market segmentation/ Economic restructuring/ Gender division of labor/ State practice/ Social networks/ Labor movements/ Decentralization/ Shoe production/ Electronics manufacture/ Spain

60. **Berger, S. 1981.** The Uses of the Traditional Sector in Italy: Why Declining Classes Survive. In *The Petite Bourgeoisie: Comparative Studies of the Uneasy Stratum*. Ed. F. Bechhofer and B. Elliott, pp. 71-89. New York: St. Martin's Press.

Berger explores the survival and reproduction of Italian small independent manufacturers and retailers which represent 90 percent of all Italian industries. Berger argues that the preponderance of traditional firms is functional to the modern sector especially when product demand is variable or when labor intensity makes subcontracting an attractive alternative. Industrial decentralization is seen as a response to increased labor costs and the expansion of union activity in large factories. Berger also argues that because the traditional sector is the principal employer of labor as well as the largest electorate it has the support of all political parties.

Class processes/ Dual sector or economy/ Small or micro-enterprises/ Subcontracting/ Decentralization/ Italy

61. **Berger, S., and M. J. Piore. 1980.** *Dualism and Discontinuity in Industrial Societies*. Cambridge, U.K.: Cambridge University Press.

Dual sector or economy/ Labor market dynamics/ Economic restructuring/ Definition/ Class processes/ Industrialized economies/ France/ Italy

62. **Berik, G. 1989.** *Born Factories: Women's Labor in Carpet Workshops in Rural Turkey*. Working Papers on Women in International Development, no. 177. East Lansing, Mich.: Michigan State University.

Berik explores the interlinkage between women's position within the home and their position in the organization of paid work through an examination of female employment in Turkish carpet workshops. Work organization in the carpet workshops is based on kinship relations that recreate household-based relations of subordination according to age and gender. While relations of control and domination by men are reinforced at work, women actively participate in these processes for both negative and positive reasons: ideology, threat of physical force, as well as perceived advantages that promise improvements in the conditions of their lives.

Gender relations/ Gender division of labor/ Gender ideology/ Disguised wage labor/ Home-based production/ Consciousness/ Piecework/ Carpet manufacture/ Turkey

63. **Berik, G., and N. Çagatay. 1992.** Industrialisation Strategies and Gender Composition of Manufacturing Employment in Turkey. In *Women's Work in the World Economy*. Ed N. Folbre, B. Bergmann, B. Agarwal, and M. Floro, pp. 41-60. New York: New York University Press.

In recent decades the view that the growing export orientation of developing economies is leading to a feminization of the labor force in low-paid, tedious, and often hazardous sectors of manufacturing industry has gained particular currency. Berik and Çagatay challenge this view in their study of Turkish manufacturing industries during the country's transition from import-substituting to export-oriented industrialization. Available data indicate that women's share of manufacturing employment remained relatively constant in Turkey despite the shift from ISI to export led industrialization. Employment indicators reveal that women's concentration in particular subsectors of manufacturing is determined more by industry characteristics (i.e., labor intensity, degree of export orientation) than by the change from one industrialization strategy to another. The authors conclude that the "widely accepted characteristics of women's manufacturing employment under export-led industrialization are not peculiar to this strategy but are more general features of women's employment in the industrialisation process."

Economic restructuring/ Labor market segmentation/ Export production/ Gender division of labor/ Women/ Turkey

64. **Berkes, F., D. Feeny, B. J. McCay, and J. M. Acheson. 1989.** The Benefits of the Commons. *Nature* 340: 91-93.

Nonmonetary exchange/ Rural/ Survival strategies

65. **Bernstein, H. 1986.** Capitalism and Petty Commodity Production. *Social Analysis* 20 (December): 11-28.

Critical review of arguments by Friedmann (1980) and Gibbon and Neocosmos (1985).

Review/ Petty commodity production/ Differentiation/ Class processes

66. ——. **1988.** Capitalism and Petty-Bourgeois Production: Class Relations and Divisions of Labour. *Journal of Peasant Studies* 15: 258-271.

Review/ Petty commodity production/ Class processes

67. **Bertaux, D., and I. Bertaux-Wiame. 1981.** Artisanal Bakery in France: How It Lives and Why It Survives. In *The Petite Bourgeoisie: Comparative Studies of the Uneasy Stratum*. Ed. F. Bechhofer and B. Elliott, pp. 155-181. New York: St. Martin's Press.

The authors investigate the persistence of small, "pre-capitalist" family production focusing on the more than 50,000 French bakeries to argue that the continuity of small-scale bread production is the result of a continual struggle by artisanal producers against attempts by large financial groups and flour mill owners to take over the huge bread market. As the authors suggest, this competition was won because of the support of baker's wives, as shopkeepers, and the stream of apprentices from poor, peasant backgrounds who aspire to become self-employed bakers as a means to social mobility. Data were drawn from life histories of approximately 180 bakers and 200 apprentices.

Unpaid labor/ Apprenticeship/ Artisanal production/ Household division of labor/ Social mobility/ Resistance/ France

68. **Berthomeiu, C., and A. Hanaut. 1980.** Can International Subcontracting Promote Industrialisation? *International Labour Review* 119: 335-349.

Subcontracting/ Economic restructuring/ Third World

69. **Bettio, F. 1988.** Sex-Typing of Occupations, the Cycle and Restructuring in Italy. In *Women and Recession*. Ed. J. Rubery, pp. 74-99. London: Routledge & Kegan Paul.

Bettio challenges human capital theory and the view of women as a flexible labor reserve vulnerable to cyclical job loss. The analysis tests the comparative vulnerability of female versus male employment, explores the pattern of sex-typing in the labor hierarchy, and discusses the role of the informal sector in comparative patterns of job instability for men and women. Cyclical vulnerability has not been the dominant characteristic of female employment in Italy. Instead, the business cycle has catalyzed restructuring of the Italian economy and led to the substitution of female labor for dwindling supplies of formal male labor and to expanding informal employment for both men and women. As female employment has grown, sex-typing and the concentration of women in the bottom rungs of the Italian labor hierarchy remains an aspect of both formal and informal work.

Labor market segmentation/ Industrial restructuring/ Gender inequality/ Gender relations/ Italy

70. **Bhatt, E. 1989.** *Grind of Work*. Ahmedabad, India: Self-Employed Women's Association.

Project assistance/ Trade unions/ Political mobilization/ Empowerment/ Home-based production/ Policy prescriptions/ Rural/ India

71. **Bicanic, I. 1987.** The Inequality Impact of the Unofficial Economy in Yugoslavia. In *The Unofficial Economy: Consequences and Perspectives in Different Economic Systems*. Ed. S. Alessandrini and B. Dallago, pp. 323-336. Aldershot, Hants, U.K.; Brookfield, Vt.: Gower Publishing.

Bicanic examines the impact of the unofficial economy on the unequal distribution of income and wealth in Yugoslavia caused by the organization of the economic system, the business cycle, and short-term economic policy. The author concludes that unofficial activities increase inequality while other activities, including moonlighting, decrease it.

Pattern or magnitude/ Illegal activity/ Moonlighting/ State practice/ Polarization/ Yugoslavia

72. **Bienefeld, M. 1975.** The Informal Sector and Peripheral Capitalism: The Case of Tanzania. *IDS Bulletin* 6 (3): 53-73.

According to Bienefeld, for the concept of the informal sector to attain analytic value it must represent a part of the economy with its own dynamic of development since this definitional problem bears on the question of accumulation and on the possibilities of developing the forces of production. Using survey data from Dar es Salaam, he describes how the urban poor are crowded into activities that share a limited ability to accumulate, a dependence on the modern sector, and linkages to the international capitalist system. These limitations highlight the unequal exchange that drains the informal sector of its surplus and benefits the modern sector.

Pattern or magnitude/ Unequal exchange/ Constraints to accumulation/ Tanzania

73. —— . **1979.** Urban Employment: A Historical Perspective. In *Casual Work and Poverty in Third World Cities*. Ed. R. Bromley and C. Gerry, pp. 27-44. New York: John Wiley & Sons.

Review/ Labor market dynamics/ Third World

74. ——. **1981.** The Informal Sector and Women's Oppression. *IDS Bulletin* 12 (3): 8-13.

The similarities and differences between the debate on the informal sector and that on women in development are examined as both debates concern groups subject to social and political discrimination. Bienefeld then examines the prospects for full employment which he uses to justify a move away from capitalism and a focus on the significance of small-scale production in processes of development. The author also argues that because gender oppression is superimposed on women's unequal access to the labor market, gender inequality is unlikely to be altered with full employment. Bienefeld therefore argues that for women to have their interests served, they should join efforts which address the problems of the informal sector.

Gender inequality/ Small or micro-enterprises/ Third World

75. **Bienefeld, M., and M. Godfrey. 1975.** Measuring Unemployment and the Informal Sector: Some Conceptual and Statistical Problems. *IDS Bulletin* 7 (3): 4-10.

The authors suggest that the concept of the informal sector has emerged from discussions of "unutilized labor power," which was shaped by analyses of growth, welfare, and political instability. The Lewis model of the 1950s, for example, focused on rural surplus labor and its transfer to capitalist production. By the 1960s, attention turned to questions of migration and urban unemployment. Conceptual difficulties and problems of measurement were broken by the debate on the informal sector in the 1970s. The authors argue, however, that the concept is still loosely defined, includes a wide variety of activities, and can only be statistically useful through disaggregation. Also necessary is a change in government policy to account for processes of accumulation and technical change in the sector and to enable understanding welfare dynamics at the household level.

Definition/ Review/ Research methods/ Policy prescriptions

76. **Bigsten, A., and S. Kayizzi-Mugerwa. 1992.** Adaptation and Distress in the Urban Economy: A Study of Kampala Households. *World Development* 20: 1423-1441.

Economic restructuring/ Survival strategies/ Structural adjustment/ Uganda

77. **Binford, L., and S. Cook. 1991.** Petty Production in Third World Capitalism Today. In *Marxist Approaches in Economic Anthropology*. Ed. A. Littlefield and H. Gates, pp. 65-90. Lanham, Md.: University Press of America.

Highlighting definitional and conceptual problems in discussions of petty commodity production, the authors propose a generic concept of PCP theorized as a form of production. Its four defining elements are: 1) exclusive production for market exchange; 2) ownership of means of production by the direct producer and the use of non-waged labor; 3) mutual independence of production units; and 4) a dominant though not exclusive dynamic of simple reproduction. The authors examine forms (peasant, peasant-artisan, and urban informal sector production) in which PCP is manifest and challenge dual economy approaches that fail to recognize both the unity of the commodity economy and the multiplicity of forms, relations and processes that may be associated with it. Real possibilities for capital accumulation and profit exist within petty commodity production, but realization is constrained by the objective positions which petty producers occupy within capitalist economies.

Review/ Petty commodity production/ Definition/ Artisanal production/ Critique of dualism/ Rural

78. **Birkbeck, C. 1978.** Self-Employed Proletarians in an Informal Factory: The Case of Cali's Garbage Dump. *World Development* 6: 1173-1185.

Through a study of garbage pickers in Cali, Birkbeck explores the hidden relations between the self-employed and the market to show how labor relations and organizational and market control of inputs and products shape processes of proletarianization. Despite some degree of entrepreneurship and innovation, garbage collectors are regulated by the market. This leads Birkbeck to conclude that these workers engage in a "refuge" occupation.

Labor processes/ Survival strategies/ Scavenging/ Class processes/ Colombia

79. —— . **1979.** Garbage, Industry, and the "Vultures" of Cali, Colombia. In *Casual Work and Poverty in Third World Cities*. Ed. R. Bromley and C. Gerry, pp. 161-184. New York: John Wiley & Sons.

Pattern or magnitude/ Relation to formal economy/ Scavenging/ Colombia

80. **Bisset, L., and U. Huws. n.d.** *Sweated Labour: Homeworking in Britain Today*. London: Low Pay Unit.

Over recent decades homeworking in industrialized economies has involved computer programming, drafting and other forms of skilled labor, as well as the more traditional, low-skill labor such as garment manufacture, knitting, and toy assembly. The authors summarize the survey findings on both new and old types of homeworking in Britain, reviewing their incidence, government and trade union policy, and the experience of producers. Interviews with 130 individuals indicate that relative to formal employment and regardless of skill level, homeworkers continue to suffer from low pay, poor terms of employment, isolation, and limited employment protection.

Home-based production/ Subcontracting/ Economic restructuring/ Worker characteristics/ Trade unions/ Policy analysis/ Britain

81. **Blades, D. 1985.** Crime: What Should Be Recorded in the National Accounts, and What Difference Would It Make? In *The Economics of the Shadow Economy*. Ed. W. Gaertner and A. Wenig, pp. 45-58. Berlin, F.R.G.; New York: Springer-Verlag.

Blades argues that national accounts bias the view of economic development because they omit the shadow economy, including both illegal activities and those legal activities carried out clandestinely in order to evade taxes. Blades suggests that illegal activities would have added, at most, only about 2.5 percent to the GDP of the United States in 1975. Since illegal activities are probably less important in other industrialized countries, the illegal part of the shadow economy is likely to be trivial.

Illegal activity/ Pattern or magnitude/ Tax evasion/ U.S.A.

82. **Blanes Jimenez, J. 1989.** Cocaine, Informality, and the Urban Economy in La Paz, Bolivia. In *The Informal Economy: Studies in Advanced and Less Developed Countries*. Ed. A. Portes, M. Castells and L. A. Benton, pp. 135-149. Baltimore, Md.; London: Johns Hopkins University Press.

The shift from the "tin connection" to the "drug connection" in Bolivia brought in its wake the expansion of informality, especially of urban underground subsistence activities. Blanes suggests that the relationship between drug traffic, clandestine economic transactions and a vulnerable formal sector depend more on the logic of clandestinity than on the dynamics of the formal sector. He focuses on cocaine production used as a family survival strategy to highlight unprecedented levels of unemployment.

Illegal activity/ Survival strategies/ Rural/ State practice/ Bolivia

83. **Blau, D. M. 1986.** Self-Employment, Earnings and Mobility in Peninsular Malaysia. *World Development* 14: 839-852.

Self-employment/ Migration/ Social mobility/ Malaysia

84. **Blim, M. L. 1990.** *Small-Scale Industrialization and Its Consequences.* New York: Praeger.

Small or micro-enterprises/ Policy analysis

85. —— **. 1992.** Small-Scale Industrialization in a Rapidly Changing World Market. In *Anthropology and the Global Factory: Studies of the New Industrialization in the Late Twentieth Century*. Ed. F. A. Rothstein and M. L. Blim, pp. 85-101. New York: Bergin and Garvey.

Globalization/ Small or micro-enterprises/ Social networks/ Italy

86. **Blincow, M. 1986.** Scavengers and Recycling: A Neglected Domain of Production. *Labour, Capital and Society / Travail, Capital et Societé* 19 (1): 94-116.
Special Issue: Rethinking Petty Commodity Production.

Blincow critically reviews the tendency to view scavengers and other petty commodity producers as forms of disguised or open wage labor rather than to recognize these as "transitional" forms of labor in early and later phases of capitalist development. PCP appears to be an ongoing form of production in and of itself rather than an indicator of disguised proletarianization.

Petty commodity production/ Scavenging/ Recycling/ Disguised wage labor

87. **Block, F., and L. Hirschorn. 1979.** New Productive Forces and the Contradictions of Contemporary Capitalism: A Postindustrial Perspective. *Theory and Society* 5: 363-396.

Economic restructuring/ Class processes/ Industrialized economies

88. **Boeschoten, W. D., and M. M. G. Fase. 1984.** *The Volume of Payments and the Informal Economy in the Netherlands, 1965-1982: An Attempt at Quantification.* Dordrecht, Netherlands: Martinus Nijhoff Publishers.

This study estimates the size of the informal economy in the Netherlands. It excludes bartering activities or other non-monetary exchanges as well as illegal or underground activities already included in the Central Bureau of Statistics.

Pattern or magnitude/ Netherlands

89. **Boissevain, J. 1974.** *Friends of Friends: Networks, Manipulators and Coalitions.* Oxford, U.K.: Basil Blackwell.

Boissevain challenges the structural-functional position in social science that gives primacy to norms and morally sanctioned social exchange in the shaping of social life. Proposed instead is a view of people as entrepreneurs who are born into sets of social relations and normative values but who actively manipulate these resources for their own benefit. The author examines networks of relatives, friends, and associates who are usually dismissed as informal or insignificant personal exchanges by social scientists to illustrate how they structure and constrain behavior. Using the personal histories of Maltese informants, Boissevain highlights the reciprocal influence exerted by biological, physical, cultural, and social factors on these networks and examines how they are manipulated for specific ends by individual actors.

Social networks/ Nonmonetary exchange/ Political mobilization/ Malta

90. **Boissevain, J., and J. C. Mitchell, eds. 1973.** *Network Analysis: Studies in Human Interaction.* The Hague, Netherlands: Mouton.

Social networks/ Research methods

91. **Boomgard, J. J., S. P. Davies, S. J. Haggblade, and D. C. Mead. 1992.** A Subsector Approach to Small Enterprise Promotion and Research. *World Development* 20: 199-212.

The authors propose a "subsector" approach to micro- and small scale enterprise (MSE) assistance that focuses on the forces determining firm competitiveness within specific product groups. Particular attention is paid to understanding the dynamics of vertical relationships between firms of different size based on case studies of sorghum beer production in Botswana and the rattan furniture industry in Indonesia. Though the subsector approach is shown to be effective in illuminating possibilities for genuinely supportive policy and project assistance, its applicability for commerce, transportation and finance activities that cut across vertical production-distribution systems is also noted.

Small or micro-enterprises/ Subcontracting/ Policy analysis/ Project assistance/ Botswana/ Indonesia

92. **Boothe, T., and A. T. Bryan. 1992.** *The Informal Sector in the Caribbean: A Comparative Study of Barbados and Jamaica*. Informal Sector Discussion Paper, no. 4. Washington, D.C.: U.S. Department of Labor, Bureau of International Labor Affairs.

Policy analysis/ State practice/ Comparative/ Barbados/ Jamaica

93. **Boris, E. 1989a.** Black Women and Paid Labor in the Home: Industrial Homework in Chicago in the 1920s. In *Homework: Historical and Contemporary Perspectives on Paid Labor at Home*. Ed. E. Boris and C. R. Daniels, pp. 33-52. Urbana, Ill.: University of Illinois Press.

Home-based production/ Women/ Racial inequality/ U.S.A.

94. —— . **1989b.** Homework and Women's Rights: The Case of the Vermont Knitters, 1980-85. In *Homework: Historical and Contemporary Perspectives on Paid Labor at Home*. Ed. E. Boris and C. R. Daniels, pp. 233-257. Urbana, Ill.: University of Illinois Press.

Home-based production/ Unpaid labor/ Household division of labor/ Survival strategies/ Self-employment/ State practice/ U.S.A.

95. **Bose, A. 1974.** *The Informal Sector in the Calcutta Metropolitan Economy*. Geneva, Switzerland: International Labour Office.

Definition/ Pattern or magnitude/ India

96. **Boulding, E. 1983.** Measures of Women's Work in the Third World: Problems and Suggestions. In *Women and Poverty in the Third World*. Ed. M. Buviníc, M. A. Lycette, and W. P. McGreevey, Baltimore, Md.: Johns Hopkins University Press.

Current methods for collecting statistics on women in development planning typically lead to a serious underestimation of women's work. Following a critical review of conventional approaches in the gathering and reporting of socioeconomic statistics, Boulding proposes a change in existing data categories in line with a basic needs approach to development measures. By emphasizing the importance of the household to meeting basic needs, this approach recognizes the inclusion of unpaid household and community work as development indicators and contributes to an important change in the focus of development work.

Women/ Unpaid labor/ Research methods/ Volunteer work

97. **Brand, V. 1986.** One Dollar Workplaces: A Study of Informal Sector Activities in Magaba, Harare. *Journal of Social Development in Africa* 1 (2): 53-74.

Pattern or magnitude/ Policy prescriptions/ Zimbabwe

98. **Brass, T. 1986.** The Elementary Structures of Kinship: Unfree Relations and the Production of Commodities. *Social Analysis* 20 (December): 56-68.

Petty commodity production/ Class processes/ Social networks/ Rural/ State practice/ Peru

99. **Breman, J. 1996.** *Footloose Labour: Working in India's Informal Sector*. Cambridge, U.K.: Cambridge University Press.

Following in the tradition of his earlier work, which provides a critical reading of the meaning and place of informal work within national economies, Breman explores the dispossessed in south Gujarat to draw attention to the increased mobility and migration of workers in recent years. Between the early 1960s and the late 1980s, according to Breman, there has been a reduction in agricultural employment and a shift from agricultural to nonagricultural casual workers, an increased casualization of agricultural labor, an increase in labor mobility, and the rise of women in low paid, unskilled nonagricultural employment. As well, there is an increase in forms of seasonal, daily, and semi- or permanent migration and the increasing replacement of local workers by migrants. Migration, moreover, is not only from rural to urban centers, but also characterizes rural employment structures. Breman also examines the important institutional mechanisms which facilitate processes of informalization and declining labor security by highlighting the segmentation of the Indian labor market. Identifying both state efforts at regulation and proletariat reactions to these initiatives in the context of the reorganization of the economy, makes this contribution among the most theoretically sophisticated and empirically rich contemporary texts on Indian labor.

Self-employment/ Migration/ Flexibilization/ Social restructuring/ Labor processes/ State practice/ Class processes/ Spatial patterns/ Political mobilization/ India

100. **Breman, J. C. 1977a.** Labour Relations in the "Formal" and "Informal" Sectors: Report of a Case Study in South Gujarat, India, Part I. *Journal of Peasant Studies* 4: 171-205.

Definition/ Pattern or magnitude/ Critique of dualism/ India

101. —— . **1977b.** Labour Relations in the "Formal" and "Informal" Sectors: Report of a Case Study in South Gujarat, India, Part II. *Journal of Peasant Studies* 4: 337-359.

Definition/ Pattern or magnitude/ Critique of dualism/ India

102. —— . **1985.** A Dualistic Labour System? A Critique of the "Informal Sector" Concept. In *Planning for Small Enterprises in Third World Cities*. Ed. R. Bromley, pp. 43-54. Oxford, U.K.: Pergamon Press. Originally published in *Economic and Political Weekly* 11 (48): 1870-1876, 11 (49): 1905-1908, 11 (50): 1939-1944.

Breman argues that attempts to demarcate the informal sector as a separate economic compartment and/or labor situation gives rise to numerous inconsistencies and difficulties as indicated by the social background, size and composition of the informal workforce in Gujarat, India. Fluctuating and discontinuous employment and the gradual transition from employment to unemployment make the informal-formal sector dichotomy problematic, whether it is seen as a buffer zone or one of structural inequality since this ignores the unity and totality of the productive system. Instead, Breman favors distinguishing between an internationally linked capitalist sector and one consisting of pre- or noncapitalist modes of production. Rather than dividing the urban system into two segments, the author argues that the concept of labor market fragmentation is more appropriate.

Review/ Critique of dualism/ Under- and unemployment/ Third World/ India

103. **Brezinski, H. 1985.** The Second Economy in the Soviet Union and Its Implications for Economic Policy. In *The Economics of the Shadow Economy*. Ed. W. Gaertner and A. Wenig, pp. 362-376. Berlin, F.R.G.: Springer-Verlag.

This article surveys the activities and determinants of the second economy in the Soviet Union. The impact of the second economy is analyzed with respect to the supply of consumer goods, the input of labor, the function of centralized planning, and the distribution of income. The second economy has a positive impact on the economy as it increases consumer goods, improves plan coordination and makes the official planning mechanism more flexible. On the other hand, it loosens planners' control, increases the role of money, and weakens socialist ethics. Brezinski concludes that, on balance, the second economy stabilizes the economy, benefits Soviet leadership, and thus leads to a certain tolerance for these activities.

Pattern or magnitude/ State practice/ U.S.S.R.

104. **Brodie, J. 1994.** Shifting the Boundaries: Gender and the Politics of Restructuring. In *The Strategic Silence: Gender and Economic Policy*. Ed. I. Bakker, pp. 46-60. London: Zed Books.

Recent feminist analyses of economic restructuring in both developed and developing countries have acknowledged the differential impact of structural adjustment policies on different genders, ethnic groups, and classes. Brodie argues, however, that simply replacing a "phallocentric" discourse and policy approach with gender-sensitive theory and research is insufficient to reverse the negative impact of restructuring on women's lives. Processes of restructuring extend beyond the economy to involve redrawing boundaries between international and national, the state and the economy, and public and private spheres of social life. From this perspective, unequal gender outcomes are not incidental results of restructuring but integral to its unfolding dynamic. Similarly, the state is not external to but centrally involved in constituting and reconstituting gender relations.

Economic restructuring/ Gender ideology/ Gender relations/ State practice/ Relation to capital/ Structural adjustment

105. **Broesterhuizen, G. A. A. M. 1985.** The Unobserved Economy and the National Accounts in the Netherlands: A Sensitivity Analysis. In *The Economics of the Shadow Economy*. Ed. W. Gaertner and A. Wenig, pp. 105-126. Berlin, F.R.G.: Springer-Verlag.

Pattern or magnitude/ Illegal activity/ Netherlands

106. **Bromley, R. 1978a.** Introduction--The Urban Informal Sector: Why Is It Worth Discussing? *World Development* 6: 1033-1039.

Bromley reviews the origin, diffusion, and deficiencies of dichotomizing formal and informal economic activities identifying nine major constraints to its use. These include the crude two sector categorization; the absence of adequate guidelines to classify activities; the assumed separateness and independence of the sectors; the belief in a uniform policy prescription for the informal sector; the use of the term as exclusively urban; the lack of clarity as to what other sectors exist; the view of the sector as having a present but no future; the tendency to confuse neighborhoods, households, people, and activities with enterprises; and the tendency to equate "the urban informal sector" with "the urban poor." Despite its many shortcomings, the concept has enjoyed wide dissemination and popularity which is a result, in part, of the "apparently feasible and politically safe" policy recommendations which international advisers, organizations, and Third World governments have adopted in its name.

Review/ Critique of dualism/ Policy analysis/ Third World

107. —— . **1978b.** The Locational Behaviour of Colombian Urban Street Traders: Observations and Hypotheses. In *The Role of Geographical Research in Latin American Research: Proceedings of the First International Congress of Latin Americanist Geographers*. Ed. W. M. Deneran, pp. 41-52. Paipa, Colombia, 8-12 August 1977. Muncie, Ind.: Conference of Latin American Geographers.

Self-employment/ Trading/ Spatial patterns/ Colombia

108. —— . **1978c.** Organization, Regulation and Exploitation in the So-called "Urban Informal Sector": The Street Traders of Cali, Colombia. *World Development* 6: 1161-1171.

Bromley contends that the ILO definition of the informal sector as enterprising, productive and unorganized is false since it implies a set of policy responses, including making available credit and technical training, to assist in incorporating these enterprises into the formal economy. Bromley finds that although street traders represent independent small entrepreneurs tied to a complex network of suppliers, moneylenders, government authorities, and customers, they are little more than "disenfranchised employees" or disguised wage earners of larger enterprises.

Definition/ Pattern or magnitude/ Self-employment/ Trading/ Disguised wage labor/ Colombia

109. —— . **1982.** Working in the Streets: Survival Strategy, Necessity or Unavoidable Evil? In *Urbanization in Contemporary Latin America: Critical Approaches to the Analysis of Urban Issues*. Ed. A. Gilbert, pp. 59-77. New York: John Wiley & Sons.

Survival strategies/ Trading/ Colombia

110. —— . **1985.** Small May Be Beautiful, But It Takes More Than Beauty to Ensure Success. In *Planning for Small Enterprises in Third World Cities*. Ed. R. Bromley, pp. 321-341. Oxford, U.K.: Pergamon Press.

Bromley reconsiders debates about small enterprises to provide recommendations for policy as well as pointers towards new lines of investigation and analysis. He argues that changes in the world economy and individual states during the last century have been accompanied by the remarkable persistence and constant readjustment of small enterprises. In Western Europe and North America, the resurgence of right-wing romanticism about small enterprises is a ploy to reinforce the importance of the private sector and state capitalism. In the Third World this attitude is replaced with corporate rapacity and government repression of informal sector business. Three broad policy alternatives are suggested to incorporate small enterprises into official decision-making: repression, tolerance, or promotion. Bromley advocates for the latter two alternatives and then examines changes in small enterprises during the transition to socialism, comparative studies of the sector, technological problems in small enterprises, and the need to evaluate government interventions and forms of organization among small enterprises.

Review/ Economic Restructuring/ Small or micro-enterprises/ Technological constraints/ Policy prescriptions/ Political mobilization/ State practice/ Industrialized economies/ Comparative/ Third World

111. —— . **1994.** Informality, de Soto Style: From Concept to Policy. In *Contrapunto: The Informal Sector Debate in Latin America*. Ed. C. A. Rakowski, pp. 131-152. Albany: State University of New York Press.

Review/ Definition/ Regulation/ State practice/ Third World

112. **Bromley, R., and C. Birkbeck. 1984.** Researching Street Occupations of Cali: The Rationale and Methods of What Many Would Call an "Informal Sector Study." *Regional Development Dialogue* 5 (2): 184-203.

Research methods/ Colombia

113. **Bromley, R., and C. Gerry, eds. 1979a.** *Casual Work and Poverty in Third World Cities*. Chichester, New York: John Wiley & Sons.

Under- and unemployment/ Urbanization/ Brazil/ India/ Colombia/ Kenya/ Senegal/ Mexico/ Philippines

114. —— . **1979b.** Who Are the Casual Poor? In *Casual Work and Poverty in Third World Cities*. Ed. R. Bromley and C. Gerry, pp. 3-23. Chichester, New York: John Wiley & Sons.

The authors eschew the division between wage and self-employment to argue for a continuum stretching from stable wage work to true self-employment. All but stable wage employment refer to ways of making a living which lack security of income and employment. The concept "poverty-in-employment" designates the ways in which the income opportunities of the poor actually promote and perpetuate poverty, insecurity, and exploitation. This phenomenon is attributed to (1) the tendency of employers to find loopholes in labor legislation; (2) the accelerating pace of worldwide technological change; (3) the increasing economic instability in most national economies; and (4) the breakdown of traditional rural economies.

Definition/ Continuum debate/ State practice/ Regulation/ Technological change/ Third World

115. **Brus, W., and K. Laski. 1985.** Repressed Inflation and Second Economy under Central Planning. In *The Economics of the Shadow Economy*. Ed. W. Gaertner and A. Wenig, pp. 377-391. Berlin, F.R.G.: Springer-Verlag.

Repressed inflation arises under central planning when excess consumer demand does not lead to appropriate price increases. If prices in the second economy increase, the excess demand would seem to disappear. In practice, this process is only partial and speculative money balances for future purchases in the first economy would arise. The accumulation of these balances is the result of the price difference ratio between the first and the second economy and of the probability of buying on the first market in the future.

State practice/ Centrally planned economies

116. **Brusco, S. 1982.** The "Emilian" Model: Productive Decentralization and Social Integration. *Cambridge Journal of Economics* 6: 167-184.

Decentralization/ Italy

117. **Brusco, S., and C. Sabel. 1981.** Artisan Production and Economic Growth. In *The Dynamics of Labour Market Segmentation*. Ed. F. Wilkinson, pp. 99-113. London: Academic Press.

Brusco and Sabel review three models of the internal organization of small firms: the artisan, the small firm in the shadow of larger ones, and independent enterprises. Such firms are part of a strategy of diversification where diversification refers to the shifting patterns of alliance between large and small industries.

Firm characteristics/ Artisanal production/ Flexible specialization/ Small or micro-enterprises/ Italy

118. **Bryant, C. D., C. J. Dudley, D. J. Shoemaker, and P. Shifflett. 1985.** Rural Occupational Diversity: Impact of Multiple Job Holding on Job Satisfaction and Traditional Life. In *The Rural Work Force*. Ed. C. D. Bryant, D. J. Shoemaker, J. K. Skipper Jr., and W. E. Snizek, pp. 223-240. South Hadley, Mass.: Bergin and Garvey.

The authors examine four questions about occupational structure in the rural United States: Do rural people hold more than two jobs? What is the relation between multiple jobs, commutation, and intention to leave the community on job satisfaction? What are the sociodemographic characteristics of multiple job holders? What is the impact of urban occupational patterns on traditional rural life? The study assumes that work specialization in rural areas is underestimated via-à-vis urban occupational patterns.

Rural/ Survival strategies/ Gender division of labor/ Multiple jobs/ Worker characteristics/ U.S.A.

119. **Bryant, C. D., D. J. Shoemaker, J. K. Skipper Jr., and W. E. Snizek, eds. 1985.** *The Rural Work Force: Non-Agricultural Occupations in America*. South Hadley, Mass.: Bergin and Garvey.

This monograph describes rural access to increasingly regulated resources and the role of work in isolated living situations. Individual chapters focus on industrial work (poultry processors and coal miners); ecological stewards (rangers, fisheries biologists); game wardens and marine law enforcement; medical delivery services to people and animals; and multiple job holding.

Rural/ Multiple jobs/ U.S.A.

120. **Bryant, W. K., and Yan Wang. 1987.** Replacing Women's Housework: A Study of Purchased Goods and Services. *Human Ecology Forum* 16: 19-22.

Unpaid labor/ U.S.A.

121. **Bryceson, D. F. 1985.** Women's Proletarianization and the Family Wage in Tanzania. In *Women, Work, and Ideology in the Third World*. Ed. H. Afshar, pp. 128-152. London: Tavistock.

Bryceson examines the contradictory forces of proletarianization and the family wage in colonial and post-colonial Tanzania. By migrating to urban areas in search of wage employment, women leave their "oppressed position" in peasant commodity production but are unable to escape sexual subordination in the wider society. Male control of the family wage leaves women with minimum wage employment under conditions of sexual discrimination.

Migration/ Gender ideology/ Gender inequality/ Tanzania

122. **Buechler, H. C., and J. Buechler. 1992.** Spanish Galician Industrialization and the Europe of 1992: A Contextual Analysis. In *Anthropology and the Global Factory: Studies of the New Industrialization in the Late Twentieth Century*. Ed. F. A. Rothstein and M. L. Blim, pp. 102-118. New York: Bergin and Garvey.

Industrial restructuring/ Rural/ Subcontracting/ Home-based production/ Small or micro-enterprises/ State practice/ Spain

123. **Bujra, J. 1982.** Prostitution, Class and the State. In *Crime, Justice, and Underdevelopment*. Ed. C. Sumner, pp. 131-150. Exeter, N.H.: Heinemann Educational Books.

Prostitution/ State practice

124. **Bunster, X. 1983.** Market Sellers in Lima, Peru: Talking about Work. In *Women and Poverty in the Third World*. Ed. M. Buvinic, M. A. Lycette, and W. P. McGreevey, pp. 92-103. Baltimore, Md.: Johns Hopkins University Press.

Bunster reports the results of interviews of twenty-one female food vendors in a low-income district of Lima. Market selling is viewed as part of a survival strategy that combines both home and market production and allows women to balance household and income-generating tasks. Although providing subsistence, market selling also exposes women to unhealthy working conditions, harassment by public officials, and exploitation by middlemen. Policies are needed to improve the situation for Lima's poor market women, yet must address their needs to balance household and economic activities.

Trading/ Survival strategies/ Double-day/ Household division of labor/ Female-headed households/ Subsistence production/ Women/ Peru

125. **Bunster, X., and E. Chaney. 1985.** *Sellers and Servants: Women Working in Lima*. New York: Praeger.

Trading/ Domestic service/ Gender division of labor/ Peru

126. **Burawoy, M. 1976.** The Function and Reproduction of Migrant Labor: Comparative Material from Southern Africa and the United States. *American Journal of Sociology* 81: 1050-1087.

Migration/ Labor market dynamics/ Comparative/ Africa/ U.S.A.

127. **—— . 1985.** *The Politics of Production: Factory Regimes under Capitalism and Socialism*. London: Verso.

Burawoy argues for the inseparability of economic, political, and ideological aspects of production, challenging distinctions drawn between economic base and superstructure in most radical studies of the labor process. He introduces the concept of production or factory regimes, embodied in institutions that regulate conflicts and resulting struggles over wages, work conditions, and worker status, to examine how different regimes shape class consciousness. A final chapter explores the relationship between changes in the global economy and the emergence of new factory regimes focusing on their implications for labor struggles in core and peripheral countries as well as in capitalist and socialist economies.

Production process/ Class processes/ Labor relations/ State practice/ Labor movements/ Consciousness/ Social restructuring/ Industrialized economies/ Centrally planned economies/ Third World

128. **Burns, S. 1977.** *The Household Economy: Its Shape, Origins and Future*. Boston, Mass.: Beacon Press.
Originally published as Burns, Scott. 1975. *Home, Inc.: The Hidden Wealth and Power of the American Household*. New York: Doubleday.

Examining the household as both a producing and consuming unit highlights the meaning and significance of money in the economy. Taking into account those who do not engage in formal work, people work for money only one out of every eight hours. Household labor is valued at one-third of the GNP and one-half of total disposable income.

Unpaid labor/ Nonmonetary exchange/ Household/ U.S.A.

129. **Buvinic, M. 1989.** Investing in Poor Women: The Psychology of Donor Support. *World Development* 17: 1045-1057.

Review/ Policy prescriptions/ Project assistance/ Women/ Third World

130. **Çagatay, N., and S. Özler. 1995.** Feminization of the Labor Force: The Effects of Long-Term Development and Structural Adjustment. *World Development* 23: 1883-1894.

Drawing from World Bank data on 165 countries in 1985 and 1990, Çagatay and Ösler test the claim that structural adjustment programs leading to greater trade openness and a declining income share of workers in manufacturing have resulted in a feminization of the workforce. They demonstrate a U-shaped relationship between women's share of employment and level of economic development, though demographic and cultural/ideological factors contribute to the degree of feminization. Structural adjustment is found to increase feminization, as declining household incomes force women to seek income-earning opportunities and as national economies become more oriented to export industries and favor low-cost, flexible labor pools.

Structural adjustment/ Gender division of labor/ Economic restructuring/ Flexibilization

131. **Campani, G. 1990.** Ethnic Minorities and New Migration Movements in Europe. *Innovation* 3: 657-672.

Migration/ Ethnicity/ Europe/ Italy

132. **Capecchi, V. 1989.** The Informal Economy and the Development of Flexible Specialization in Emilia-Romagna. In *The Informal*

Economy: Studies in Advanced and Less Developed Countries. Ed. A. Portes, M. Castells, and L. A. Benton, pp. 189-215. Baltimore, Md.; London: Johns Hopkins University Press.

This article describes the informal economy in Emilia-Romagna, an Italian region characterized by the relatively recent development of flexible industrialization and by the even more recent expansion of the tertiary sector. The analysis focuses on the socioeconomic history of this region since 1900, a method which facilitates systematic comparison across regions.

Pattern or magnitude/ Industrial restructuring/ Flexible specialization/ Comparative/ Italy

133. **Carson, C. S. 1984a.** The Underground Economy: An Introduction, Parts I-III. *Survey of Current Business* 64 (May): 21-37.

Definition/ Pattern or magnitude/ Research methods/ Industrialized economies/ U.S.A.

134. —— . **1984b.** The Underground Economy: An Introduction, Part IV. *Survey of Current Business* 64 (July): 106-119.

Definition/ Illegal activity/ Research methods/ Industrialized economies/ U.S.A.

135. **Cassel, D., and U. Cichy. 1987.** The Shadow Economy and Economic Policy in East and West: A Comparative System Approach. In *The Unofficial Economy: Consequences and Perspectives in Different Economic Systems*. Ed. S. Alessandrini and B. Dallago, pp. 127-146. Aldershot, Hants, U.K.; Brookfield, Vt.: Gower Publishing.

This paper examines the growth of shadow economies in Western and Eastern industrialized countries. In both economic systems the general cause is to be found in the state's failure to respond to the preferences of private households. In the West, the rising burden of taxation worsens conditions on the supply side. In the East, the growing shadow economy suppresses inflation which leads to shortages of and a permanent excess demand for input factors, especially labor. The authors conclude that the shadow economy's growth is limited and cyclical in the West, but persistent in the East because of the basic mechanisms of socialist planning.

State practice/ Comparative/ Centrally planned economies/ Industrialized economies

136. **Castells, M., and A. Portes. 1989.** World Underneath: The Origins, Dynamics, and Effects of the Informal Economy. In *The Informal Economy: Studies in Advanced and Less Developed Countries*. Ed. A. Portes, M. Castells, and L. A. Benton, pp. 11- 40. Baltimore, Md.; London: Johns Hopkins University Press.

The authors reject concepts of economic dualism and social marginality and define informality as a form of production within the formal economy. An international survey indicates that the informal economy is universal, heterogenous and rapidly expanding. Three features of this economy are discussed: its integration in national economies given the formation of decentralised networks of production and distribution; the vulnerability of informal workers; and the tendency to tolerate or even stimulate informal economic activities to resolve potential social conflicts and promote political patronage. The authors conclude that informalization is intrinsic to global processes of economic restructuring in the 1980s.

Review/ Definition/ Economic restructuring/ Worker characteristics/ State practice/ Relation to formal economy/ Comparative/ Industrialized economies/ Third World

137. **Chadeau, A. 1985.** Measuring Household Activities: Some International Comparisons. *The Review of Income and Wealth* 31: 237-253.

Unpaid labor/ Nonmonetary exchange/ Research methods

138. **Chadeau, A., and C. Roy. 1986.** Relating Household Final Consumption to Household Activities: Substitutability or Complementarity Between Market and Non-market Production. *Review of Income and Wealth* 32: 387-407.

Unpaid labor/ Dual sector or economy/ France

139. **Chan, S. 1983.** Young Women and Development in Africa: Some Generally Unconsidered Considerations. *Community Development Journal* 18: 257-262.

Women/ Migration/ Policy prescriptions/ Africa

140. **Charmes, J. 1990.** A Critical Review of Concepts, Definitions and Studies in the Informal Sector. In *The Informal Sector Revisited*. Ed. D. Turnham, B. Salomé, and A. Schwarz, pp. 10-48. Paris, France: Development Centre, Organisation for Economic Co-operation and Development.

Review/ Definition/ Third World

141. —— . **1996.** Progress in Measurement of Informal Employment. *Regional Development Dialogue* 17 (1): 18-30.

Pattern or magnitude/ Research methods

142. **Chaudhuri, T. D. 1989.** A Theoretical Analysis of the Informal Sector. *World Development* 17: 351-355.

Drawing from the work of Fields on migration dynamics and Stark on informal sector modeling, Chaudhuri develops a theoretical framework for analyzing formal and informal sector linkages. His proposed model differs from that of Stark in one important respect; rather than assume an dependent and subsidiary relationship to the formal sector, expansion in the informal sector, measured in terms of output and employment, is shown to be possible even when the formal economy contracts. Implied by this model is the inherent stability of the informal sector.

Relation to formal economy/ Pattern or magnitude

143. **Chen, M. A., ed. 1996.** *Beyond Credit: A Subsector Approach to Promoting Women's Enterprises*. Ottawa, Canada: Aga Khan Foundation Canada.

Written by practitioners, development consultants, and researchers, this volume addresses approaches for assisting women in micro-enterprises. Their "participatory subsector approach" avoids exclusive emphasis on credit provision, includes attention to numerous dimensions of micro-enterprise development (including organizing), shapes interventions according to the specific conditions of the particular subsector, and places women in charge of defining their own needs and intervention priorities. Case studies of successful initiatives are presented from India, Bangladesh, Nigeria, Ghana, Philippines, Chile, and Canada.

Women/ Gender relations/ Small or micro-enterprises/ Project assistance/ Empowerment/ India/ Bangladesh/ Nigeria/ Ghana/ Philippines/ Chile/ Canada

144. **Chen, M. A. 1989.** A Sectoral Approach to Promoting Women's Work: Lessons from India. *World Development* 17: 1007-1016.

Chen argues for a sectoral approach to best analyze and promote women's work, particularly work not usually included in statistics or policies related to the formal economy. She describes how this has been done for women engaged in dairy and silk production in India.

Women/ Home-based production/ Policy prescriptions/ India

145. **Chickering, A. L., and M. Salahdine, eds. 1991.** *The Silent Revolution: The Informal Sector in Five Asian and Near Eastern Countries*. San Francisco, Calif.: ICS Press.

The informal sector is examined as an indicator of the good health of an economy, a positive phenomenon in economic development which builds on the creative forces of small, less regulated enterprises.

Review/ State practice/ Policy analysis/ Small or micro- enterprises/ Morocco/ Philippines/ Sri Lanka/ Thailand/ Bangladesh

146. **Christensen, K. 1989.** Home-Based Clerical Work: No Simple Truth, No Single Reality. In *Homework: Historical and Contemporary Perspectives on Paid Labor at Home*. Ed. E. Boris and C. R. Daniels, pp. 183-197. Urbana, Ill.: University of Illinois Press.

Home-based production/ Household division of labor/ Clerical work/ U.S.A.

147. **Chu, Y. W. 1992.** Informal Work in Hong Kong. *International Journal of Urban and Regional Research* 16: 420-441.

Informal work is defined as income generating activity which is not regulated by contract yet subject to domination by capitalist relations of production. Recent literature highlighting the links between informal work and formal production has challenged the marginality of informal work to capitalist development. Focusing on homework, ambulatory work, subcontracting and out-processing, Chu provides evidence of the role played by each type of work in keeping wages low, reducing production costs, and increasing flexibility in Hong Kong's industrial sector. Both political processes related to labor legislation and socioeconomic processes in the development of capitalism are shown to shape the informal sector's development. While informality has contributed to the success of Hong Kong's export industries, long-term developments are more ambiguous.

Pattern or magnitude/ / Relation to capital/ Home-based production/ Subcontracting/ Economic restructuring/ Flexibilization/ Hong Kong

148. **Chugh, R. L., and J. S. Uppal. 1986.** *Black Economy in India*. New Delhi, India: Tata McGraw-Hill.

Definition/ Pattern or magnitude/ Illegal activity/ State practice/ Policy analysis/ India/ Third World/ Industrialized economies/ Centrally planned economies

149. **Clark, G., ed. 1988.** *Traders versus the State: Anthropological Approaches to Unofficial Economies*. Boulder, Colo.; London, U.K.: Westview Press.

Nine papers examine patterns of informal vending of food and other consumer goods in Peru, Tanzania, Ghana, Nigeria, Hong Kong, India, and the United States. The papers explore the relations between state institutions and street vendors. Clark's introduction provides a brief review of distinctions between the "informal sector" and "petty commodity production" frameworks. Employing an anthroplogical perspective that stresses the vantage point of vendors themselves, the volume's major purpose is to achieve a better understanding of the parallels and divergences in informal economic activity in different local, national, and historical contexts.

Review/ Petty commodity production/ Trading/ State practice/ Peru/ Tanzania/ Ghana/ Nigeria/ Hong Kong/ India/ U.S.A.

150. **Cohen, D. 1985.** The People Who Get in the Way: Poverty and Development in Jakarta. In *Planning for Small Enterprises in Third World Cities*. Ed. R. Bromley, pp. 219-232. Oxford, U.K.: Pergamon Press.

Based on field research conducted in 1972, Cohen argues that while the majority of low-income residents of Jakarta are thought to get in the way of development, they are actually intimately involved in it. Politics and Indonesian economic change cannot be fully understood without the perspective of this low income group who, although uninvolved in planning, figure prominently in tertiary occupations which skim money from the industrial sector for nonproductive activities. Politically, their passive posture is linked to three factors: (a) the absence of improvement in their standard of living; (b) the lack of thought given to social change and the government's role in it; and (c) the uncritical acceptance of one's position in society.

State practice/ Survival strategies/ Marginalization/ Indonesia

151. **Cole, W. E., and B. Fayissa. 1991.** The Urban Subsistence Labor Force: Toward a Policy-Oriented and Empirically Accessible Taxonomy. *World Development* 19: 779-789.

Fuzziness persists around the concept of the informal sector, often obscuring actual conditions of employment faced by the working poor. To improve on the concept, Cole and Fayissa propose a taxonomic system that focuses on labor force units rather than firms to highlight the importance of subsistence labor as a analytic category for addressing issues of poverty. This framework allows for new insights into wage determinants, constraints on labor moblity, and intersectoral linkages.

Definition/ Under- and unemployment/ Labor market dynamics/ Relation to formal economy/ Policy analysis/ Third World

152. **Colijn, L. 1987.** Some Proposed Methodologies to Quantify the Influence of Macroeconomic Disequilibrium on the Size of the Second Economy in Poland. In *The Unoffical Economy: Consequences and Perspectives in Different Economic Systems*. Ed. S. Alessandrini and B. Dallago, pp. 337-345. Aldershot, Hants, U.K.; Brookfield, Vt.: Gower Publishing.

Colijn offers a method for estimating the influence of macroeconomic disequilibrium on the size of the second economy in Soviet-type economies. Using Polish data, a hypothesis is examined suggesting that because of exogenous shocks, excess demand develops in the first economy, and an inflationary gap arises which is partially spent in the second economy. The increase in second economy incomes results in the inflationary demand which originated in the first economy. The result is an increase in income inequality. The approach represents an amalgam of Keynesian and Kaleckian insights.

Relation to formal economy/ State practice/ Polarization/ Research methods/ Poland

153. **Collins, J. L. 1990.** Unwaged Labor in Comparative Perspective: Recent Theories and Unanswered Questions. In *Work without Wages*. Ed. J. L. Collins and M. Giminez, pp. 3-45. Albany, N.Y.: State University of New York Press.

In this introductory essay the author provides a review of the literature on unwaged labor. Collins draws attention to the diversity of unwaged relations, the debate on peasant relations, contemporary discussions of simple commodity production, and the domestic labor debate to provide a theoretical assessment of the field.

Review/ Unpaid labor/ Petty commodity production/ Household/ Household division of labor/ Comparative

154. **—— . 1991.** Housework and Craftwork within Capitalism: Marxist Analyses of Unwaged Labor. In *Marxist Approaches in Economic Anthropology*. Ed. A. Littlefield and H. Gates, pp. 91-99. Lanham, Md.: University Press of America.

Collins examines the relationship between unwaged labor and the process of surplus value generation as well as the nature of the social relations that organize unwaged work. Though affecting capitalist accumulation by reproducing the workforce as well as maintaining a reserve of docile female labor, unwaged housework and community work is located "outside value" given the construction of gender and other social relations. This contrasts with the case of petty commodity production, which is distinctly if indirectly valorized by market processes. In both cases, however, a purely economistic approach is inadequate for understanding production as shaped by a system of social relations integral to capitalist development.

Unpaid labor/ Gender relations/ Gender ideology/ Petty commodity production/ Reserve army of labor/ Relation to capital

155. **Collins, J. L., and M. Gimenez, eds. 1990.** *Work without Wages: Domestic Labor and Self-Employment within Capitalism*. Albany, N.Y.: State University of New York Press.

Collins and Gimenez bring together a range of articles exploring the economic significance of household-based production for both family consumption and exchange. Particular attention is given to the articulation of women's domestic labor and home-based activities and the restructuring of the global economy. Following two theoretical essays by each editor exploring contemporary themes in analyses of unwaged work, the individual chapters draw attention to the salience of livelihood strategies, domestic politics, petty commodity production among Mexican artisanal hosueholds, struggles over reproduction, and changes in the relationship between unpaid domestic labor and wage employment.

Unpaid labor/ Household/ Household division of labor/ Rural/ Gender ideology/ Petty commodity production/ Artisanal production/ Survival strategies/ Relation to capital/ Class processes/ Social reproduction/ Self-provisioning/ Self-employment/ U.S.A./ Spain/ Mexico/ Caribbean

156. **Connolly, P. 1985.** The Politics of the Informal Sector: A Critique. In *Beyond Employment: Household, Gender and Subsistence*. Ed. N. Redclift and E. Mingione, pp. 55-91. Oxford, U.K.: Basil Blackwell.

Connolly compares the origins and use of the informal sector concept in advanced capitalist countries and in Latin America to argue that the acceptance of the informal sector is not theoretically coherent. In the West, for example, a focus on the "underground" or "parallel" economy corresponds to the loss of fiscal revenues arising from the nonobservance of legal and institutional norms. In Latin America, in contrast, the term refers to widespread urban poverty where, for instance, in Mexico the term is used to mystify the causes of poverty and legitimize the state's economic and social welfare policies. In empirical research, apart from unfavorable labor conditions, no common characteristic provides a basis for categorization. The author argues that the concept should be rejected in favor of a focus on the dynamics of global capitalist accumulation with a particular emphasis on the reserve army of labor, the reproduction of the labor force, the family life cycle, the value of women's work, and urban social movements.

Review/ Definition/ Survival strategies/ State practice/ Relation to capital/ Worker characteristics/ Reserve army of labor/ Processes of accumulation/ Comparative/ Latin America/ Mexico

157. **Contini, B. B. 1983.** Labour Market Segmentation and the Development of the Parallel Economy: The Italian Experience. *Oxford Economic Papers* 3: 401-412.

Gender division of labor/ Labor market segmentation/ Italy

158. **Cook, S. 1984a.** Peasant Economy, Rural Industry and Capitalist Development in Oaxaca Valley, Mexico. *Journal of Peasant Studies* 12: 3-40.

While early scholars of capitalist development recognized the role of home-based rural production in industrialization, recent theorists have emphasized the impossibility of expanding artisanal production beyond the logic of simple reproduction. Cook examines the general characteristics of labor-intensive small-scale and home-based industries and describes their major markets and factors influencing the incidence and configuration of rural industrial production to challenge generalized assumptions about processes of accumulation. He highlights a distinct process of capital accumulation and class formation among Oaxaca's rural commodity producers which, though constrained by inequality in the global economy, harbor a real potential for capitalist change in less developed countries.

Petty commodity production/ Class formation/ Artisanal production/ Handicrafts/ Processes of accumulation/ Home-based production/ Firm characteristics/ Rural/ Mexico

159. —— . **1984b.** Rural Industry, Social Differentiation, and the Contradictions of Provincial Mexican Capitalism. *Latin American Perspectives* 11 (4): 60-85.

Cook examines various small-scale, labor-intensive, noncapitalist industrial commodity producing industries in Oaxaca to argue that this sector contributes to subsistence, provides surplus external capital, as well as generates capital from within that can lead to a transformation from simple commodity to capitalist forms of production. This means that petty commodity production has the potential for capital accumulation and social differentiation.

Class formation/ Processes of accumulation/ Petty commodity production/ Rural/ Mexico

160. **Corcoran, M. P. 1991.** Informalization of Metropolitan Labour Forces: The Case of Irish Immigrants in the New York Construction Industry. *Irish Journal of Sociology* 1: 31-51.

Ethnicity/ Migration/ Construction industry/ Labor processes/ Economic restructuring/ Industrialized economies/ U.S.A.

161. **Cornford, J. 1981.** Conclusion: The Revival of Self-Help? In *Can I Have It In Cash?: A Study in Informal Institutions and Unorthodox Ways of Doing Things*. Ed. S. Henry, pp. 192-197. New York: St. Martin's Press.

Cornford argues that the irregular economy is the revival of patterns of "making out" rendered illicit by systems of modern public administration which often depend on arbitrary distinctions between employment and unemployment. The author argues that a majority of British people enjoy a standard of living far superior to that of previous generations and share the perception that present economic difficulties are transitory. While this has changed people's consciousness in favor of alternatives to the official economy, future developments will depend upon alternative work opportunities amidst the continuing decline in regular employment. Whatever the outcome, it is recommended that there be dispersion of political influence and wealth so that self-help does not become the excuse for a prosperous majority to turn its back on the sick, disabled, poor and unemployed.

State practice/ Survival strategies/ Consciousness/ Welfare/ Social restructuring/ Britain

162. **Cornuel, D., and B. Duriez, with Marc Foudrignier. 1985.** Local Exchange and State Intervention. In *Beyond Employment: Household, Gender and Subsistence*. Ed. N. Redclift and E. Mingione, pp. 165-188. Oxford, U.K.: Basil Blackwell.

This article describes how informal exchange, like formal exchange, is used as a way to minimize cost where the advantage of the former is its unregulated and flexible nature. This advantage is offset by the risks associated with unregulated work and the costs of maintaining the social networks which make these exchanges possible. Once established, however, informal exchange also creates and reinforces social cohesion. As the state bears the responsibility of maintaining social cohesion nationally, it generally opposes informal exchange and co-opts informal activities within the framework of public services, regulation, or control.

Social networks/ State practice/ Nonmonetary exchange/ France

163. **Cruise O'Brien, R. 1972.** Urban Unemployment in Africa. *Journal of Modern African Studies* 10: 109-112.

This short article provides an account of the conference on urban unemployment in Africa held at the University of Sussex in 1971--the forum where the "informal sector" as a concept was first introduced. The three major conference themes were (1) the definition of the problem and its relation to income distribution; (2) education and labor migration; and (3) the social and political implications of employment. This report identifies the participating institutions and provides summaries of the papers presented by John Weeks, Samir Amin, Keith Hart, Michael Todaro, and others.

Definition/ Under- and unemployment/ Policy prescriptions/ Migration/ Africa

164. **Cummings, S., ed. 1980.** *Self-Help in Urban America: Patterns of Minority Business Enterprise*. New York: Kennikat Press.

This edited volume examines patterns of economic development among immigrants in the United States. Focusing on the collective responses to urban industrial life, the essays examine self-help institutions and mutual benefit societies.

Ethnicity/ Migration/ Social networks/ U.S.A.

165. **Dallago, B. 1987.** The Underground Economy in the West and the East: A Comparative Approach. In *The Unofficial Economy: Consequences and Perspectives in Different Economic Systems*. Ed. S. Alessandrini

and B. Dallago, pp. 147-163. Aldershot, Hants, U.K.; Brookfield, Vt.: Gower Publishing.

Dallago argues that underground production is present in labor-intensive and less standardized activities where economies of scale are irrelevant and technology permits the decomposition of production into smaller units. He attributes the underground economy's existence to shortages in Soviet-type economies, whereas within capitalist economies it may be linked to capitalist efforts to decrease costs and increase demand, as well as by efforts to increase personal incomes and secure employment. Underground enterprises have both system-specific advantages and disadvantages in comparison with regular enterprises, and may often be integrated for their mutual advantage.

Relation to formal economy/ Comparative/ Industrialized economies/ Centrally planned economies

166. —— . **1990.** *The Irregular Economy: The "Underground" Economy and the "Black" Labour Market.* Aldershot, Hants, U.K.: Darthmouth Publishing House; Gower Publishing.

Current discussions of the irregular economy build upon an interest in irregular labor market activities in the United States and Italy, including those which concern tax evasion and its consequences. Whether defined as irregular, subterranean, submerged, parallel, hidden, occult, informal, unofficial, shadow, illegal, criminal, second, clandestine, or black, underground economic activities are so routine as to constitute a genuine alternative to regular employment. Dallago argues that underground activities began during a period of rising unemployment when trade unions were able to resist reductions in wages. In Italy, this resulted in a shift from formal work to irregular activity rather than in a withdrawal of female or male labor. This period also witnessed the decentralization of production attributed to a rapid rise in the cost of labor without a change in the structure of production or technology. This increased the tendency for firms to purchase goods and services from small enterprises, often those operating in the irregular economy. Dallago also examines the growing number of migrant workers whose economic participation is not reflected in labor statistics and tax and social security payments.

Definition/ Migration/ Tax evasion/ Decentralization/ Comparative/ U.S.A./ Italy/ U.S.S.R./ Hungary

167. **Danes, S. M., M. Winter, and M. B. Whiteford. 1987.** Level of Living and Participation in the Informal Market Sector among Rural Honduran Women. *Journal of Marriage and the Family* 49: 691-639.

The authors examine factors that affect Honduran women's market participation and their impact on household income. The authors conclude that women who engage in informal work have little formal education and tend to represent female-headed households.

Women/ Survival strategies/ Female-headed households/ Education/ Honduras

168. **Dangler, J. F. 1986.** Industrial Homework in the Modern World Economy. *Contemporary Crises* 10: 257-279.

Home-based production/ Subcontracting/ Labor processes/ Comparative

169. **—— . 1989.** Electronic Subassemblers in Central New York: Nontraditional Homeworkers in a Nontraditional Homework Industry. In *Homework: Historical and Contemporary Perspectives on Paid Labor at Home*. Ed. E. Boris and C. R. Daniels, pp. 147-164. Chicago, Ill.: University of Illinois Press.

Home-based production/ Industrial restructuring/ Electronics manufacture/ U.S.A.

170. **Daniels, A. K. 1987.** Invisible Work. *Social Problems* 34: 403-415.

Unpaid labor/ Gender ideology/ Household division of labor/ U.S.A.

171. **Daniels, C. R. 1989.** Between Home and Factory: Homeworkers and the State. In *Homework: Historical and Contemporary Perspectives on Paid Labor at Home*. Ed. E. Boris and C. R. Daniels, pp. 13-32. Chicago, Ill.: University of Illinois Press.

State practice/ Home-based production/ U.S.A.

172. **Daohuai, D., J. Zhenji, Z. Zhunying, and S. Suoda. 1988.** Building a New Countryside: Chinese Women in Rural Enterprises. In *Daughters in Industry: Work, Skills and Consciousness of Women Workers in Asia*. Ed. N. Heyzer, pp. 69-104. Kuala Lumpur, Malaysia: Asian and Pacific Development Centre.

This paper provides an overview of rural differentiation and rural industrialization in China through a comparison of a prosperous and backward region of the country. The study focuses on women's labor and their opportunities for work.

Rural/ Gender division of labor/ Small or micro-enterprises/ Differentiation/ Comparative/ China

173. **Das, V. 1984.** Informal Sector in Socialist Economies: A Reexamination of the Relationship of the Informal Sector to Development. *Regional Development Dialogue* 5 (2): 123-134.

Das criticizes urban dualism which views informality as either necessary and inevitable for modernization, or as a sector exploited by international capitalism as it enters production in the Third World. As an alternative, Das examines informality as petty capitalism which coexists with and is an independent form of market exchange within socialism or capitalism.

Critique of dualism/ Class processes/ Relation to formal economy/ Third World/ Centrally planned economies

174. **Davies, R. 1979.** Informal Sector or Subordinate Mode of Production? A Model. In *Casual Work and Poverty in Third World Cities*. Ed. R. Bromley and C. Gerry, pp. 87-104. New York: John Wiley & Sons.

Davies argues that an "adequate" definition of the informal sector must recognize that it represents a peripheral, underdeveloped and dependent mode of production, existing within a social formation it cannot directly influence. Drawing upon data from Zimbabwe, the author highlights characteristics of the informal sector: indigenous ownership, ease of entry, nonmonopolistic, small-scale, noninstitutionalized price setting mechanisms, intensive use of labor, and illegality. The sector's origin is linked to its absorption of the "reserve-army" and to the demand for informal goods and services not met by the formal sector. Its continued existence is traced to its role in keeping formal sector wages low through low-cost labor supply, de facto social security, and the provision of low-cost goods and services. The maintenance of the informal sector is the "optimum" capitalist strategy.

Definition/ Relation to formal economy/ Reserve army of labor/ Third World/ Zimbabwe

175. **Davies, W. J. 1987.** *Black Entrepeneurial Experience and Practice in Port Elizabeth*. Development Studies Working Paper, no. 36. Grahamstown, South Africa: Institute of Social and Economic Research, Rhodes University.

Small or micro-enterprises/ Racial inequality/ Ethnicity/ State practice/ South Africa

176. **De Gijsel, P. 1985.** A Macroeconomic Analysis of Black Labour Demand and Supply. In *The Economics of the Shadow Economy*. Ed. W. Gaertner and A. Wenig, pp. 218-226. Berlin, F.R.G.: Springer-Verlag.

De Gijsel examines the relationship between tax and wage-employment rates. Taking into account the risk of being fined, firms maximize their expected profits and workers their expected utility by determining the optimal demand for and supply of homogenous legal and black labor inputs. Results show how a change in the tax rate, in the black and legal wage rate, and in the probability of being fined affect individual and market demand for and supply of both illegal and legal labor. Employment in the black labor market rises if the tax rate increases, provided that the probability of being fined does not exceed a critical level. Black market employment also rises if the probability of being fined is lowered and if the demand for total labor is constrained by firm rationing in the product market or in inflexible legal wage rates.

Labor market dynamics/ Tax evasion

177. **De Grazia, R. 1980.** Clandestine Employment: A Problem of Our Times. *International Labour Review* 119: 549-563.

Review

178. ——. **1984.** *Clandestine Employment: The Situation in the Industrialised Market Economy Countries*. Geneva, Switzerland: International Labour Office.

Pattern or magnitude/ France/ Italy/ Germany/ Sweden/ Britain/ U.S.A./ Japan

179. **De Oliveira, F. 1985.** A Critique of Dualist Reason: The Brazilian Economy since 1930. In *Planning for Small Enterprises in Third World Cities*. Ed. R. Bromley, pp. 65-95. Oxford, U.K.: Pergamon Press.

Critique of dualism/ Small or micro-enterprises/ Brazil

180. **De Soto, H. 1989.** *The Other Path: The Invisible Revolution in the Third World*. New York: Harper & Row.
First publ. in collaboration with Enrique Ghersi, Mario Ghibellini, and el Instituto Libertad y Democracia (ILD), with title *El otro sendero: la revolucion informal*. Lima: Editorial El Barranco, 1986.

Since the early 20th century, rural migration to Peru's urban centers has been accompanied by a growing number of informal enterprises. De Soto examines the role of informal entrepreneurs in housing, transport and trade to highlight the reasons for this development and argues that behind their rise is the belief in systematic government intervention on behalf of select business groups to ensure successful industrialisation. Such intervention is biased against urban, migrant, small-scale entrepreneurs who are constrained by lower productivity levels than those in the formal economy. Though extralegal, informal entrepreneurs avoid anarchy by creating new institutions to facilitate economic activity. This "invisible revolution" suggests an alternative path towards economic development which contrasts with proposals offered by Peru's radical left. De Soto recommends a reform of the country's legal system as well as the reform of other institutions which affect economic production. He concludes by advocating for decentralization and deregulation to realize alternative forms of production.

Pattern or magnitude/ State practice/ Policy analysis/ Small or micro-enterprises/ Entrepreneurship/ Housing/ Trading/ Transportation/ Peru

181. **Delphy, C. 1984a.** *Close to Home: A Materialist Analysis of Women's Oppression*. Trans. and ed. Diana Leonard. London: Hutchinson.

A collection of papers published between 1970 and 1981 presents Delphy's analysis of a feminist understanding of housework as unpaid work. Ten papers and an introduction explore the concept of the domestic mode of production, the economic basis of marriage and household formation, and the role of intrafamily social divisions and hierarchies in structuring women's subordinated position within the wider economy and society.

Gender ideology/ Household/ Household division of labor/ Unpaid labor/ Relation to capital

182. —— . **1984b.** Housework or Domestic Work. In *Close to Home: A Materialist Analysis of Women's Oppression*. C. Delphy, pp. 78-92. London: Hutchinson.

This paper examines the definition of housework. The author argues that housework should be defined as a work relationship rather than a series of tasks. To facilitate this line of analysis, the concept of domestic work should replace housework.

Unpaid labor/ Household/ Gender ideology/ Gender relations

183. **Denison, E. F. 1982.** Is US Growth Understated Because of the Underground Economy? Employment Ratios Suggest Not. *Review of Income and Wealth* 28: 1-16.

It is conventionally argued that growth of the underground economy results in increasingly understated economic statistics, in particular those reflecting national income and GNP. However, Denison uses a ratio of employment to population to argue that there is no evidence to suggest that there has been an understatement of these statistics.

Pattern or magnitude/ Research methods/ U.S.A.

184. **Denton, J. A. 1985.** The Underground Economy and Social Stratification. *Sociological Spectrum* 5: 31-42.

Definition/ Polarization/ U.S.A.

185. **Díaz, A. 1993.** *Restructuring and the New Working Classes in Chile: Trends in Waged Employment, Informality and Poverty, 1973-1990.* 25pp. UNRISD Discussion Paper, no. DP47. Geneva, Switzerland: United Nations Research Institute for Social Development.

Díaz examines change in employment and industrial development during the "neoliberal experiment" in Chile between 1973 and 1990. While high unemployment, poverty, and high rates of participation in public emergency work programs as well as non waged, informal work characterized the early years of this period in the 1970s, the decades since have seen a steady rise in rate of waged work coupled with a decline in numbers of workers in the informal (i.e., self-employed and unwaged) sector. Also indicated is an increase in small and medium-sized enterprises and greater concentration of industrial growth in small and medium-sized cities. While the informal sector as a distinct sector of the economy appears to have shrunk, evidence suggests growing segmentation of labor markets and growing informality of labor-capital relations. Though more people are engaged in waged work than in previous decades, a growing share of the workforce faces highly precarious employment security characterized by intermittent unemployment and frequent job switching within and between firms, often of small to medium size. Accordingly, growing inequality in the Chilean population in terms of income and job prospects is also indicated. In sum, social restructuring in Chilean society with the neoliberal experiment has brought new forms of informality, facilitated by fundamental changes in state regulation of economic activity.

Economic restructuring/ Social restructuring/ Labor market segmentation/ Class processes/ Differentiation/ State practice/ Chile

186. **Dick, H. W., and P. J. Rimmer. 1980.** Beyond the Formal/ Informal Sector Dichotomy: Towards an Integrated Alternative. *Pacific Viewpoint* 21: 26-41.

Two geographers review and critique economic dualism and argue that the concept of informal sector is attractive to policymakers who are committed to the rapid growth of the modern capitalist sector through foreign aid and investment. Thirteen characteristics suggested by Sethuraman to identify informal enterprises are critically examined and their application to specific sites challenged on the basis of a lack of analytic coherence. As an alternative, the authors propose an "integrated conceptual framework" which disaggregates the organization dichotomy into management, ownership and scale. These criteria are linked to the technology dichotomy which is also disaggregated into motive power, scale and level. This framework is used to promote "decorporation" or the spread of small scale technologies suited to the resources of noncorporate organizations. The policy of decorporation is envisioned as a counter to distortions in relative factor prices and a way to promote efficiency and equity in resource allocation.

Critique of dualism/ Policy analysis/ Appropriate technology/ Third World

187. **Ditton, J. 1977.** Perks, Pilferage and the Fiddle: The Historical Structure of Invisible Wages. *Theory and Society* 4: 39-71.

Ditton examines the concepts of pilfering and perks and conceptualizes these as in-kind wages. The distinction between these concepts is that perks are benefits accorded white collar workers while pilfering refers to blue collar strategies used to increase real wages. The author also notes how customary rights to bonuses and resource access among peasants vis-à-vis feudal lords have been transformed into perks and pilfering in contemporary industrialized setting.

Nonmonetary exchange/ Pilfering/ Industrialized economies

188. **Dobosiewicz, Z. 1987.** The Role of Unofficial Economy in North African Countries. In *The Unofficial Economy: Consequences and Perspectives in Different Economic Systems*. Ed. S. Alessandrini and B. Dallago. Aldershot, Hants, U.K.; Brookfield, Vt.: Gower Publishing.

Unofficial economies in North African countries are linked to attempts by producers to diminish costs, particularly taxes, and to workers need for employment. Unofficial employment is critically important particularly in situations of rapid urbanization. Dobosiewicz argues that the unofficial economy is a transitory phenomenon which will disappear with economic development but, as a transitional strategy, permits the survival of many people despite unfavorable working conditions. From the point of view of production, it also plays an important part in producing cheap goods for the poor majority.

Survival strategies/ Egypt/ Algeria/ Tunisia/ Morocco

189. **Dunlop, Y., and A. Stretton. 1984.** *A Decomposition of Changes in Full-time Employment, 1971-76 and 1976-81*. Technical Paper, no. 20. Canberra, Australia: Bureau of Labor Market Research.

Labor market dynamics/ Research methods/ Australia

190. **Durand-Lasserve, A. 1987.** Land and Housing in Third World Cities: Are Public and Private Strategies Contradictory? *Cities* 4: 325-338.

Housing/ Policy analysis/ Third World

191. **Dwyer, D. J., and V. F. S. Sit. 1986.** Small-Scale Industries and Problems of Urban and Regional Planning: A Hong Kong Case Study. *Third World Planning Review* 8 (2): 99-119.

Small or micro-enterprises/ Spatial patterns/ Policy analysis/ Hong Kong

192. **Eades, J. S. 1985.** If You Can't Beat `Em, Join `Em: State Regulation of Small Enterprises. In *Planning for Small Enterprises in Third World Cities*. Ed. R. Bromley, pp. 203-218. Oxford, U.K.: Pergamon Press.

Comparing Papua-New Guinea, West Africa and Singapore, Eades explores state practices which affect their degree of control over small enterprises. He argues that these countries vary in their form of economy as well as in official attitudes towards small enterprises. Focused on trade, the discussion suggests four sets of factors that explain differences in state policies: (a) the presence or absence of a well-developed division of labor, coupled with the specialization of production and inter-regional trade in the precolonial period; (b) the presence or absence of a settler community involved in primary production; (c) links with the surrounding region, especially the rural hinterland; and (d) the present form of integration into the world economy. An analysis of state legislation and of the social organization of state agents suggests that the degree of control over small enterprises is greater when the degree of overlap between the social networks of small-scale entrepreneurs and state agents is minimal, and where rigid enforcement is monitored by a powerful interest group anxious to avoid any erosion of its dominant position in the economic and political system.

State practice/ Economic restructuring/ Social networks/ Small or micro-enterprises/ Production process/ Trading/ Regulation/ Papua New Guinea/ West Africa/ Singapore

193. **Eaton, P. J. 1992.** Rural-urban Migration and Underemployment among Females in the Brazilian Northeast. *Journal of Economic Issues* 26: 385-395.

Eaton argues that female migration to Brazil's northeast is a search for informal rather than formal or modern sector employment. This finding contrasts with those of Todaro, a researcher well known for his work on Brazil.

Migration/ Women/ Brazil

194. **Edwards, R. 1979.** *Contested Terrain: The Transformation of the Workplace in the Twentieth Century*. New York: Basic Books.

The roots of labor conflict lie in capitalist production where labor power is sold to employers oriented towards capital accumulation, and where employers compel production through various forms of control despite worker resistance. Edwards traces the development of simple, technical and bureaucratic forms of control in U.S. labor and industrial history, and examines the relationship between bureaucratic control, the process of labor market segmentation and its institutionalization in the twentieth century. As he demonstrates, segmentation has led to a fractionalized working class which limits possibilities for a unified working-class movement. Instead, "class-fraction politics" promote an expanded government role in stimulating the economy and mediating conflict. Although capitalists push to enlarge the role of administrative power in the political arena and mitigate workplace democracy, growing tensions harbor potential for a unified challenge to bureaucratic control.

Labor market segmentation/ Production process/ Class processes/ Labor relations/ Social restructuring/ Labor movements/ U.S.A.

195. **Edwards, R. C., M. Reich, and D. M. Gordon, eds. 1976.** *Labor Market Segmentation*. Lexington, Mass.: Lexington Books.

Labor market segmentation/ Production process/ Racial inequality/ Gender division of labor/ U.S.A.

196. **Ekpenyong, S. 1992.** The Burden on Urban Women and Children in the Nigerian Economy Due to Structural Adjustment Enforced by the International Monetary Fund. *Philosophy and Social Action* 18 (4): 17-28.

Women/ Survival strategies/ Structural adjustment/ Nigeria

197. **Elkan, W. 1976.** Concepts in the Description of African Economies. *Journal of Modern African Studies* 14: 691-699.

Critique of dualism/ Africa

198. **El-Shakhs, S. 1984.** On City-Size and the Contribution of the Informal Sector: Some Hypotheses and Research Questions. *Regional Development Dialogue* 5 (2): 77-81.

This study correlates city size with the economic contribution of the informal sector by disaggregating the latter into two sets of activities: 1) essential production and service functions which substitute or supplement those in the formal sector; and 2) peripheral, income-generating non-productive services that are almost never performed by the formal sector. Evidence suggests that small cities have simpler, more traditional economies that are dominated by informal sector activities. Thus, the relative share of the informal sector could be expected to diminish with the increased functional complexity of the urban economy, itself the result of increased market size and changes in market characteristics.

Definition/ Urbanization/ Dual sector or economy

199. **Elson, D., and R. Pearson. 1980.** *The Latest Phase of the Internationalisation of Capital and Its Implications for Women in the Third World*. IDS Discussion Paper, no. 150. Sussex, U.K.: University of Sussex.

Elson and Pearson examine how firms financed by international capital increasingly employ female workers to produce low-cost goods for export. They highlight an emergent pattern in international capital accumulation to show how gendered relations in the labor market of Third World economies lead to the proliferation of "world market factories"where high levels of production are achieved not through technological development, but by submitting the factory workforce to a high degree of labor intensity. The marked preference for females in the international labor force can only be explained as a function of their subordination as a gender, representing a set of social and cultural relations which facilitate their exploitability as workers. The conditions of their employment thus subject women to new forms of subordination, even as older forms are weakened by women's increased participation in the wage labor market.

New international division of labor/ Gender division of labor/ Export production/ Third World

200. **Emmerij, L. 1974.** A New Look at Some Strategies for Increasing Productive Employment in Africa. *International Labour Review* 110: 199-218.

Policy analysis/ Africa

201. **Evers, H. D., and R. Korff. 1986.** Subsistence Production in Bangkok. *Development* 4: 50-55.

Survival strategies/ Unpaid labor/ Household division of labor/ Subsistence production/ Thailand

202. **Evers, H. D., and O. Mehmet. 1994.** The Management of Risk: Informal Trade in Indonesia. *World Development* 22: 1-9.

The authors report the results of a large-scale survey on the informal sector in Central Java. They discuss risk-avoidance strategies of informal traders which include maintaining small inventories to avoid pressures of local social obligations, obtaining formal trading licenses to avoid eviction, formation of cooperatives, and selling of goods on commission for formal firms. A broad tendency toward formalization of informal trading is noted, and the impacts of various government policies and programs (deregulation, licensing, human resources training, credit) are briefly reviewed.

Trading/ Industrial restructuring/ Indonesia

203. **Evers, H., W. Clauss, and D. Wong. 1984.** Subsistence Reproduction: A Framework for Analysis. In *Households and the World Economy*. Ed. J. Smith et al., pp. 17-22. Beverly Hills, Calif.: Sage.

This paper redresses the preoccupation of economics with production and circulation by concentrating on the process of household reproduction. The authors distinguish between primary reproduction, which is the reproduction of labor power and human life in general, and secondary reproduction, which is the reproduction of the social and economic order to ensure either its continued existence as a social formation or its propitious transformation. The informal sector combines subsistence production and petty commodity production to help maintain low reproduction costs for labor which subsidize formal sector production. The paper concludes by discussing various methodological problems in the analysis of primary reproduction.

Unpaid labor/ Household division of labor/ Household/ Subsistence production/ Subsidy to capital/ Research methods

204. **Eviota, E. U. 1986.** The Articulation of Gender and Class in the Philippines. In *Women's Work: Development and the Division of Labor by Gender*. Ed. E. Leacock and H. I. Safa, pp. 194-206. South Hadley, Mass.: Bergin & Garvey.

Eviota explores the articulation of gender and class under dependent development in the Philippines. As landlessness now affects close to half of the rural labor force, women face a double burden in their need to perform both household tasks and poorly paid work as share tenants, seasonal laborers, and agribusiness employees. Facing growing impoverishment, women dominate the flow of migrants to the city where they find themselves overwhelmingly concentrated in low-paid service jobs. Female migrants also are more likely than males to end up in the informal sector, where they form about 60 percent of the workforce and combine work with household responsibilities. This balancing act entails great hardships, particularly for those who are the only adult income earners.

Gender division of labor/ Survival strategies/ Migration/ Female-headed households/ Double-day/ Rural/ Philippines

205. —— . **1992.** *The Political Economy of Gender*. London: Zed Books.

Following a broad historical discussion of the political economy of the Philippines, Eviota examines various configurations of women's changing employment. Following a discussion of formal sector employment in the agricultural, industrial and service economy, she explores subsistence activities, domestic service, and petty trade and production. However, unlike many who pose these latter activities as outside of the formal economy, Eviota argues instead that they are not always separate and distinct from other economic activities. Rather, some informal sector work of women is integrated into industrial organizations by means of work that stretches vertically from salaried and waged employees to casual laborers, subcontractors, piece works and scavengers. Informal work includes as well, recycling, and the sex trade.

Gender division of labor/ Relation to formal economy/ Gender ideology/ Production process/ Class processes/ Social restructuring/ Rural/ State practice/ Subsistence production/ Domestic service/ Trading/ Philippines

206. **Fapohunda, E. R. 1978.** Women at Work in Nigeria: Factors Affecting Modern Sector Employment. In *Human Resources and African Development*. Ed. U. G. Damachi and V. P. Diejomaoh, pp. 220-241. New York: Praeger.

Women/ Gender division of labor/ Nigeria

207. **Fapohunda, O. J. 1980.** Urbanisation and Employment in Developing Countries: The Role of the Informal Sector. *Labour and Society* 5: 31-48.

Urbanization/ Migration/ Labor market dynamics/ Policy analysis/ Third World

208. —— . **1985.** *The Informal Sector of Lagos: An Inquiry into Urban Poverty and Employment*. Lagos, Nigeria: University Press.

Fapohunda explores the relationship between urban migration and patterns of informal work, identifies enterprise characteristics, highlights labor and employment issues such as length of employment, absorptive capacity of different firms, and worker characteristics, including educational and wage differentials, and elaborates the linkages between formal and informal sector enterprises. She includes in her analysis self-employed petty entrepreneurs and traders but excludes work undertaken within the household economy.

Migration/ Firm characteristics/ Worker characteristics/ Survival strategies/ Relation to formal economy/ Nigeria

209. **Feige, E. L. 1979.** How Big Is the Irregular Economy? *Challenge* 22 (November-December): 5-13.

Pattern or magnitude/ Research methods/ U.S.A.

210. **—— . ed. 1981.** *The Underground Economies: Tax Evasion and Information Distortion*. Cambridge, U.K.: Cambridge University Press.

Underground economies are generally thought to consist of economic activities and the incomes derived from them that circumvent or otherwise elude government regulation, tax or observation. This includes both illegal work and work done "off- the-books".

Definition/ Tax evasion

211. **—— . 1985.** The Meaning of the "Underground Economy" and the Full Compliance Deficit. In *The Economics of the Shadow Economy*. Ed. W. Gaertner and A. Wenig, pp. 19-36. Berlin, F.R.G.; New York: Springer-Verlag.

This paper proposes a taxonomic framework to clarify differences and interconnections among the variety of descriptive terms presently employed by those who study the underground economy. Feige distinguishes between economic, fiscal and social concepts of income and then employs these distinctions to explore the current controversies surrounding the dramatic growth of government deficits. The concept of a full-compliance deficit is defined and given empirical content and is then related to other deficit measures. The relationship of a full-compliance deficit to issues of tax evasion and social fraud also are explored.

Definition/ Tax evasion/ Policy analysis/ U.S.A.

212. —— . **1987.** The Anatomy of the Underground Economy. In *The Unofficial Economy: Consequences and Perspectives in Different Economic Systems*. Ed. S. Alessandrini and B. Dallago, pp. 83- 106. Aldershot, Hants, U.K.; Brookfield, Vt.: Gower Publishing.

Feige examines the methods employed to measure the size and growth of the "underground" economy distinguishing between its economic and fiscal characteristics. As he argues, unrecorded income reflects an understatement of total income because of income earned in the underground economy. Unreported fiscal income, in contrast, is an understatement of total taxable income. The article also examines official estimates of unrecorded income to conclude that official estimates understate unrecorded income. Finally, Feige highlights the consequences of these distinctions for interpretations of federal budget deficits.

Definition/ Pattern or magnitude/ Research methods

213. **Feldman, S. 1991.** Still Invisible: Women in the Informal Sector. In *Women and International Development Annual*. Ed. R. S. Gallin and A. Ferguson, pp. 59-88. Boulder, Colo.: Westview Press.

Feldman examines how the disillusionment with modernization theory has helped recognize informal activities as an analytical category and framework for organizing development assistance. Poverty alleviation models, dual economy theory and its critiques, and theories of petty commodity production examine the relationship between formal and informal sectors, focusing particularly on the latter's distinctiveness as a relatively autonomous, if subordinated, sector within the wider economy. Much of this research remains problematic because it assumes an undifferentiated labor pool and ignores the centrality of gender relations in shaping informal activity. A focus on the labor process and global accumulation addresses these limitations.

Review/ Relation to formal economy/ Gender relations/ Unpaid labor

214. **Felt, L. F., and P. R. Sinclair. 1992.** "Everyone Does It": Unpaid Work in a Rural Peripheral Region. *Work, Employment and Society* 6: 43-64.

Unpaid labor/ Rural/ Canada

215. **Ferber, M. A. 1987.** *Women and Work, Paid and Unpaid*. New York: Garland Publishing.

Annotations are provided for 1,031 works focusing primarily on the economics of women and work, with some reference to relevant literature from other fields. Materials cited date primarily since 1960 and reflect original research. The bibliography is presented in six major sections: General Works; The Family; Labor Force Participation; Occupational Distribution; Earnings and the Female-Male Pay Gap; Discrimination; Unemployment; Women in Individual Occupations; Women Throughout the World.

Bibliography/ Gender division of labor/ Household division of labor/ Gender inequality/ Under- and unemployment/ Labor market dynamics

216. **Ferman, L. A., and L. Berndt. 1981.** The Irregular Economy. In *Can I Have It In Cash?: A Study of Informal Institutions and Unorthodox Ways of Doing Things*. Ed. S. Henry, pp. 26-42. New York: St. Martin's Press.

This paper classifies goods and services production and distribution as the regular, irregular, and social economy, based on whether the activity is accounted for by conventional economic measures and on whether money is used as the medium of exchange. Using household survey data from Detroit, Michigan, the authors argue that although individual exchanges may be small, taken as a whole, the social and irregular economy provide goods and services often unavailable or difficult to obtain in the regular economy. The irregular and social economies also distribute goods produced in the regular economy to local or marginal markets as well as consumes, distributes, and maintains products made in the regular economy. The authors argue that because informal work offers opportunities to cope with changing circumstances, this work should be included in analyses of the labor force. They also argue that the irregular economy is neither a product of recession and high unemployment nor of excessive tax rates, but a consequence of the bureaucratic apparatus protecting the regular economy.

Unpaid labor/ Nonmonetary exchange/ Social networks/ Survival strategies/ Relation to formal economy/ State practice/ Industrialized economies/ U.S.A.

217. **Ferman, L. A., L. E. Berndt, and S. Henry, eds. 1993.** *Work beyond Employment in Advanced Capitalist Countries: Class and Contemporary Perspectives on the Informal Economy*. 2 vols. Lewiston, N.Y.: Edwin Mellen Press.

These volumes bring together papers on various aspects of informal economic activity and provide an overview of the development of the concept in industrialized societies. Volume 1 reviews early conceptions of informal activity and engages ethnographic research approaches to gauge the size and extent of informal work. Volume 2 explores recent revisions of earlier concepts and theory as well as addresses the concept's overall validity and usefulness in the study of advanced capitalism. Together, the volumes "reveal the developing debate" on the informal sector in industrialized societies.

Review/ Definition/ Pattern or magnitude/ Unpaid labor/ Labor processes/ Industrialized economies/ Italy/ U.S.A.

218. **Ferman, L. A., and P. R. Ferman. 1973.** The Structural Underpinnings of the Irregular Economy. *Poverty and Human Resources Abstracts* 8: 3-17.

This paper argues that the irregular economy is caused by the imperfect distribution of goods and services and by job discrimination and other forms of labor market exclusion.

Labor market segmentation/ Industrialized economies

219. **Ferman, L. A., S. Henry, and M. Hoyman. 1987.** Issues and Prospects for the Study of Informal Economies: Concepts, Research Strategies, and Policy. *Annals of the American Academy of Political and Social Science* 493: 154-172.

Review/ Research methods/ Policy analysis/ Industrialized economies

220. **Fernández-Kelly, M. P. 1989.** International Development and Industrial Restructuring: The Case of Garment and Electronics Industries in Southern California. In *Instability and Change in the World Economy*. Ed. A. MacEwan and W. K. Tabb, pp. 147-165. New York: Monthly Review Press.

Reviewing the reorganization of production in the garment and electronics industries, Fernández-Kelly examines industrial restructuring in the United States. To regain global competitiveness, these industries increasingly rely upon informal labor arrangements such as subcontracting and homework to retain low production costs. Contrary to the previous focus on the Third World, Fernández-Kelly argues that global processes of industrial restructuring target women, immigrants, and refugees as providers of cheap labor.

Industrial restructuring/ Migration/ Ethnicity/ Subcontracting/ Home-based production/ Refugees/ Garment manufacture/ Electronics manufacture/ U.S.A.

221. —— . **1994.** Towanda's Triumph: Social and Cultural Capital in the Transition to Adulthood in the Urban Ghetto. *International Journal of Urban and Regional Research* 18: 88-111.

Fernández-Kelly examines the interplay between cultural and social capital in shaping the livelihood status and prospects of poor urban residents from Baltimore. Livelihood status is shaped by the physical environment of urban spaces as well as by collective constructions of social class, race, and gender. She argues that restructuring may offer immigrant families opportunities for upward mobility but close opportunities for poor African American households. Interviews reveal that among informants pregnancy is seen as one of the few means available for girls to become adult.

Survival strategies/ Ethnicity/ Racial inequality/ Social networks/ U.S.A.

222. **Fernández-Kelly, M. P., and A. M. Garcia. 1985.** The Making of an Underground Economy: Hispanic Women, Home Work, and the Advanced Capitalist State. *Urban Anthropology* 14: 59-90.

Home-based production/ Subcontracting/ Gender division of labor/ State practice/ Industrial restructuring/ Ethnicity/ U.S.A.

223. —— . **1989a.** Hispanic Women and Homework: Women in the Informal Economy of Miami and Los Angeles. In *Homework: Historical and Contemporary Perspectives on Paid Labor at Home*. Ed. E. Boris and C. R. Daniels, pp. 165-182. Chicago, Ill.: University of Illinois Press.

Home-based production/ Women/ Survival strategies/ U.S.A.

224. ——. **1989b.** Informalization at the Core: Hispanic Women, Homework, and the Advanced Capitalist State. In *The Informal Economy: Studies in Advanced and Less Developed Countries*. Ed. A. Portes, M. Castells, and L. A. Benton, pp. 247-264. Baltimore, Md.; London: Johns Hopkins University Press.

Miami and Los Angeles are characterized by an expanding Hispanic population and the coexistence of large industries and small manufacturing operations operating outside government legislation. This study explores the extent to which the advanced capitalist state, through the actions of local and federal agencies, contributes to the expansion of the underground economy. The authors also examine the garment industry to highlight the degree of internal variation in how households adapt to changing economic relations and an increasingly fragmented labor market.

Industrial restructuring/ State practice/ Ethnicity/ Household division of labor/ Gender division of labor/ Home-based production/ Garment manufacture/ Social mobility/ U.S.A.

225. **Fevre, R. 1989.** Informal Practices, Flexible Firms and Private Labour Markets. *Sociology* 23: 91-109.

Firm characteristics/ Flexibilization/ Social networks/ Industrial restructuring/ Wales/ Britain

226. **Fields, G. 1990.** Labour Market Modelling and the Urban Informal Sector: Theory and Evidence. In *The Informal Sector Revisited*. Ed. D. Turnham, B. Salomé, and A. Schwarz, pp. 49-69. Paris, France: Development Centre, Organisation for Economic Co-operation and Development.

Fields reviews the development of the concept of the informal sector and its integration into major labor market models. Growing recognition of the diversity of informal sector activities coupled with Fields's own fieldwork in Malaysia and Costa Rica reveal that certain types of informal work actually provide higher remuneration than formal sector employment and those involved in such activities generally do so by choice rather than necessity. Moreover, rather than as an alternative to informal work, formal employment provides the capital and training for undertaking successful informal enterprises. This suggests the presence of two qualitatively different sectors within the wider informal economy: the "easy-entry informal sector" and "upper-tier informal sector." The former conforms to most conventional assumptions about informality, free-entry, low wage, and undesirable types of employment, while the latter requires considerable capital and offers higher wages and more preferable employment than available in the formal sector.

Pattern or magnitude/ Research methods/ Labor market dynamics/ Firm characteristics/ Malaysia/ Costa Rica/ Third World

227. **Fischer, C. S. 1982.** *To Dwell among Friends: Personal Networks in Town and City*. Chicago, Ill.: University of Chicago Press.

Social networks/ Nonmonetary exchange/ Ethnicity/ U.S.A.

228. **Fisher, N. W. F. 1983a.** *An Assessment of the Informal Labour Market in Australia*. Technical Paper, no. 7. Canberra, Australia: Bureau of Labour Market Research.

Pattern or magnitude/ Research methods/ Australia

229. **—— . 1983b.** *An Expenditure Approach to Estimation of the Hidden Economy and Informal Labour Market*. Working Paper, no. 12. Canberra, Australia: Bureau of Labor Market Research.

Pattern or magnitude/ Research methods

230. **Fitzpatrick, P., and L. Blaxter. 1975.** Colonialism and the Informal Sector. *Australian and New Zealand Journal of Sociology* 11: 42-46.

State practice/ Rural/ Papua New Guinea

231. **Foo, G. H. C., and L. Y. C. Lim. 1989.** Poverty, Ideology and Women Export Factory Workers in Asia. In *Women, Poverty and Ideology*. Ed. H. Afshar and B. Agarwal, pp. 212-232. London: Macmillan.

Foo and Lim take issue with the conventional view of Asia's female export industry workers as poor, ideologically backward, and torn by traditional values which challenge employment outside the home. Research on Malaysian female workers in multinational firms reveals that women are not poor by local standards and that factory employment provides them a means to enhance their consumption.

They also suggest that while women workers are concentrated in low-paid factory jobs, this inequity derives not from the dynamic of factory employment per se, but from gender inequality within the wider society. As Foo and Lim conclude, the new income opportunities and the more individualistic, egalitarian ideology promoted by factory employment is a progressive rather than purely exploitative development in Asian women's lives and society.

Export processing zones/ Women/ Gender inequality/ Gender ideology/ Asia

232. **Forbes, D. K. 1978.** Urban-Rural Interdependence: The Trishaw Riders of Ujung Pandang. In *Food, Shelter and Transport in Southeast Asia and the Pacific*. Ed. P. J. Rimmer, D. Drakakis-Smith, and T. G. McGee, pp. 219-236. Department of Human Geography Monograph, no. 12. Canberra, Australia: Australian National University.

Migration/ Urbanization/ Rural/ Survival strategies/ Transportation/ Indonesia

233. —— . **1979.** *The Pedlars of Ujung Pandang*. Centre for Southeast Asian Studies Working Paper, no. 17. Melbourne, Australia: Monash University.

Pattern or magnitude/ Trading/ Indonesia

234. —— . **1981.** Production, Reproduction, and Underdevelopment: Petty Commodity Producers in Ujung Pandang, Indonesia. *Environment and Planning A* 13: 841-856.

In this study of the relationship among petty commodity, peasant and capitalist relations of production in Indonesia, Forbes argues that the transfer or economic surplus from petty commodity production into the capitalist sector supports the wage labor force in the formal sector but limits the possibility of capital accumulation among petty commodity producers. This maintains the subsistence-oriented and impoverished position of petty commodity producers. The result is a lack of class consciousness among these producers which, when coupled with their subordinated position vis-à-vis existing capitalist groups, limits the possibilities for effective improvement in their position.

Petty commodity production/ Relation to formal economy/ Unequal exchange/ Constraints to accumulation/ Consciousness/ Self-provisioning/ Indonesia

235. **Fortuna, J. C., and S. Prates. 1989.** Informal Sector versus Informalized Labor Relations in Uruguay. In *The Informal Economy: Studies in Advanced and Less Developed Countries*. Ed. A. Portes, M. Castells, and L. A. Benton, pp. 78-94. Baltimore, Md.: London: Johns Hopkins University Press.

Based on surveys of the footwear and recycling industries, the authors describe informal labor relations in Montevideo. These experiences reveal how restructuring and the expansion of informal activities are not limited to circumstances or periods characterized by low economic growth. Rather, such activities also can be found during expansive economic cycles and in sectors which are distinguished by high levels of development.

Industrial restructuring/ Shoe production/ Recycling/ Uruguay

236. **Fourcade, B., and G. Tahar. 1990.** Wage-Employment, Self-Employment and Employment Promotion: The Malian Example. *Labour and Society* 15: 365-377.

Policy analysis/ Rural/ Mali

237. **Fowler, D. A. 1978.** *The Informal Sector of Freetown (Sierra Leone)*. Geneva, Switzerland: International Labour Office.
Pattern or magnitude/ Sierra Leone

238. **Frankmann, M., and E. Charle. 1973.** Employment in the Service Sector in Sub-Saharan Africa. *Journal of Modern African Studies* 11: 201-210.

Trading/ Policy prescriptions/ Africa

239. **Franz, A. 1985.** Estimates of the Hidden Economy in Austria on the Basis of Official Statistics. *Review of Income and Wealth* 31: 325-336.

By definition, the hidden economy eludes observation by means of official statistics. However, estimates of work in the hidden economy usually include nonrecorded self-employment and moonlighting and exclude criminal behavior. Franz estimates that 3.7 percent of Austrian GDP is produced in the hidden economy.

Pattern or magnitude/ Research methods/ Moonlighting/ Austria

240. **Freedman, M. 1976.** *Labor Markets: Segments and Shelters*. New York: Universe.

Labor market segmentation/ U.S.A.

241. **Frey, B. S., and W. W. Pommerehne. 1984.** The Hidden Economy: State and Prospects for Measurement. *Review of Income and Wealth* 30: 1-23.

The authors analyze methods employed in estimating the hidden economy. Reasons for increased attention to activities in the hidden economy of developed countries include: 1) the interpretation of the informal sector as a reaction to overburdening of individuals and firms; 2) the concern that a growth in hidden economic activities may lead to a decrease in tax receipts if there is a change in the allocation of labor between taxed and untaxed sectors; and 3) the concern over inappropriate economic policy if based on incorrect measures of economic health.

Pattern or magnitude/ Research methods/ State practice/ Industrialized economies

242. **Frey, B. S., and H. Weck. 1983a.** Estimating the Shadow Economy: A "Naive" Approach. *Oxford Economic Papers* 35: 23-44.

Pattern or magnitude/ Research methods

243. **—— . 1983b.** What Produces a Hidden Economy? An International Cross-Section Analysis. *Southern Economic Journal* 49: 822-832.

Policy analysis/ Comparative/ Industrialized economies

244. **Friedmann, H. 1986.** Patriarchal Commodity Production. *Social Analysis* 20 (December): 47-55.

Friedmann highlights the place of family enterprises, particularly family farms, in advanced capitalist countries, analyzing the internal labor process they embody. Understood as a form of simple commodity production, family enterprises reflect a unity of property and labor within the context of generalised circulation of commodities. Yet, because these enterprises involve families, their analysis requires close attention to how particularistic, cooperative ties associated with family life evolve with the development of capitalist relations. While patriarchal relations accompany the *separation* of family and employment for households assuming wage dependent status under capitalism, for simple commodity producers, the transformation of patriarchy occurs *within* this production form: The commodization and specialization of farm production results in a distinct separation between women's non-commodified domestic labor and men's responsibility for market production. Despite this division, the success of family farms requires close cooperation between spouses as farm property (land and expensive equipment) reinforces both spousal and intergenerational family ties. However, contradictions between relations of property and labor and between patriarchy and egalitarian self-direction can transform possibilities for restructuring households along principles other than the cash nexus, patriarchy and property ownership.

Petty commodity production/ Labor processes/ Household division of labor/ Gender relations/ Rural/ Household

245. **Friedmann, J., and M. Salguero. 1988.** The Barrio Economy and Collective Self-Empowerment in Latin America. *Comparative Urban and Community Research* 1: 3-37.

Grass-roots social movements emerging in wake of failed development models suggest the potential for redemocratization of society and economy in Latin America. Friedmann and Salguero propose a framework for assessing and contributing to this potential that centers on the barrio economy which is the territorial basis for working class life and livelihood, and a center for counterhegemonic practice neither colonized by capital nor subservient to the state. The authors examine various linkages between economic practices, actors and sectors including forward linkages to the market economy, embodied in production relationships between household-based or micro- enterprises and large urban and international firms; backward linkages to dynamics of sociability and conviviality; and lateral linkages within the barrio, embodied in producer and consumer cooperatives that often lead to political engagement with local governments.

Survival strategies/ Social networks/ Political mobilization/ Relation to formal economy/ Economic restructuring/ Spatial patterns/ Latin America

246. **Friedmann, J., and F. Sullivan. 1974.** The Absorption of Labor in the Urban Economy: The Case of Developing Countries. *Economic Development and Cultural Change* 22: 385-413.

Labor market dynamics/ Policy analysis/ Third World

247. **Fröbel, F., J. Heinrichs, and O. Kreye. 1980.** *The New International Division of Labour: Structural Unemployment in Industrialised Countries and Industrialisation in Developing Countries*. Cambridge, U.K.; Paris: Cambridge University Press and Editions de la Maison des Sciences de l'Homme.
First published with title *Die neue internationale Arbeitsteilung: Struktrelle Arbeitslosigkeit in den Industrieländern und die Industrialisierung der Entwicklungsländern*. Reinbek bei Hamburg, Germany: Rowohlt, 1977.

While regions of Latin America, Africa, and Asia have long been integrated into the world economy as suppliers of agricultural and raw materials, they are increasingly becoming the site for the production of manufactured goods competitive in the late twentieth century world economy. Argue the authors, this development heralds a new international division of labor in which growing unemployment in industrialized countries is accompanied by growing industry-oriented foreign investment in the developing world. The argument is developed through exploration of empirical evidence documenting the decline of German textile and garment industries, increasing employment abroad by German companies, and export-oriented industrialization in developing countries, as exemplified by free trade zones and world market factories. While establishing new sites of manufacturing growth, present trends in late twentieth century capitalism bode not only structural unemployment in the industrialized world, but also continued "uneven and dependent development in the under-developed countries."

New international division of labor/ Export production/ Export processing zones/ Subcontracting/ Comparative/ Garment manufacture/ Third World/ Germany

248. **Fuentes, A., and B. Ehrenreich. 1984.** *Women in the Global Factory.* Boston, Mass.: South End Press.

Fuentes and Ehrenreich review recent trends in the global economy where multinational firms increasingly rely on the labor of women. This expansion of female employment is concentrated in new free trade and export processing zones, common in Asia and other Third World regions, as well as in expanding maquiladora and sweatshop production in North America. The authors conclude that one strategy for effective struggle against the exploitative conditions of these trends is to create links between women across the globe.

New International division of labor/ Gender division of labor/ Trade unions/ Export processing zones/ Worker characteristics

249. **Fuller, A. M. 1983.** Part-Time Farming and the Farm Family: A Note for Future Research. *Sociologia Ruralis* 23: 5-9.

Rural/ Unpaid labor/ Multiple jobs/ Household division of labor/ Industrialized economies

250. **Funkhouser, E. 1996.** The Urban Informal Sector in Central America: Household Survey Evidence. *World Development* 24 (11): 1737-1751.

Using household survey data from five Central American countries four patterns of employment and income structures in formal and informal enterprises are identified; whether the sector represents a refuge or dynamic one; that informal workers are among the youngest, the oldest, the least educated, and female members of the labor force; that human capital returns are lower than returns to education in the formal sector; and that male-female earning differentials are much higher in the informal sector than for formal sector workers. A country's "level of development" also shapes the pattern of informal employment. This point relates to questions of labor market regulation where, in Nicaragua, the direct control of wages alters the structure of earnings in favor of the informal sector. In Costa Rica, in contrast, with higher levels of development and lower levels of unemployment there is a smaller informal sector.

Pattern or magnitude/ Worker characteristics/ Education/ Labor market dynamics/ Gender inequality/ Gender division of labor/ Comparative/ Guatemala/ Honduras/ El Salvador/ Nicaragua/ Costa Rica

251. **Gaertner, W., and A. Wenig, eds. 1985.** *The Economics of the Shadow Economy*. Berlin, Germany: Springer-Verlag.

These papers respond to the growing size and role of unreported economic activities in industrialized countries. They address six themes: 1) conceptual questions concerning the definition of the shadow economy; 2) empirical evidence of its presence, size and nature in several countries of Europe and North America; 3) theoretical approaches to macroeconomic policy and microeconomic analysis; 4) implications for national fiscal and monetary policy; 5) role of household production in the informal economy; and 6) the role of the hidden economy in socialist countries of Eastern Europe.

Definition/ Pattern or magnitude/ Policy analysis/ Home-based production/ Survival strategies/ Domestic service/ Relation to formal economy/ U.S.A./ Switzerland/ Hungary/ Britain/ Belgium/ Austria/ Canada/ U.S.S.R./ Netherlands/ Germany/ Centrally planned economies/ Industrialized economies

252. **Galasi, P. 1985.** Peculiarities and Limits of the Second Economy in Socialism (the Hungarian Case). In *The Economics of the Shadow Economy*. Ed. W. Gaertner and A. Wenig, pp. 353-361. Berlin, Germany: Springer-Verlag.

Pattern or magnitude/ Hungary/ Centrally planned economies

253. **Galasi, P., and E. Sik. 1988.** Invisible Incomes in Hungary. *Social Justice* 15 (3-4): 160-178.

Pattern or magnitude/ State practice/ Hungary

254. **Galasi, P., and G. Sziráczki, eds. 1985a.** *Labour Market and Second Economy in Hungary*. Frankfurt, F.R.G.; New York: Campus Verlag.

State practice/ Labor market dynamics/ Hungary

255. ——. **1985b.** Introduction: Development and Tendencies, Labour Market and Second Economy. In *Labour Market and Second Economy in Hungary*. Ed. P. Galasi and G. Sziráczki, pp. 9-24. Frankfurt, F.R.G.; New York: Campus Verlag.

The authors argue that the second economy in Hungary is neither identical to the small capitalist sector nor to the shadow economy in capitalist countries. Their purpose is to identify the constraints that characterize and determine the development of activities in the second economy by focusing on the relationship between the state and this sector. The state stimulates expanding output in the second economy and tries to eliminate the negative and unintended effects accompanying its growth. The two objectives, however, are not reconcilable which results in a particular form of growth where increasing illegitimacy, capital and income formation, and stagnant productivity go hand in hand.

State practice/ Constraints to accumulation/ Hungary

256. **Galasi, P., and G. Sziráczki. 1990.** *Small Enterprises and Business Work Partnerships in Hungary*. Discussion Papers, DP/29/ 1990. Geneva, Switzerland: International Institute for Labour Studies.

Small or micro-enterprises/ Subcontracting/ Centrally planned economies/ Hungary

257. **Garvey, B. 1991.** Patrimonial Economics and Informal Bureaucracies: Public Administration and Social Reality in the Least Developed Countries of the 1990s: A Review Article. *Public Administration and Development* 11: 591-600.

Garvey notes the importance of two recent streams of analysis for assessing future trends in public administration in less developed countries. Current discussions characterize informal work as dynamic economic activity that avoids the constraints of state regulation. A parallel literature highlights the ineffectual and/or outright predatory role of the state in economic development, due to self-enriching exploitative behavior by ruling elites, administrative incapacity, and the pressures of international trade and politics. As bureaucracies come under increasing challenge from various sectors, a more appropriate alternative for ensuring social cohesion while realizing gradual improvements in living standards is likely to be a decentralized form of government building on "prebureaucratic" structures, systems and measures for administrative organizing.

Review/ State practice/ Africa/ South Asia/ Latin America

258. **Gatchalian, J. C., M. M. Gatchalian, C. J. Almeda, and N. O. Barranco. 1986.** *Nature, Consequences, and Prospects of Underground Employment in Four Cities of Metro Manila.* Quezon City, Metro Manila, Philippines: University of the Philippines.

Pattern or magnitude/ Philippines

259. **Gates, H. 1991.** "Narrow Hearts" and Petty Capitalism: Small Business Women in Chengdu, China. In *Marxist Approaches in Economic Anthropology*. Ed. A. Littlefield and H. Gates, pp. 13- 36. Lanham, Md.: University Press of America.

Noting the resurgence of petty capitalism in the form of proliferating household and micro-enterprises in rural and urban China since the reforms of the 1980s, Gates surveys small business women in Chengdu to assess the possibility of business growth and the ability to accommodate domestic responsibilities with income- earning economic activity. Most of these women obtain capital from informal sources rather than formal bank loans. Though current patterns resemble petty capitalist traditions characteristic of prerevolutionary China where harsh conditions of male domination prevailed, socialist emphasis on the desirability of women's work has helped to gain greater acceptance of women as paid workers. In other respects, however, state law reinforces patriarchal gender relations, increasing the potential for the growing commoditization of women's labor.

Women/ Industrial restructuring/ Home-based production/ Small or micro-enterprises/ Double-day/ Gender ideology/ China

260. **Gaughan, J., and L. Ferman. 1987.** Toward an Understanding of the Informal Economy. *Annals of the American Academy of Political and Social Science* 493: 15-24.

Nonmonetary exchange/ Unpaid labor/ Social networks/ Rural/ Third World/ Industrialized economies

261. **Geertz, C. 1963.** *Peddlers and Princes: Social Change and Economic Modernization in Two Indonesian Towns*. Chicago, Ill.: University of Chicago Press.

Geertz describes the economies of two towns in central Java and southwestern Bali, a comparison which reveals a contrast between the bazaar and trade-based pattern of business development on Java and the concentration of entrepreneurial activity among traditional political elites in Bali. Important underlying similarities also are present in the sociocultural position of each entrepreneurial group which suggests that despite different characteristics, a similar role facilitates the initiation of both towns into sustained economic growth. The study also suggests the variation possible in this process, providing an important lesson for countries marked by wide cultural and social diversity in the face of economic modernization.

Trading/ Social networks/ Entrepreneurship/ Indonesia

262. **Gereffi, G., and L. Cheng. 1992.** *The Contrasting Roles of the Informal Sector in East Asian and Latin American Development*. Discussion Paper Series on the Informal Sector, No. 6. Washington, D.C.: U.S. Department of Labor, Bureau of International Labor Affairs.

In contrast to the informal sector in Latin America, Gereffi and Cheng argue that problems of unemployment and state overregulation play little or no role in promoting its development in East Asia. More significant in the proliferation of home-based or underground units in the export-oriented economies of Taiwan and Hong Kong are the extant sociocultural conditions which support dense subcontracting networks, political tolerance of underground firms garner clientelistic electoral support, the competitiveness of flexible subcontracting arrangements for unstable or volatile markets, and the dominance of large import-export traders who cull from large numbers of small domestic subcontractors. These cases highlight the embeddedness of economic activities that fall outside the state's mandate. For Mexico this implies the need for policies to promote exports, enhance domestic subcontracting networks and upgrade worker skills.

Small or micro-enterprises/ Subcontracting/ Social networks/ Export production/ State practice/ Policy prescriptions/ Flexibilization/ Comparative/ Hong Kong/ Singapore/ South Korea/ Taiwan/ Mexico

263. **Gerry, C. 1974.** *Petty Producers and the Urban Economy: A Case Study of Dakar*. Geneva, Switzerland: International Labour Office.

Petty commodity production/ Migration/ Senegal

264. —— **. 1978a.** Petty Production and Capitalist Production in Dakar: The Crisis of the Self-Employed. *World Development* 6: 1147-1160.

Gerry critiques functional dualism and marginality as the two dominant approaches in analyses of the informal sector and argues that petty commodity production must be viewed within the context of a changing economic structure. This requires recognizing the limitations placed on Third World capitalist economies which, because of the unequal relationship between these economies, international capital and aid-giving agencies, generate relations of subordination. Processes of underdevelopment, according to Gerry, accelerate processes of differentiation among the urban self-employed which lead to the polarization and progressive impoverishment of those on the "margins."

Relation to capital/ Differentiation/ Petty commodity production/ Self-employment/ Critique of dualism/ Polarization/ Marginalization/ Senegal

265. —— **. 1978b.** Underemployment, Petty Production and Government Promotion Schemes in Senegal. *IDS Bulletin* 9 (3): 11-16.

Gerry argues that petty producers are not homogeneous and that each strata related differently to dominant forms of capitalist production and distribution. Two trends within the evolution of petty production and its external relationships are discussed: the continuing process of differentiation among petty producers, some of whom manage to graft themselves onto the structure of industry and lose virtually all but formal control of their own process of production; and the impoverishment of the mass of petty producers unable to secure urban subsistence. The underemployment of the latter highlights the disfunctionality of relations between capitalist/industrial and petty production and signifies an underlying dualism. The fact that petty production cannot participate in the development process except in a dependent and subordinate way has serious consequences for state intervention which include (a) a laissez-faire policy; (b) the selective promotion of selected industries; and (c) positive promotion coupled with a reappraisal of the economy where small-scale activities are encouraged to contribute and share in a "real process of development."

Differentiation/ Petty commodity production/ Dual sector or economy/ Policy analysis/ Under- and unemployment/ State practice/ Senegal

266. ——. **1979.** Small-Scale Manufacturing and Repairs in Dakar: A Survey of Market Relations within the Urban Economy. In *Casual Work and Poverty in Third World Cities*. Ed. R. Bromley and C. Gerry, pp. 229-250. Chichester, New York: John Wiley & Sons.

This study of petty production in Dakar of shoe and furniture makers, tailors, and mechanics/metalworkers illuminate relations between dominant and subordinate groups in the urban economy. Data on backward linkages indicate that the development of capitalist industries in Senegal provide petty producers and "traditional" artisans with three inputs: (a) initial training, (b) tools, equipment and raw materials, and (c) markets. Analyses of forward linkages show that only in metalwork do petty producers participate in the large-scale capitalist commercial and industrial circuits. Producers integrated into the capitalist market or into state industries enjoy production stability and continuity though they too do not make a significant contribution to raising incomes. Despite government efforts to promote small enterprises, few petty producers make the transition from one scale and form of production to another.

Self-employment/ Relation to formal economy/ Differentiation/ Small or micro-enterprises/ State practice/ Shoe production/ Senegal

267. —— . **1985a.** Wagers and Wage-Working: Selling Gambling Opportunities in Cali, Colombia. In *Planning for Small Enterprises in Third World Cities*. Ed. R. Bromley, pp. 155-170. Oxford, U.K.: Pergamon Press.

Gerry summarizes worker-enterprise relations in the "gambling sector" of Colombia's third largest city to suggest that neither the lumpenproletariat nor the self-employed characterize *loteros* or sellers of wagers. *Loteros* and allied vendors are not outside the capitalist labor market, but are incorporated into the process of capitalist accumulation where the reproduction of working relations combine capitalist forms of exploitation with petite bourgeois, individualist levels of consciousness. Under these conditions, workers are more accurately characterized as "disguised wage workers," employed to ensure that a larger than "normal" share of the costs which enable accumulation are borne by labor.

Relation to capital/ Disguised wage labor/ Illegal activity/ Colombia

268. —— . **1985b.** The Working Class and Small Enterprises in the UK Recession. In *Beyond Employment: Household, Gender and Subsistence*. Ed. N. Redclift and E. Mingione, pp. 288-316. Oxford, U.K.: Basil Blackwell.

The current world recession has accelerated the internationalization of capital and the relocation of production as new types of small enterprises have proliferated and as capitalist firms try to reduce labor costs by "externalization." Gerry examines state initiatives to restructure and regulate these organizational and institutional forms to show their consistency with the interests of the ruling class. Moving beyond Gorz's (1982) conclusion that these new small enterprises will create a struggle for political space, Gerry argues that the struggle also will involve the distribution of the surplus produced by such enterprises.

State practice/ Industrial restructuring/ Small or micro-enterprises/ Unequal exchange/ Political mobilization/ Britain

269. —— . **1987.** Developing Economies and the Informal Sector in Historical Perspective. *Annals of the American Academy of Political and Social Science* 493: 100-119.

Review/ Labor processes/ Survival strategies/ Unpaid labor/ Third World

270. **Gerry, C., and C. Birkbeck. 1981.** The Petty Commodity Producer in Third World Cities: Petit Bourgeois or "Disguised Proletarian"? In *The Petite Bourgeoisie: Comparative Studies of the Uneasy Stratum*. Ed. F. Bechhofer and B. Elliott, pp. 121-154. New York: St. Martin's Press.

Gerry and Birkbeck argue that despite the utility of the Marxian concept of class, the notion of a petite bourgeoisie is problematic because it does not allow for the possibility of contradictory class locations, and because it tends to locate workers not defined as "true" proletarians among the bourgeoisie. The paper disaggregates petty commodity producers into three types: (1) direct wage laborers, (2) disguised wage workers, and (3) the truly self- employed. Evidence from Senegal and Colombia demonstrate that the "self-employed" are actually disguised wage workers unable to accumulate capital. The pattern of class formation which results is supported by ideological factors, such as the illusion of independence, which generates support for capitalism notwithstanding constraints to upward mobility.

Petty commodity production/ Self-employment/ Disguised wage labor/ Social mobility/ Constraints to accumulation/ Class formation/ Senegal/ Colombia

271. **Gerry, C., and R. Bromley. 1979.** Where Do We Go from Here? In *Casual Work and Poverty in Third World Cities*. Ed. C. Gerry and R. Bromley, pp. 305-310. New York: John Wiley & Sons.

Policy prescriptions/ Third World

272. **Gershuny, J. I. 1977.** Post-Industrial Society: The Myth of the Service Economy. *Futures* 9: 103-114.

This essay critiques Daniel Bell's thesis that postindustrial society is characterized by the increasing concentration of expenditure on services rather than material goods. Gershuny argues that in the UK expenditures on material goods is increasing rather than decreasing, and that the growth of tertiary sector employment is the result of an emerging division of labor which passes on the planning, forecasting, and organizational functions associated with the production of manufactured goods from artisans to white and pink collar workers. Thus, a large proportion of those in the tertiary sector are persons involved in manufacturing rather than in services.

Industrial restructuring/ Britain

273. —— . **1978.** *After Industrial Society? The Emerging Self-Service Economy*. Atlantic Highlands, N.J.: Humanities Press.

Industrial restructuring/ Nonmonetary exchange/ Unpaid labor/ Industrialized economies

274. —— . **1979.** The Informal Economy: Its Role in Post-Industrial Society. *Futures* 11: 3-15.

Gershuny argues that services once provided in the "formal" economy of developed countries are being informalized. OECD data on the "productivity gap" suggest that jobs lost in manufacturing have not been replaced by new jobs in services but have been partially replaced by low-wage informal employment. Underground, household, and communal activities also have been enabled by the declining costs of capital equipment. The author develops a nonlinear model of development where transformations to and from the formal, household, communal, and underground economies occur with changes in technology, labor supply, and public regulation. He argues that while government can ignore, suppress or promote informal sources of income earning, its promotion is preferable because a dual economy policy can combine the efficiency of formal production with the less efficient use of labor in informal activity. Informal activity is estimated to represent 10 to 25 percent of GNP.

Industrial restructuring/ Home-based production/ Relation to formal economy/ Dual sector or economy/ Pattern or magnitude/ Policy analysis/ Technological change/ Industrialized economies

275. —— . **1983.** *Social Innovation and the Division of Labour*. Oxford, U.K.: Oxford University Press.

Gender division of labor/ Relation to formal economy

276. —— . **1985.** Economic Development and Change in the Mode of Provision of Services. In *Beyond Employment: Household, Gender and Subsistence*. Ed. N. Redclift and E. Mingione, pp. 128-164. Oxford, U.K.: Basil Blackwell.

In the context of the shift from manufacture to service production, Gershuny examines the effects of sociotechnical innovations on the provision of services to explain changes in patterns of paid employment. Using data from eight western European countries on patterns of time and money expenditure, the article applies a model of innovation to the provision of services. The industrialization of service production involves the subdivision of tasks, capital intensification, and the pursuit of economies of scale such that part of final production is displaced outside the formal economy. The authors also examine changes in labor productivity in the context of new household technologies.

Industrial restructuring/ Technological change/ Relation to formal economy/ Industrialized economies

277. —— . **1987.** Technology, Social Innovation, and the Informal Economy. *Annals of the American Academy of Political and Social Science* 493: 49-63.

Technological change/ Home-based production/ Research methods/ Canada/ Netherlands/ Norway/ Britain/ U.S.A.

278. —— . **1988.** Time, Technology and the Informal Economy. In *On Work: Historical, Comparative and Theoretical Approaches*. Ed. R. E. Pahl, pp. 579-597. Oxford, U.K.: Basil Blackwell.

Gershuny reviews the informal economy and discusses historical changes in the organization of production. He highlights historical shifts of work between the formal and informal sectors of the economy. He explores the various kinds of work that constitute daily life to elaborate a complex definition of work. He then examines the way people use their time to investigate the changing mix of production and consumption activities.

Unpaid labor/ Social reproduction/ Household division of labor/ Technological change/ Industrialized economies

279. **Gershuny, J. I., and R. E. Pahl. 1981.** Work Outside Employment: Some Preliminary Speculations. In *Can I Have It in Cash?: A Study of Informal Institutions and Unorthodox Ways of Doing Things*. Ed. S. Henry, pp. 73-88. New York: St. Martin's Press.

Given the decline in formal employment in Britain, the authors argue that a rethinking of the meaning of work and the economy is necessary for the formulation of appropriate policy formulation. A review of economic trends indicates that productivity in manufacturing has grown faster than demand, that labor productivity has increased without a growth in total output, and that the expansion in services has relied upon state resources. These trends do not augur well for decreasing unemployment, especially given the needs of women and unskilled workers. The authors note that policies supporting formal employment have been either unsuccessful or politically objectionable. Thus, for workers, unemployment can only be met by informal work which has the advantages of autonomy, variety, and greater use of personal skills. Moreover, since some form of dual economy is inevitable, policies must be devised which adapt the informal economy to socially progressive ends.

Industrial restructuring/ Dual sector or economy/ Britain

280. **Gilbert, A., ed. 1982.** *Urbanization in Contemporary Latin America: Critical Approaches to the Analysis of Urban Areas*. Chichester, U.K.: John Wiley & Sons.

Urbanization/ Survival strategies/ Dual sector or economy/ Latin America

281. **Gilbert, A., and J. Gugler. 1992.** *Cities, Poverty, and Development: Urbanization in the Third World*. Oxford, U.K.: Oxford University Press.

Noting the regional fragmentation of urbanization studies, Gilbert and Gugler review current theories on urbanization and poverty to assess their applicability to diverse settings in the Third World. Placing the process of urbanization within context of a world system, they discuss patterns of agglomeration, regional imbalances in growth, complex process of urban rural linkages through migration, and the implications of urban migration for labor markets, particularly in terms of un-, under-, and informal sector employment. Issues of urban housing, the dynamics of urban social organization, and political conflicts and social movements are addressed in separate chapters. In conclusion, the value of formulating spatial policy to resolve poverty in the absence of genuine social and economic reform is shown to be problematic.

Urbanization/ Migration/ Under- and unemployment/ Spatial patterns/ Social networks/ Housing/ Political mobilization/ Third World

282. **Gindling, T. H. 1991.** Labor Market Segmentation and the Determination of Wages in the Public, Private-Formal and Informal Sectors in San Jose, Costa Rica. *Economic Development and Culture Change* 39: 585-605.

Labor market segmentation occurs when institutional barriers prevent workers in the informal economy or in private, formal sector services from assuming positions in high sectors of the economy. A model is developed to explore three related hypotheses: 1) that wage equations are different in different sectors; 2) that observationally identical workers have higher expected income in upper than in lower sectors; and 3) that worker mobility between sectors is limited. Data from workers in public, private-formal and informal employment in transportation and service industries of San José support the hypothesis that segmentation exists between both the urban public and private-formal and the private-formal and informal sectors.

Labor market segmentation/ Worker characteristics/ Social mobility/ Relation to formal economy/ Transportation/ Trading/ Costa Rica

283. **Ginsburgh, V., Ph. Michel, F. P. Schioppa, and P. Pestieau. 1985.** Macroeconomic Policy in the Presence of an Irregular Sector. In *The Economics of the Shadow Economy*. Ed. W. Gaertner and A. Wenig, pp. 194-217. Berlin, F.R.G.: Springer-Verlag.

This paper examines the policy implications of the presence of both an observed regular and an unobserved irregular sector. It develops a two-sector model in which the regular sector is subject to fixed prices and wages, while irregular sector wages fluctuate freely. A number of regimes are shown to be possible and for each the paper examines the effects of different policies on regular as well as overall employment. Ignoring the existence of the irregular sector can lead to employment policies which ultimately reduce the overall level of employment.

Dual sector or economy/ State practice/ Industrialized economies

284. **Glatzer, W., and R. Berger. 1985.** Household Composition, Social Networks and Household Production. In *The Economics of the Shadow Economy*. Ed. W. Gaertner and A. Wenig, pp. 330-351. Berlin, F.R.G.; New York: Springer-Verlag.

This article describes household production of goods and services for self-consumption and for exchange in West Germany. Household production includes daily housework chores to housing construction and childcare as well as the care of the aged. Household production thus includes economic value and non-material contributions to individual welfare. The article examines selected aspects of household production in relation to the performance of the market system and the welfare state highlighting the effects of household composition, income, social class, and the age of household members on household production activities.

Survival strategies/ Home-based production/ Unpaid labor/ Social networks/ Worker characteristics/ Social reproduction/ Germany

285. **Godard, F. 1985.** How Do Ways of Life Change? In *Beyond Employment: Household, Gender and Subsistence*. Ed. N. Redclift and E. Mingione, pp. 317-337. Oxford, U.K.: Basil Blackwell.

Godard analyzes the relationship between the state, political movements and consciousness in Western Europe in the context of the "autonomization" of civil society and the creation of new social relations. The decline of the welfare state and of large-scale institutions of production and management has been accompanied by new forms of production organization, including the recomposition of relations within the home. Recent work rejects analysis which takes the family as a mode of reproduction as its starting point, and, instead, examines the household as a sphere of both production and reproduction.

Social restructuring/ Survival strategies/ Labor processes/ Consciousness/ Household division of labor/ Social reproduction/ Industrialized economies

286. **Goddard, V. 1981.** The Leather Trade in the Bassi of Naples. *IDS Bulletin* 12 (3): 30-35.

Goddard argues that outwork and the high incidence of small units of production in Italy must be understood as part of the process of decentralized production. In Naples, men and women play different roles within this process and these differences can only be understood through analyses of the sexual division of household labor and gender roles. Thus, gender determines differential access to resources such as capital, labor and personal networks which are central to an individual's prospects as worker, employer or producer. While men may manipulate these networks to establish themselves as petty entrepreneurs, women are constrained by them and remain dependent both within and outside the factory.

Subcontracting/ Industrial restructuring/ Gender division of labor/ Social networks/ Household division of labor/ Italy

287. **Gordon, D. M., R. Edwards, and M. Reich. 1982.** *Segmented Work, Divided Workers: The Historical Transformation of Labor in the United States*. New York: Cambridge University Press.

Highlighting the quiescence of the U.S. workforce in the face of steadily eroding worker welfare since the 1970s, the authors identify the factors behind this pattern through an analysis of complex relationships usually neglected in conventional accounts and dual labor market theories. Overlapping stages of proletarianization, homogenization, and segmentation have characterized the development of the labor process and labor markets under U.S. capitalism since the early 1900s. The study describes these stages focusing on the links between long swings in economic activity, structures of accumulation in the United States, and the organization and structure of work and U.S. labor markets. Interactions between these factors have produced qualitative transformations in the labor process, and labor force segmentation since the 1920s has served to forge and deepen materially based divisions among American workers. Such divisions limit the emergence of a unified working class movement and consolidate the position of capital over labor.

Production process/ Labor market segmentation/ Class processes/ Labor relations/ Processes of accumulation/ Consciousness/ U.S.A.

288. **Gorz, A. 1982.** *Farewell to the Working Class: An Essay on Post-Industrial Socialism*. London: Pluto Press.

In a nine-part essay calling for the abolition of work performed for pay, Gorz challenges basic concepts in Marxist theory on capitalist development. The primacy of the production process in defining social relations, and the conceptualization of the working class as the sole source of revolutionary power is challenged since workers' have decreasing power in face of increasing automation. Instead, he argues that the new revolutionary force is the emergent "non-class of post industrial proletarians" comprised of growing numbers of people with no job security engaged both simultaneously and successively in a wide variety of unrelated paid activities. He emphasizes the possibility of a postindustrial revolution and the necessary conditions for its success including an appreciation of the women's movement which must assert the centrality of noneconomic values to society.

Economic restructuring/ Class processes/ Political mobilization/ Gender ideology/ Consciousness/ Industrialized economies

289. **Gottlieb, B. H., ed. 1981.** *Social Networks and Social Support*. Beverly Hills, Calif.: Sage.

Nonmonetary exchange/ Social networks

290. **Grancelli, B. 1987.** Political Trade-Offs, Collective Bargaining, Individual Tradings: Some Remarks on Industrial Relations in Italy. In *The Unofficial Economy: Consequences and Perspectives in Different Economic Systems*. Ed. S. Alessandrini and B. Dallago, pp. 257-270. Aldershot, Hants, U.K.; Brookfield, Vt.: Gower Publishing.

Grancelli interprets the informal economy in Italy as playing a crucial role in social and economic stabilization. He begins with a discussion of Italy's industrial relations where "neo- corporatist" and "neo-liberalist" solutions have been unable to solve the contradiction between the need for economic accumulation and intense social conflict. The existence of economic stability is explained in terms of the development of subcontracting and small enterprises which has created flexible and innovative local employment and the practice of moonlighting which served as a social shock absorber. The "rusting" of political institutions and the "polycentrism of social power" also brought trade unions to a crisis of representation which has been resolved by the opening up of the informal economy where individual identity can be affirmed.

Flexibilization/ Small or micro-enterprises/ Industrial restructuring/ Moonlighting/ Subcontracting/ State practice/ Labor movements/ Consciousness/ Italy

291. **Granovetter, M. 1984.** Small Is Bountiful: Labor Markets and Establishment Size. *American Sociological Review* 49: 323-334.

Small or micro-enterprises/ Firm characteristics/ U.S.A./ Sweden/ Japan

292. **Gray, J. 1987.** Conference on the Comparative Study of the Informal Sector: Harpers Ferry West Virginia, October 1986. *International Journal of Urban and Regional Research* 11: 421- 423.

Definition/ Survival strategies/ State practice/ Comparative

293. **Greenfield, H. I. 1993.** *Invisible, Outlawed, and Untaxed: America's Underground Economy*. Westport, Conn.: Praeger.

Defining the underground economy as the production and distribution of goods and services that are not directly reflected in national income and product accounts, Greenfield determines its size in the United States. Various methods are outlined to identify the size and sources of unreported income. The size of different illegal sectors (drugs, gambling, prostitution, smuggling) is estimated, and indicators for rates of informal labor force participation are given. The author argues that the size of the underground economy has been much smaller than has been claimed in recent literature, and U.S. economic indicators suggest robust growth, probably leading to diminished though not eliminated role of the underground economy in the future.

Review/ Pattern or magnitude/ Illegal activity/ Research methods/ U.S.A.

294. **Greenstreet, M. 1981.** When Education Is Unequal. *IDS Bulletin* 12 (3): 14-18.

Greenstreet examines factors which account for the importance of women in the urban informal sector in Ghana. Women find urban trading a suitable occupation because the traditional division of labor between the sexes means that women have a dual responsibility for home and outside employment. For the majority, trading is the only occupation that enable women to fulfill their various functions as wife, mother, and income earner. The formal schooling of females have lagged behind that of males, and many illiterate women occupy lower status jobs in the informal sector.

Double-day/ Gender inequality/ Women/ Trading/ Education/ Ghana

295. **Gringeri, C. E. 1994.** *Getting By: Women Homeworkers and Rural Economic Development*. Lawrence: University Press of Kansas.

In recent decades, home assembly work has emerged as an increasingly frequent development strategy in the rural United States. In a study of two communities in Iowa and Wisconsin, Gringeri investigates this phenomenon from the perspective of homeworkers and explores state involvements in promoting home-based production as a rural development strategy. A review of local economic history highlights developments leading to the establishment of home-based subcontracting arrangements with a supplier for General Motors in both areas. Interview results and field observations are presented to describe conditions of work, motivations for participation, and labor constraints. Homeworkers, particularly women, engage in home-based production to augment household income while maintaining other household responsibilities. Gringeri proposes the need to understand industrial homework as a rural development strategy subsidized by the labor of growing numbers of rural women.

Home-based production/ Subcontracting/ Worker characteristics/ Economic restructuring/ Rural/ U.S.A.

296. **Grootaert, C. 1992.** The Position of Migrants in the Urban Informal Labour Markets in Côte d'Ivoire. *Journal of African Economies* 1 (3): 416-445.

Grootaert describes formal and informal sectors of urban labor markets in Côte d'Ivoire, highlighting the role of migrant status in influencing worker access to each sector. The study reveals the heterogeneity of the informal sector, which is most accurately described less in terms of firm size than in terms of self-employed versus employee status of the workers involved. Also challenged is the notion that the informal sector serves mainly as a transitory springboard to formal employment. Only informal employees are shown to comprise a more unstable part of the informal sector, and often undergo an eventual transition to self-employed status.

Pattern or magnitude/ Worker characteristics/ Labor market dynamics/ Self-employment/ Côte d'Ivoire

297. **Grosh, B., and G. Somolekae. 1996.** Mighty Oaks from Little Acorns: Can Microenterprise Serve as the Seedbed of Industrialization? *World Development* 24 (12): 1879-1890.

Grosh and Somolekae explore strategies for promoting dynamic industrial growth through support for microenterprises. Small informal firms and microenterprises are conceptualized as a potential "seedbed for industrialization" capable of supporting the health of the wider industrial sector, including medium- and large-size businesses. Specific policy alternatives are examined, and the importance of growth as well as savings by small firms is emphasized. The authors argue for macro-level policy reform rather than firm-level interventions to enhance overall growth. Policy interventions include not merely mitigating overregulation but also state promotion of the institutional infrastructure supporting business development.

Small or micro-enterprises/ Processes of accumulation/ Regulation/ Policy prescriptions/ Third World

298. **Grossman, G. 1977.** The "Second Economy" of the USSR. *Problems of Communism* 26 (September-October): 25-40.

Pattern or magnitude/ U.S.S.R.

299. —— **. 1989.** Informal Personal Incomes and Outlays of the Soviet Urban Population. In *The Informal Economy: Studies in Advanced and Less Developed Countries*. Ed. A. Portes, M. Castells, and L. A. Benton, pp. 150-172. Baltimore, Md., London: Johns Hopkins University Press.

Based on a survey of more than one thousand immigrant Soviet families to the United States. about urban informal sector employment in the U.S.S.R., Grossman describes their size and the distribution of their earnings. Informal income is defined as that derived from productive informal activity and from illegal earnings from embezzlement, misappropriation, and the misuse of state-owned production facilities. Informal outlays refer to the purchase or acquisition of goods and services outside formal channels.

Illegal activity/ Pattern or magnitude/ U.S.S.R.

300. **Grossman, G., and V. Treml. 1987.** Measuring Hidden Personal Income in the USSR. In *The Unofficial Economy: Consequences and Perspectives in Different Economic Systems*. Ed. S. Alessandrini and B. Dallago, pp. 285-296. Aldershot, Hants, U.K.; Brookfield, Vt.: Gower Publishing.

This paper examines the survey methodology used in a research project to collect data from recent Soviet immigrants on the underground economy in the U.S.S.R. Estimates of the size of unofficial income as a supplement to official earnings and on household composition, income, wealth and expenditure are offered, but these estimates are provisional since food purchases in rural areas and family-grown food were excluded.

Pattern or magnitude/ Worker characteristics/ Research methods/ U.S.S.R.

301. **Guhathakurta, S. 1993.** Economic Independence through Protection? Emerging Contradictions in India's Small-Scale Sector Policies. *World Development* 21: 2039-2054.

An important component of the Indian government's policies to promote development of the small-scale industrial sector has been to reserve specific items for exclusive production by small enterprises. Guhathakurta criticizes the policy through a case study of the metal furniture manufacturing industry. While government policy has resulted in some expansion of manufacturing activity to small scale and artisanal units in economically backward areas, these small units have in most cases evolved as inefficient subsidiaries of large firms to whom the real benefits of the policy have largely accrued. Alternative policies are needed that focus less on regulation and more on creating supportive networks and market conditions which allow small producers to find appropriate niches without compromising industrial growth.

Small or micro-enterprises/ Artisanal production/ Policy analysis/ Subcontracting/ India

302. **Guisinger, S., and M. Irfan. 1980.** Pakistan's Informal Sector. *Journal of Development Studies* 16: 412-426.

Pattern or magnitude/ Pakistan

303. **Gupta, S. B. 1992.** *Black Income in India*. New Delhi, India: Sage Publications.

Gupta defines black income as income that is either illegally obtained or legally obtained yet not reported. Links between the growth of black income in India and political corruption are examined, and two general arenas through which black income is garnered are identified: evasion of taxes, excise duties and other fees associated with government administration; and smuggling, black marketeering, bribery, pilferage, and other forms of corruption. The study estimates the level of black income and reviews various government policies to deter or control the sector. The general failure of these policies may be traced to corruption in Indian politics and government bureaucracy, as wealth generated through black income sources accrues to those already economically well-established or politically well-connected.

Pattern or magnitude/ Pilfering/ Policy analysis/ Polarization/ India

304. **Gutmann, P. 1978.** Off the Books. *Across the Board* 15 (August): 8-14.

Pattern or magnitude/ Policy prescriptions/ U.S.A.

305. —— . **1979.** Statistical Illusions, Mistaken Policies. *Challenge* 22 (November-December): 14-17.

Pattern or magnitude/ Policy prescriptions/ U.S.A.

306. —— . **1985.** The Subterranean Economy, Redux. In *The Economics of the Shadow Economy*. Ed. W. Gaertner and A. Wenig, pp. 2-18. Berlin, F.R.G.; New York: Springer-Verlag.

This paper examines the "subterranean economy" in the United States defined as productive activity that "escapes the ministrations of the tax collector and largely that of the statistician." Guttman estimates that it contributes 14-15 percent to the GNP, involves approximately 28 million people, and expands in response to high taxes, extensive government regulations, the prohibition of illegal activity, the fear of losing welfare benefits, and its flexible use of labor. The policy implications emphasize (a) erroneous official statistics, (b) mistakes in government policy, (c) false reporting on household surveys, (d) a breakdown in the tax system, and (e) small business dependence on subterranean income. Gutmann argues that governments should revise current statistics and economists need to reexamine their monetary, micro-economic, and tax theories.

Pattern or magnitude/ Tax evasion/ Policy prescriptions/ U.S.A.

307. **Hackenberg, R. A. 1980.** New Patterns of Urbanization in Southeast Asia: An Assessment. *Population and Development Review* 6: 391-419.

Urbanization/ Malaysia/ Thailand/ Philippines/ Indonesia

308. **Hadjicostandi, J. 1990.** Façon: Women's Formal and Informal Work in the Garment Industry in Kavala, Greece. In *Women Workers and Global Restructuring*. Ed K. Ward, pp. 64-81. Ithaca, N.Y.: ILR Press, School of Industrial and Labor Relations, Cornell University.

Garment manufacture/ Gender division of labor/ Export production/ Piecework/ Home-based production/ Household/ Household division of labor/ Gender relations/ Greece

309. **Hakim, C. 1988.** Homeworking in Britain. In *On Work: Historical, Comparative and Theoretical Approaches*. Ed. R. E. Pahl, pp. 609-632. Oxford, U.K.: Basil Blackwell.

Home-based production/ Britain

310. **Halperin, R. H. 1990.** *The Livelihood of Kin: Making Ends Meet the Kentucky Way*. Austin, Tex.: University of Texas Press.

Drawing from ethnographic fieldwork in rural Kentucky, Halperin highlights the dynamic of "the Kentucky way"—a complex of local knowledge and practices that allows rural people a sense of autonomy and control over their livelihood within capitalist American society. Integral to this complex is a multiplicity of livelihood strategies involving wage labor, the use of state services and payments, and unpaid, home-based economic activities. Carefully cultivated kin and friendship networks provide access to goods and services outside the formal market. Regional and periodic marketplace systems also play a key role as alternative economic institutions for generating needed household cash from the sale of family-produced goods. The study illustrates the complex dynamics of rural resistance to capitalism and dependency on the state.

Multiple jobs/ Unpaid labor/ Home-based production/ Social networks/ Survival strategies/ Rural/ Farmer's markets/ Resistance/ U.S.A.

311. **Halter, M., ed. 1995.** *New Migrants in the Marketplace: Boston's Ethnic Entrepreneurs*. Amherst: University of Massachusetts Press.

Six case studies of entrepreneuralism among Soviet Jewish, West Indian, Greek, Latino, Khmer, and Haitian neighborhoods of the Boston metropolitan area explore pattern of small business development in each ethnic context. Highlighted is the role of various social and cultural institutions characterizing each community. The authors identify the significance of small and microenterprises in providing employment to co-ethnic residents and in providing economic and social resources that enable the younger generation to advance into professional employment. Also highlighted is the structure of sociocultural resources which may constrain business development.

Small or micro-enterprises/ Ethnicity/ Social networks/ Migration/ Social mobility/ U.S.A.

312. **Hansen, K. T. 1980.** The Urban Informal Sector as a Development Issue: Poor Women and Work in Lusaka, Zambia. *Urban Anthropology* 9: 199-225.

Women/ Trading/ Policy analysis/ Zambia

313. **Hansohm, D., and K. Wohlmuth. 1987.** Promotion of Rural Handicrafts as a Means of Structural Adjustment. *Scandinavian Journal of Development Alternatives* 6: 170-190.

Structural adjustment/ Small or micro-enterprises/ State practice/ Rural/ Handicrafts/ Sudan

314. **Hansson, I. 1987.** Optimal Income Taxation and the Untaxed Sector. In *The Unofficial Economy: Consequences and Perspectives in Different Economic Systems*. Ed. S. Alessandrini and B. Dallago, pp. 311-321. Aldershot, Hants, U.K.; Brookfield, Vt.: Gower Publishing.

Hansson examines the specific problem of tax evasion, its consequences, and the optimal redistributive income tax when untaxed income is included. A two-sector general equilibrium model of an open economy is presented where two agents exist: an individual and a government collecting taxes and redistributing transfers. When the untaxed sector is considered, the optimal tax rate appears higher than when this sector is excluded, as in traditional models. The explanation given is that the tax base acts as a signal for capacity in the untaxed sector, and that income tax provides insurance for variations in capacity in the taxed as well as in the untaxed sector.

Policy analysis/ Tax evasion/ Industrialized economies

315. **Harding, P., and R. Jenkins. 1989.** *The Myth of the Hidden Economy*. Milton Keynes, U.K.: Open University Press.

Harding and Jenkins reject the concept of a hidden economy and note that by conceiving informal and noneconomic work as a discrete economic sphere, even when multiple intersections between formal and informal activity are recognized, findings are contradictory. Efforts to measure the sector through survey and secondary data fail to substantiate assertions about its growing size or presence. An alternative conceptualization is proposed which builds on the perceptions and accounts of relevant actors regarding their own activities and emphasizes a continuity between formality and informality where activities are seen to differ in degree rather than kind. Also recognized is the centrality of informal economic activities to developed capitalist economies, as well as the close, if contradictory, relationship of informal activities to principles of capitalism.

Review/ Definition/ Critique of dualism/ Relation to formal economy/ Continuum debate/ Research methods/ Industrialized economies

316. **Harper, M. 1996.** Urban Planning and the Informal Sector. *Regional Development Dialogue* 17 (1): 97-112.

Policy prescriptions/ Trading/ Malaysia

317. **Harris, C. C. 1983.** Social Transitions and the Deconstruction of the Family: Reflections on Research into the Domestic Circumstances of the Victims of Economic Change. *Tocqueville Review* 5 (2): 365-381.

Survival strategies/ Social networks/ Household division of labor/ Social restructuring/ Wales

318. **Harrison, B. 1974.** The Theory of the Dual Economy. In *The Worker in "Postindustrial" Capitalism: Liberal and Radical Responses*. Ed. B. Silverman and M. Yanowitch, pp. 267-287. New York: Random House.

Dual sector or economy/ Review/ Racial inequality/ U.S.A.

319. **Harrison, F. V. 1991.** Women in Jamaica's Urban Informal Economy: Insights from a Kingston Slum. In *Third World Women and the Politics of Feminism*. Ed. C. T. Mohanty, A. Russo, and L. Torres, pp. 173-196. Bloomington, Ind.: Indiana University Press.

Harrison describes the position and role of women in Jamaica's urban informal economy where their economic activities are disproportionately concentrated. Emphasizing the intersection of gender and class inequality in capitalist development at both national and international levels, she identifies possibilities for change through political activism. She notes that activism is constrained by sexism which inhibits women's political behavior in the informal economy and the political development of the casual work force overall.

Labor market segmentation/ Gender ideology/ Women/ Trading/ Political mobilization/ Jamaica

320. **Harriss, B. 1978.** Quasi-Formal Employment Structures and Behaviour in the Unorganized Urban Economy, and the Reverse: Some Evidence from South India. *World Development* 6: 1077-1086.

Labor market dynamics/ India

321. **Harriss, J. 1982a.** Character of an Urban Economy: Small- scale Production and Labour Markets in Coimbatore [1]. *Economic and Political Weekly* 17: 945-954.

Petty commodity production/ Differentiation/ Small or micro-enterprises/ India

322. —— . **1982b.** Character of an Urban Economy: Small-Scale Production and Labor Markets in Coimbatore [2]. *Economic and Political Weekly* 17: 993-1002.

Differentiation/ Small or micro-enterprises/ Petty commodity production/ India

323. —— . **1982c.** *Studies of Small-Scale Enterprise and Urban Labour in South India.* School of Development Studies Occasional Paper, no. 19. Norwich, U.K.: University of East Anglia.

Small or micro-enterprises/ Subcontracting/ India

324. —— . **1985.** Our Socialism and the Subsistence Engineer: The Role of Small Enterprises in the Engineering Industry of Coimbatore, South India. In *Planning for Small Enterprises in Third World Cities*. Ed. R. Bromley, pp. 137-154. Oxford, U.K.: Pergamon Press.

Focusing on the engineering industry in Tamil Nadu, Harriss examines 15 relatively large factories and 175 small enterprises or workshops and finds that small units have strong forward and backward linkages to the large-scale sector, primarily through subcontracting arrangements. These linkages are not homogenous since their subordination and exploitation depend upon their bargaining power, itself shaped by their providing specialized services or having secure access to finance. While most workshops have been able to accumulate capital and expand, their growth potential is constrained by their dependent status. The persistence of small production units can be attributed to the interests of large-scale capital to control the labor process by fighting unionization and to reduce labor costs by avoiding labor legislation. Harriss concludes that the policy claims of encouraging small-scale production have not been attained, except under circumstances when a more democratic structure of ownership extends bourgeois interests.

Subcontracting/ Small or micro-enterprises/ State practice/ Trade unions/ Constraints to accumulation/ India

325. **Hart, K. 1970.** Small-Scale Entrepreneurs in Ghana and Development Planning. *Journal of Development Studies* 6: 104-120.

Hart assesses the contribution of small-scale, part-time, indigenous entrepreneurs to Ghana's economic development and suggests that economic planners have obscured their significance in economic planning because of their western ethnocentric focus and their preoccupation with firms and businessmen. This has led to a failure to differentiate among service sector activity and to unreliable data on individuals who, in the absence of an advanced capital market, invest savings in productive and profitable self-managed enterprises.

To minimize risk and escape bureaucratic control, small entrepreneurs in local development projects display diversified interests that make the homogenization of their efforts dubious.

Small or micro-enterprises/ Transportation/ Trading/ Housing/ Policy analysis/ Ghana

326. —— . **1973.** Informal Income Opportunities and Urban Employment in Ghana. *Journal of Modern African Studies* 11: 61-89.

Hart describes the economic activities of the low-income, urban subproletariat of Accra's labor force into which unskilled and illiterate migrants are drawn. Price inflation, inadequate wages, and a growing surplus labor pool have caused a high degree of informal income-generating activities among this population where job duplication, petty capitalism and multiple informal jobs are used to augment family income. Hart calls for a rethinking of employment policy, a redefinition of those defined as unemployed, and recommends the use of an input-output matrix to chart income flows within the urban economy.

Dual sector or economy/ Definition/ Worker characteristics/ Multiple jobs/Migration/ Survival strategies/ Ghana

327. **Haruo, N. 1996.** Planning for Employment in the Urban Informal Sector. *Regional Development Dialogue* 17 (1): 185-192.

Pattern or magnitude/ Policy analysis/ Policy prescriptions/ Asia

328. **Haulk, C. J. 1980.** Thoughts on the Underground Economy. *Economic Review (Federal Reserve Bank of Atlanta)* March/April: 23-27.

Policy analysis/ U.S.A.

329. **Hauser, P. M. 1982.** Urbanisation and Development. *Development* 2: 8-9.

Urbanization/ Dual sector or economy/ Policy analysis

330. **Hawrylyshyn, O. 1976.** The Value of Household Services: A Survey of Empirical Estimates. *Review of Income and Wealth* 22: 101-131.

Unpaid labor/ Research methods/ Industrialized economies

331. —— . **1977.** Towards a Definition of Non-Market Activities. *Review of Income and Wealth* 23: 79-96.

Hawrylyshyn highlights the economic value of nonmarket activities and notes that nonmarket household work crosses the boundary between noneconomic and economic work. He classifies household activities which meet biological needs and market activities as paid work. Productive nonmarket activities include housework and child care, but exclude voluntary time and leisure-pleasure.

Unpaid labor/ Social reproduction/ Research methods/ Industrialized economies

332. **Heck, R. 1987.** A Profile of Home-Based Workers. *Human Ecology Forum* 16: 15-18.

Heck describes the characteristics of U.S. home-based workers based on the 1984 Panel Study of Income Dynamics. She also identifies selected advantages and disadvantages of home-based work from the point of view of the individual.

Home-based production/ Worker characteristics/ U.S.A.

333. **Heertje, A. 1987.** Some Observations on the Welfare Economic Aspects of the Unofficial Economy. In *The Unofficial Economy: Consequences and Perspectives in Different Economic Systems*. Ed. S. Alessandrini and B. Dallago, pp. 303-310. Aldershot, Hants, U.K.; Brookfield, Vt.: Gower Publishing.

Official and unofficial work as well as transactions within and outside the market are part of the economy, although resources are allocated within economic units in response to an individual's preference for the noninterference of government. Depending on the transaction costs associated with market allocation, such as taxes and regulation, and the benefits of internal allocation or mutual trust, this may have a positive welfare effect. In modern economies the informal sector grows when the allocative function of the price mechanism is weakened. We now face a "schizophrenic" dual economy with tendencies toward full and underemployment as well as Pareto and non-Pareto optimality.

Dual sector or economy/ Welfare/ Industrialized economies

334. **Hegedus, A. 1987.** Some Problems of the Expansion of the Second Economy in Hungary. In *The Unofficial Economy: Consequences and Perspectives in Different Economic Systems*. Ed. S. Alessandrini and B. Dallago, pp. 297-301. Aldershot, Hants, U.K.; Brookfield, Vt.: Gower Publishing.

Hedegus examines the contradictory economic and political effects of Hungary's second economy. While shortages have been reduced, inflation has increased as has the shift of the workforce from the first to the second economy in response to the impact on different social strata of recent policy initiatives. The second economy offers opportunities to those able to mobilize unused personal capital while also contributing to declines in living standards among those unable to do so. Hegedus also argues that when mainstream social activity is diverted to nonpolitical areas, political pluralism is deprived of its social basis and divides pro- and antireformist factions.

State practice/ Hungary

335. **Heinze, R. G., and T. Olk. 1982.** Development of the Informal Economy: A Strategy for Resolving the Crises of the Welfare State. *Futures* 14: 189-204.

Industrial restructuring/ Home-based production/ Unpaid labor/ Policy analysis/ Welfare/ Germany

336. **Hemmer, H. R., and C. Mannel. 1989.** On the Economic Analysis of the Urban Informal Sector. *World Development* 17: 1543-1552.

The authors identify linkages between the informal and formal sector and suggest that the former is the more dynamic sector, able to generate more products and services than the formal sector. The interconnections between these sectors mean that policies affecting one sector are likely to affect the other.

Relation to formal economy/ Policy analysis/ Third World

337. **Henry, S. 1981.** Introduction. In *Can I Have It in Cash?: A Study of Informal Institutions and Unorthodox Ways of Doing Things*. Ed. S. Henry, pp. 1-23. New York: St. Martin's Press.

Henry examines why informal institutions have been overlooked in the literature and suggests that the social sciences must reintegrate the study of everyday social life into social theory and recognize that informal and formal institutions are complementary parts of a single system. He proposes a typology of informal economies based on their relationship to official institutions. Henry concludes that: informal institutions are an integral part of the official economy, but also mask its failures; they provide grounds for governments and those in the formal economy to off-load their more difficult functions and avoid social change; informal institutions are subject to the worst problems of formal institutions; and not everyone has equal access to informal institutions. The absence of political reform means that participants benefit at the expense of those unable to compete in informal exchange.

Review/ State practice/ Social networks/ Social restructuring/ Industrialized economies

338. ——. **1982.** The Working Unemployed: Perspectives on the Informal Economy and Unemployment. *Sociological Review* 30 (3): 460-477.

Henry focuses on the relationship between the informal economy and unemployment and, expanding upon the work of Ferman, Gershuny, Pahl, and Henry, he categorizes discussions of informality into two opposing perspectives. In one, the informal economy represents an alternative form of work which has the potential to absorb unemployment, is a vehicle for entrepreneurial innovation, and can operate as the vanguard for an alternative society. In the other perspective, informality is envisioned as masking its dependence on the dominant market economy where it operates as no more than a temporary buffer or survival mechanism for the poor.

Review/ Entrepreneurship/ Relation to formal economy/ Industrialized economies

339. ——. **1987.** The Political Economy of Informal Economies. *Annals of the American Academy of Political and Social Science* 493: 137-153.

Relation to formal economy/ Industrialized economies

340. ——. **1988.** Can the Informal Economy Be Revolutionary? Toward a Dialectial Analysis of the Relations between Formal and Informal Economies. *Social Justice: A Journal of Crime, Conflict and World Order* 15: 29-60.

Relation to formal economy/ Political mobilization/ Industrialized economies

341. **Henwood, F., and I. Miles. 1987.** The Experience of Unemployment and the Sexual Division of Labour. In *Unemployed People: Social and Psychological Perspectives*. Ed. D. Fryer and P. Ullah, pp. 94-110. Milton Keynes, U.K.: Open University Press.

This paper reviews relations between unemployment, poverty, and poor health to examine the psychological consequences of unemployment: loss of social contacts, status, the organization of time, and a collective purpose. The authors argue for a distinction between men's and women's experience of unemployment when comparing formal and domestic economic activities.

Gender division of labor/ Social networks/ Britain

342. **Herman, B., and W. Stoffers, eds. 1996.** *Unveiling the Informal Sector: More Than Counting Heads*. Aldershot, Hants, U.K.: Avebury.

This volume contains a series of papers presented at an International Seminar on Informal Sector Employment Statistics held in 1995. Seminar objectives were to share experiences of accurate measurement of informal sector size and structure and thus support better employment policy formulation. Individual papers reflect current ILO-recommended measurement methodologies, major questions concerning adequate data collection, as well as discussons of informal sector size and characteristics in a number of countries, including Pakistan, India, Turkey, Brazil, Cosa Rica, Nigeria, Tanzania, the United States and various European countries.

Pattern or magnitude/ Research methods/ Pakistan/ India/ Turkey/ Brazil/ Costa Rica/ Nigeria/ Tanzania/ U.S.A./ Europe

343. **Hermann, G., and S. Soeffer. 1984.** For Fun and Profit: An Analysis of the American Garage Sale. *Urban Life* 12: 397-421.

Review/ Garage sales/ U.S.A.

344. **Heyzer, N. 1981a.** Towards a Framework of Analysis. *IDS Bulletin* 12 (3): 3-7.

Based on case studies from several Third World countries, Heyzer argues that the concentration of women in the informal sector and their form of work, particularly those who are married with young children, result from the interaction of four factors: (a) the changing requirements of the labor process in different branches of production and at certain phases of economic reorganization, (b) differential labor absorption and the creation of an age-specific female workforce, (c) the value of female labor power, and (d) the relationship between women's domestic role and the gender division of wage labor.

Gender division of labor/ Gender ideology/ Worker characteristics/ Double-day/ Labor market segmentation/ Relation to capital/ Third World

345. ——. **1981b.** Women, Subsistence and the Informal Sector: Towards a Framework of Analysis. IDS Discussion Paper, no. 163. Sussex, U.K.: Institute of Development Studies.

Heyzer traces the development of the informal sector debate, from its conception in the early 1970s through its revival in the late 1970s within a mode of production framework. Heyzer argues that the mode of production analysis is a better tool for explaining the mechanisms which link the informal sector to the larger economic arena because it helps to reveal factors which explain women's concentration and forms of participation in informal work.

Review/ Relation to formal economy/ Labor market segmentation/ Gender division of labor/ Third World

346. ——. **1982.** From Rural Subsistence to an Industrial Peripheral Work Force: An Examination of Female Malaysian Migrants and Capital Accumulation in Singapore. In *Women and Development: The Sexual Division of Labor in Rural Societies*. Ed. L. Benería, pp. 179-202. New York: Praeger.

Migration/ Gender division of labor/ New international division of labor/ Self-provisioning/ Singapore/ Malaysia

347. **Heyzer, N., and G. Sen, eds. 1994.** *Gender, Economic Growth and Poverty: Market Growth and State Planning in Asia and the Pacific*. New Delhi: Kali for Women.

Fourteen papers examine the development experiences of Asian-Pacific countries from a gender equity perspective to engage current debates on the roles of the market and the state in development. The authors propose alternative options that make women's empowerment central to development policy and process. Three major concerns frame the discussions: 1) identifying the types of market growth, state-led development and interventions needed to reduce poverty and promote gender equity; 2) examining the relationship between market growth and poverty, market growth and gender equity, and poverty alleviation efforts and gender equity; and 3) exploring ways in which states and markets might be transformed to strengthen poor women's entitlements and their status as people rather than merely as dependents or targets. Major lessons drawn include the ongoing insecurity faced by poor women dependent on both informal and formal markets for livelihood despite progress in the macroeconomy, and the erosion of women's access to needed resources during the past decade due to increasing commercialization and the state's withdrawal from ensuring service delivery.

Gender inequality/ State practice/ Women/ Empowerment/ Project assistance/ Comparative/ Korea/ Sri Lanka/ Papua New Guinea/ India/ Pakistan/ Thailand/ Vietnam/ Centrally planned economies/ Asia

348. **Hilhorst, J. 1984.** City-Size and the Informal Sector. *Regional Development Dialogue* 5 (2): 86-95.

Hilhorst employs neoclassical economics to model the relationship between the size of a city and the size of the informal sector. The size of the urban economy is measured by its total income and by its population size. No relation was found between city size and the informal sector when using a measure of total income. When urban size is measured, the level of informal sector output tends to go up with size as long as the given wage rate for the labor aristocracy remains below a certain level. This result will hold when the informal sector is more labor-intensive than the formal sector and when its goods have a lower price elasticity than those produced by the formal sector.

Urbanization/ Pattern or magnitude/ Dual sector or economy

349. **Hodson, R. 1978.** Labor in the Monopoly, Competitive and State Sectors of Production. *Politics and Society* 8: 429-480.

Hodson critiques the theory of the dual labor market and extends the concepts of monopoly and competitive sectors of capitalist production to an analysis of the labor force.

Critique of dualism/ Industrialized economies

350. **Hofmann, M. 1986.** The Informal Sector in an Intermediate City: A Case in Egypt. *Economic Development and Cultural Change* 34: 263-277.

Pattern or magnitude/ Migration/ Egypt

351. **Holmes, J. 1986.** The Organization and Locational Structure of Production Subcontracting. In *Production, Work, Territory: The Geographical Anatomy of Industrial Capitalism*. Ed. A. J. Scott and M. Storper, pp. 80-106. Boston, Mass.: Allen and Unwin.

Holmes examines the role of subcontracting and labor market segmentation in the organization of industrial production in advanced capitalist economies, focusing particularly on what these forms of production suggest about industry location. He reviews how interfirm linkages are traditionally examined, identifies different forms of subcontracting, and analyzes the form, causes, and dynamics of subcontracting based on data from the Canadian automotive, electronics and clothing industries. Holmes concludes that an adequate explanation of subcontracting must consider the structure of technology and work organization, the nature of product markets, control over the labor process, and labor supply conditions.

Subcontracting/ Labor market segmentation/ Spatial patterns/ Production process/ Industrial restructuring/ Electronics manufacture/ Garment manufacture/ Industrialized economies/ Canada

352. **Hongladarom, C., W. Isarankura, and V. F. Sit. 1988.** Increasing the Absorptive Capacity of the Urban Economy. *Regional Development Dialogue* 9 (4): 134-159.

Pattern or magnitude/ Spatial patterns/ Trading/ Thailand

353. **Hosier, R. H. 1987.** The Informal Sector in Kenya: Spatial Variation and Development Alternatives. *Journal of Developing Areas* 21: 383-402.

Pattern or magnitude/ Spatial patterns/ Kenya

354. **Hossain, H. 1987.** Capitalist Penetration into Handicrafts Manufacture: An Historical Review of Women's Work for the Market in Bangladesh. In *Invisible Hands: Women in Home-Based Production*. Ed. A. Menefee-Singh and A. Kelles-Viitanen, pp. 165-174. New Delhi: Sage.

Hossain examines women's involvement in home-based commodity production and the limited benefits derived from this activity. The development of urban and export markets for handcrafted goods, particularly handwoven cloth, transform once relatively fluid task sharing into deepening gender-based differentiation, allocating low-paid, time-consuming, and strenuous activities almost exclusively to women. With industrialization of indigenous cloth production during the nineteenth and early twentieth centuries, men were employed as machine operators and women were excluded from the industrial workplace. Recent trends reveal that with economic stagnation women's paid work became a growing imperative for household survival where the handicraft sector, marked by relatively easy entry, suitability for home-based production, and the need for traditional female skills, once again became a source of women's paid work. However, potential opportunities for further skill formation, organizing, and direct market penetration are constrained by the gender differentiation of work and the hierarchy of control over the sector exerted by nonproducers. Marketing agents, who include middle-class women as well as men endowed with access to credit, supplies, and market links, form an entrepreneurial class in control of rural production. Urban-based exporters, with access to subsidized credit and overseas market opportunities, capture most of the profit from overseas sales and place the risks related to meeting production and quality specifications on direct producers. Given these unequal relations, direct handicraft producers may derive some income from their work, but lack the means to improve their productivity over the long term.

Artisanal production/ Gender division of labor/ Class formation/ Labor market segmentation/ Home-based production/ Handicrafts/ Export production/ Subcontracting/ Survival strategies/ Constraints to accumulation/ Credit/ Bangladesh

355. **House, W. J. 1984a.** Labor Market Segmentation: Evidence from Cyprus. *World Development* 12: 403-418.

Labor market segmentation/ Cyprus

356. —— **. 1984b.** Nairobi's Informal Sector: Dynamic Entrepreneurs or Surplus Labor. *Economic Development and Cultural Change* 32: 277-302.

Definition/ Entrepreneurship/ Self-employment/ Kenya

357. —— **. 1987.** Labor Market Differentiation in a Developing Economy: An Example from Urban Juba, Southern Sudan. *World Development* 15: 877-897.

House examines the determinants of income differences, employment opportunities, and labor market differentiation in Juba, Sudan. Indices of human capital play a significant role in labor market outcomes, but imperfections in credit access and ethnic biases in the labor market lead to highly skewed income distribution. A dualistic conception of the labor market fails to predict the diverse outcomes found in Juba's economy or explain why half the households below the poverty line are headed by persons in the formal sector. The data suggest that a dispersed and flexible urban wage structure is responsive to large numbers of migrant job seekers, that open unemployment is negligible, and that the flexibility and absorptive capacity of the labor market contributes to an efficient and equitable transfer of labor from the subsistence rural economy to a dynamic urban one. House concludes that improving the school system is most critical in efforts to reduce poverty.

Critique of dualism/ Worker characteristics/ Migration/ Policy prescriptions/ Credit/ Polarization/ Education/ Sudan

358. **House, W. J., G. K. Ikiara, and D. McCormick. 1993.** Urban Self-Employment in Kenya: Panacea or Viable Strategy? *World Development* 21: 1205-1223.

Increasingly, the promotion of viable self-employment is being regarded as a policy priority for the Kenyan government in dealing with problems of slow growth, economic crises, and structural adjustment. The authors describe current patterns of self-employment to highlight earnings, age and experience levels of the self-employed workforce. The authors then examine the specific constraints hindering successful self-employment. These include the lack of financial and physical resources, market constraints in the demand for goods and services and the supply of needed materials, and legal barriers related to licensing, zoning, employee-employer relations, taxation, debt collection, copyright, and trade. Alternative policy and project assistance approaches to realize the expansion of successful self-employment are suggested.

Pattern or magnitude/ Worker characteristics/ Self-employment/ Policy analysis/ Legislation/ State practice/ Project assistance/ Kenya

359. **Hoyman, M. 1987.** Female Participation in the Informal Economy: A Neglected Issue. *Annals of the American Academy of Political and Social Science* 493: 64-82.

A review of ethnographic, survey-based, and statistical accounts of informal sector reveals that female participation is significantly greater than that of males based on the number of individuals, amount of time spent, and estimated dollar value of activities performed. A growing share of female informal workers occupy a "dual loyalty" status: they are forced into irregular, home-based work in additional to formal sector employment in order to accommodate both household income and maintenance needs. Government policy should expand the availability of reliable day care; expand possibilities for flex-time and other arrangements sensitive to women's household work; extend government protection; and expand opportunities for adequate remuneration of informal work.

Gender division of labor/ Double-day/ Policy prescriptions/ Women/ U.S.A.

360. **Huber, J. 1985.** Conceptions of the Dual Economy. *Technological Forecasting and Social Change* 27: 63-73.

Dual sector or economy/ Industrialized economies/ Centrally planned economies/ Third World

361. **Humphrey, J. 1996.** Responses to Recession and Restructuring: Employment Trends in the Sao Paulo Metropolitan Region, 1979-87. *Journal of Development Studies* 33 (1): 40- 62.

Humphrey explores the gender differential effects of recession and restructuring in Sao Paulo households. Women bear the major costs of these processes particularly in terms of labor market opportunities and incomes.

Economic restructuring/ Industrial restructuring/ Household/ Gender division of labor/ Gender inequality/ Regulation/ Brazil

362. **Humphrey, J., and Hubert Schmitz. 1996.** The Triple C Approach to Local Industrial Policy. *World Development* 24 (12): 1859-1877.

Mounting evidence from both developing and developed countries indicate that clustering and networking assist the development of small and medium sized manufacturers in a competitive market. According to the authors, the "Triple C," cumulative, collective, and customer-oriented approach to local industrial policy can strengthen the competitive advantage of small manufacturers.

Industrial restructuring/ Small or micro-enterprises/ Comparative

363. **Illich, I. 1979.** Are We Now Going to Colonize the Informal Sector? *International Development Review / Revue du Developpment International / Revista del Desarrollo Internacional* 21 (4): 9-14.

Unpaid labor/ Labor processes

364. **—— . 1981.** *Shadow Work.* Boston, Mass.: Marion Boyars.

This collection of essays examines the rise of what the author refers to as the shadow economy, which refers to transactions that are not in the monetized sector and yet do not exist in preindustrial societies.

Unpaid labor/ Labor processes/ Gender division of labor

365. **International Bank for Reconstruction and Development. 1978.** *Employment and Development of Small Enterprises: A Sector Policy Paper.* Washington, D.C.: World Bank.

This report examines the potential role of small-scale enterprises (SSEs) for employment generation in developing countries.

Emphasis is placed on the role of the World Bank in encouraging and supporting such enterprises.

Small or micro-enterprises/ Policy prescriptions/ Self- employment/ Third World

366. **International Conference of Labour Statisticians. 1992.** *Statistics of Employment in the Informal Sector: Third Item of the Agenda.* Report III of the 15th International Conference of Labour Statisticians held 19-28 January 1993 in Geneva, Switzerland. Geneva, Switzerland: ILO.

Pattern or magnitude/ Research methods

367. **International Labor Office (ILO). 1972.** *Employment, Incomes and Equality: A Strategy for Increasing Productive Employment in Kenya,*. Geneva, Switzerland: International Labor Office.

Addressing the broad issue of employment in both Kenya and other developing country contexts, this 600-page study emphasizes the need to address the problem of poverty-level incomes earned by producers who work extremely long hours. In a departure from earlier analyses, focused on expanding formal sector employment, this study suggests policies that complement economic growth and correct key regional and sectoral imbalances. Three areas of imbalance are emphasized; the rate of population growth and technology; infrastructural development and other resources between urban centers and rural peripheries; and the resources available in each sector. Discussion addresses questions related to population, technology, agriculture and rural development, industry and construction, services, education, labor markets, income, fiscal management, socioeconomic equity, as well as informal sector development. In contrast to understandings of the traditional sector, the informal sector is seen as economically efficient and profit-making even if constrained by small size, limited capital and technology, and poor links with the formal sector. Resolving these constraints will require better linkages between between formal and informal sectors in order to facilitate informal sector investment, productivity and wages.

Policy analysis/ Dual sector or economy/ Under- and unemployment/ Technological constraints/ Appropriate technology/ Rural/ Kenya

368. **Isachsen, A., and S. Strom. 1985.** The Size and Growth of the Hidden Economy in Norway. *Review of Income and Wealth* 31: 21- 38.

In their study of the hidden economy in Norway, the authors suggest that hidden labor, which includes unreported income from moonlighting, constitutes about half of the estimated 4 to 6 percent of GDP. Their survey also indicates that 35 percent of the adult population bought or sold hidden labor services within the past year and among all respondents, 2.3 percent think this practice is increasing. Shortening the workweek to alleviate unemployment is thought to increase the supply of hidden labor.

Pattern or magnitude/ Moonlighting/ Norway

369. **Iwuji, E. C., and A. E. Okorafor. 1978.** Small-Scale Industry and Employment Generation in Nigeria. In *Human Resources and African Development*. Ed. U. G. Damachi and V. P. Diejomah, pp. 273-287. New York: Praeger.

Small or micro-enterprises/ Self-employment/ Nigeria

370. **Jackson, G., G. Masnick, R. Bolton, S. Bartlett, and J. Pitkin. 1981.** *Regional Diversity: Growth in the United States, 1960-90.* Boston, Mass: Auburn House.

This report by the Joint Center for Urban Studies divided the United States into regions to document changes in population and the economy across place.

Spatial patterns/ Migration/ U.S.A.

371. **Jackson, P., and S. Walsh. 1987.** Unemployment and the Family. In *Unemployed People: Social and Psychological Perspectives*. Ed. D. Fryer and P. Ullah, pp. 194-216. Milton Keynes: Open University Press.

Under- and unemployment/ Survival strategies/ Britain

372. **Jelin, E. 1977.** Migration and Labor Force Participation of Latin American Women: The Domestic Servants in the Cities. In *Women and National Development: The Complexities of Change*. Ed. Wellesley Editorial Committee, pp. 129-141. Chicago, Ill.: University of Chicago Press.

Latin American literature shows that women migrate to cities more often than men, that female migrants have higher labor force participation rates than native city dwellers, and that they are more likely than natives to be engaged in domestic service. Understanding these patterns requires an examination of the relationship between women's labor force participation and household organization. For housewives accompanying husbands in search of urban employment, the fluidity of the informal labor market in domestic service makes it possible to enter or leave part-time paid employment as a simple extension of their domestic subsistence tasks. For young women first entering the urban labor market, domestic work can sometimes be a bridge to jobs in industry or personal services. In most cases, however, it is viewed as preceding the goal of starting one's own family. The availability of domestic service work is assured, moreover, due to the nature of housework and the interest middle class women have in creating space for leisure or paid employment outside the home.

Gender division of labor/ Domestic service/ Migration/ Survival strategies/ Double-day/ Latin America

373. **Jellenick, L. 1978.** Circular Migration and the Pondok Dwelling System: A Case Study of Ice Cream Traders in Jakarta. In *Food, Shelter and Transport in Southeast Asia and the Pacific*. Ed. P. Rimmer, D. W. Drakakis-Smith, and T. G. McGee, pp. 135-154. Department of Human Geography Monograph, no. 12. Canberra: Australian National University.

Migration/ Unpaid labor/ Trading/ Indonesia

374. **Jenkins, R. 1984.** Divisions over the International Division of Labour. *Capital and Class* 22: 28-57.

Jenkins reviews recent discussions on the new international division of labor noting flaws in theories which separate the sphere of exchange and production separately. He argues instead for a framework that focuses on circuits of capital during processes of internationalization which depend on the need to increase surplus value and depreciate constant capital through changes in production techniques, the centralization of capital, and the elimination of least profitable forms of accumulation. Depending on conditions characteristic of particular industries and countries, specific strategies include such measures as the relocation of production to lower wage regions, and involve the internationalization of productive capital as well as commodity and money capital. Jenkins also questions the call for building a unified international proletariat and argues instead that organizing strategies depend on specific processes of restructuring within different industries and countries.

Economic restructuring/ Labor processes/ Class processes/ Labor movements/ Third World

375. **Jensen, L., G. T. Cornwell, and J. L. Findeis. 1995.** Informal Work in Nonmetropolitan Pennsylvania. *Rural Sociology* 60 (1): 91-107.

Survey data reveal factors shaping participation in informal work in rural Pennsylvania and indicate the widespread participation in informal income-generating activities across different household income levels. While informal earnings do not contribute substantively to average household income, they do help poor families survive economic crises. The impact on informal work of other factors, including sociodemographic variables, rurality, and characteristics of the formal labor supply are also explored.

Pattern or magnitude/ Rural/ Survival strategies/ Social networks/ Household/ U.S.A.

376. **Jessen, J., W. Siebel, C. Siebel-Rebelli, U. J. Walther, and I. Weyrather. 1987.** The Informal Work of Industrial Workers: Present Situation, Trend Prognosis and Policy Implications. In *The Unofficial Economy: Consequences and Perspectives in Different Economic Systems*. Ed. S. Alessandrini and B. Dallago, pp. 271-282. Aldershot, Hants, U.K.; Brookfield, Vt.: Gower Publishing.

This paper examines household strategies based on interviews with 120 shipyard workers in northern Germany. Informal work is a common phenomenon which is part of a moral economy guided by norms of solidarity and mutual exchange. The authors argue that the informal economy does not represent a distinct alternative to the official economy or provide a means for the transformation of the capitalist system. Rather, it complements formal, paid work and thus is not a resource-saving strategy on which to base unemployment or social policy.

Survival strategies/ Social networks/ Relation to formal economy/ Nonmonetary exchange/ Germany

377. **Jiggins, J. 1989.** How Poor Women Earn Income in Sub-Saharan Africa and What Works against Them. *World Development* 17: 953-963.

Rapidly growing population, development policies which have been urban-biased and largely ineffective, and falling terms of trade have placed increasing pressures on rural households, particularly sub-Saharan African women. Sketching various forms of poverty facing rural households, Jiggins describes their specific effects on household composition and labor processes. While the informal economy, mainly in trade, offers a venue for women to ensure family survival, women's success as informal entrepreneurs is often blocked by a number of factors, including male interference, lack of infrastructure, competition with state enterprises and other traders, and lack of access to credit.

Women/ Survival strategies/ Trading/ Credit/ Rural/ Household/ Policy analysis/ Project assistance/ Sub-Saharan Africa

378. **Johnson, L. C., and R. E. Johnson. 1983.** *The Seam Allowance: Industrial Home Sewing in Canada*. Toronto, Canada: Women's Press.

Home-based production/ Subcontracting/ Household division of labor/ Ethnicity/ State practice/ Policy analysis/ Canada

379. **Jolly, R., and R. Cruise O'Brian. 1972.** Urban Unemployment in Africa: Report on a Conference Held at the Institute of Development Studies, University of Sussex, 12-16 September, 1971. *Manpower and Unemployment Research in Africa* 5 (1): 26-30.

Under- and unemployment/ Migration/ Africa

380. **Jules-Rosette, B. 1982.** Women's Work in the Informal Sector: A Zambian Case Study. Women in International Development Working Paper, no. 3. East Lansing, Mich.: Michigan State University.

Jules-Rosette examines women's occupational careers and socioeconomic adjustment in Lusaka, Zambia, an area marked by high rates of urban migration and restricted opportunities for women's formal employment. The exclusion of women from the urban wage labor force has created alternative occupations such as self-employed petty traders, craft producers, and small entrepreneurs which is often temporary and a way to commercialize traditional skills. The analysis suggests an important link between urban and rural development processes and highlights the need for policy planners to account for the short-term entrepreneurial options that migrant women generate in the urban context.

Labor market segmentation/ Migration/ Self-employment/ Trading/ Artisanal production/ Handicrafts/ Policy prescriptions/ Women/ Zambia

381. **Kabra, K. N. 1982.** *The Black Economy in India: Problems and Policies*. Delhi, India: Chanakya Publications.

Pattern or magnitude/ State practice/ Policy analysis/ India

382. —— . **1995.** The Informal Sector: A Reappraisal. *Journal of Contemporary Asia* 25 (2): 197-232.

In a broad review of major streams of thought on the informal sector, its characteristics, and causal factors, Kabral argues the need to conceptualize informality as encompassing new and evolving rather than archaic and stagnant forms of production. The first two sections of the essay review important literature as well as more recent empirical studies to highlight key attributes of informal economic activity. Informal work is described as highly diverse, connected but subordinated to advanced sectors of the economy, and representing a lower stage of economic development. Subsequent discussion emphasizes that rather than representing residual or unstable aspects of industrialization, informality clearly coexists with dominant and standard organizational forms that have failed to become generalized. These developments, moreover, clearly reflect the unevenness of capitalist development, particularly in late capitalism, and offer evidence of the "empirical reality of *capitalisms*." Kabral concludes with suggestions for appropriate state policies to help informal workers overcome the constraints and difficulties that keep them at a disadvantaged position vis-à-vis the formal sector.

Review/ Class processes/ Economic restructuring

383. **Kahn, J. S. 1982.** From Peasants to Petty Commodity Production in Southeast Asia. *Bulletin of Concerned Asian Scholars* 14 (1): 3-15.

Petty commodity production/ Economic restructuring/ Southeast Asia

384. **Kahveci, E., T. Nichols, and N. Sugur. 1996.** The Shoe-Shine Boys of Izmir. In *Work and Occupation in Modern Turkey*. Ed E. Kahveci, N. Sugur, and T. Nichols, pp. 38-71. London: Mansell Publishing.

The authors present a description of children working as shoe-shiners in Izmir, Turkey. Socioeconomic conditions, including educational experience, family migration history, and parental occupation, are detailed. Also discussed are motivations for engaging in shoe shining as well as typical hours, earnings and conditions of work. The paper concludes with profiles of four children and a father.

Child labor/ Worker characteristics/ Turkey

385. **Kandiyoti, D. 1987.** Emancipated but Unliberated? Reflections on the Turkish Case. *Feminist Studies* 13: 317-338.

Gender ideology/ State practice/ Social networks/ Turkey

386. **—— . 1988.** Bargaining with Patriarchy. *Gender and Society* 2: 274-290.

Kandiyoti argues for a focus on patriarchy's specific forms across different sociocultural and temporal contexts. Using women's resistance strategies as a point of entry, two systems of male dominance are contrasted, one from sub-Saharan Africa and the other from the Middle East, East and South Asia. A review of development project literature for sub-Saharan Africa shows that women, facing less corporate forms of householding that grant relative autonomy to the mother-child unit under polygyny, engage in open resistance to trends that lower the value of female labor and appropriate its products. In the Middle East, East and South Asia, where "classic patriarchy" prevails in the form of distinctly corporate male-headed household entities, women accommodate male dominance in their defense of institutions like dowry, purdah and virilocal spousal arrangements which reinforce extant hierarchies of authority. In this context, women manipulate male affection rather than openly confront them. Thus, women strategize differently within the constraints of the "patriarchal bargain," a bargain subject to change through historical transformation and as new strategies and forms of consciousness are born of complex and contradictory personal and political struggles.

Gender ideology/ Survival strategies/ Resistance/ Comparative/ Sub-Saharan Africa/ Asia/ Middle East

387. **Kannappan, S., ed. 1977.** *Studies of Urban Labour Market Behaviour in Developing Areas*. Geneva, Switzerland: International Institute for Labour Studies.

Labor market dynamics/ Dual sector or economy/ Policy analysis/ Sudan/ Japan/ Ethiopia/ Singapore/ Brazil/ Kenya/ Indonesia/ Yugoslavia

388. —— . **1984.** Tradition and Modernity in Urban Employment in Developing Nations. *Regional Development Dialogue* 5 (2): 55-62.

Kannappan argues against the modern-traditional or formal- informal sector dichotomy and proposes instead a perspective that includes family, caste, ethnic, and religious affinities as independent sources of differentiation. These variables are discussed with reference to wage employment, rural-urban migration, self-employment and enterprise formation to show that since these affinities are unequally distributed, public policy must be used to improve urban infrastructure on a generalized basis. Moreover, given a heterogeneous labor force and variable productivities, growth-inducing income and profit-maximizing activities cut across the modern-traditional dichotomy.

Critique of dualism/ Survival strategies/ Migration/ Ethnicity/ Self-employment/ Policy analysis/ Social networks/ Third World

389. **Kasfir, N. 1983.** State, Magendo, and Class Formation in Uganda. *Journal of Commonwealth and Comparative Politics* 21: 84-103.

State practice/ Class formation/ Uganda

390. **Kassim, A., and Jomo K. S. 1991.** Social Dimensions of Industrialization in Malaysia. *Regional Development Dialogue* 12 (1): 45-64.

Economic restructuring/ Migration/ Gender division of labor/ Housing/ Malaysia

391. **Kazi, S., and B. Raza. 1990.** The Duality in Female Employment in Pakistan. *South Asia Bulletin* 10 (2): 1-8.

Kazi and Raza review Pakistani women's changing participation in work and occupational status during the 1970s and 1980s. National statistics and survey data reveal a pattern of low female labor force participation in most professions and well-paid industrial sector work, and their expanding participation in poorly remunerated agricultural work, services, and subcontracted, home-based and other types of informal activities. This pattern derives from deliberate employer policies to exploit women as a cheap and compliant labor force; cultural norms that designate "proper" female activities; growing poverty and the need for additional household income; and the lack of education and skills among the majority of women. The result is a marked division in female employment as economic trends place more and more women into the work force.

Gender division of labor/ Gender ideology/ Women/ Pakistan

392. **Kemper, R. V. 1981.** Obstacles and Opportunities: Household Economics of Tzintzuntzan Migrants in Mexico City. *Urban Anthropology* 10: 231-229.

Survival strategies/ Social networks/ Migration/ Mexico

393. **Kenedi, J. 1981.** *Do It Yourself: Hungary's Hidden Economy*. London: Pluto Press.

Written as a first person story, this book provides a firsthand glimpse into Hungary's "private sector." Since all enterprises in Hungary are, in theory, state-owned, craft workers and artisans must rely on informal networks and arrangements in order to work around the heavy taxation and restrictions placed on them by the state.

State practice/ Social networks/ Tax evasion/ Hungary

394. **Kennedy, P. 1976.** Cultural Factors Affecting Entrepreneurship and Development in the Informal Economy in Ghana. *IDS Bulletin* 8 (2): 17-21.

Institutional or cultural constraints that affect informal sector growth include the demands of kinship and community that weaken the capacity for accumulation, the pattern of market demand, and the willingness of people to seek regular employment and accept its rules. These constraints cannot be understood solely in terms of the endemic survival capacity of precapitalist elements because they are constituted by the economic realities of a dependent Third World economy where culture-structure interactions perpetuate self-employment and make it difficult for entrepreneurs to secure a permanent and disciplined workforce. Entrepreneurs who start in the informal sector and develop large firms can be regarded as intermediaries whose position was enabled by both particular cultural attributes and their differential access to material resources.

Entrepreneurship/ Constraints to accumulation/ Self-employment/ Differentiation/ Social networks/ Ghana

395. —— . **1983.** Workers in Petty Production, Accra, Ghana: Towards Proletarianization? *Labour, Capital and Society / Travail, Capital et Societé* 16: 64-93.

Petty commodity production/ Differentiation/ Ghana

396. **Keyes, W. 1982.** Manila Scavengers: The Struggle for Urban Survival. In *The Philippine Poor I: Two Monographs*. Ed. M. S. Fernandez, pp. 1-56. Quezon City, Philippines: Institute of Philippine Culture, Ateneo de Manila University.

Self-employment/ Scavenging/ Philippines

397. **Kibria, N. 1989.** Patterns of Vietnamese Refugee Women's Wagework in the U.S. *Ethnic Groups* 7: 297-323.

Home-based production/ Ethnicity/ Migration/ Refugees/ Women/ U.S.A.

398. **King, K. 1974.** Kenya's Informal Machine Makers: A Study of Small Scale Industry in Kenya's Emerging Artisan Society. *World Development* 2: 9-28.

Pattern or magnitude/ Small or micro-enterprises/ Policy prescriptions/ Kenya

399. —— . **1975.** Skill Acquisition in the Informal Sector of an African Economy: The Kenya Case. *Journal of Development Studies* 11: 108-122.

King examines the informal educational system by which low-income Kenyans acquire skills in carpentry, tinsmithing, sheet metal work, automobile mechanic crafts, and panel beating. The lack of vocational training in the formal school system helped establish unofficial fee-paying apprenticeships from craftsmen who assist trainees start their own workshop and develop product types and innovative uses of scrap materials. King also highlights problems faced by rural craftsmen, including the limited demand for goods because of low agricultural incomes, an inability to access the urban apprentice system, and licensing restrictions.

Apprenticeship/ Education/ Rural/ Artisanal production/ Kenya

400. —— . **1979.** Petty Production in Nairobi: The Social Context of Skill Acquisition and Occupational Differentiation. In *Casual Work and Poverty in Third World Cities*. Ed. R. Bromley and C. Gerry, pp. 217-228. New York: John Wiley & Sons.

Petty commodity production/ Self-employment/ Differentiation/ Worker characteristics/ Kenya

401. —— . **1990.** Research, Policy and the Informal Sector: African Experience. In *The Informal Sector Revisited*. Ed. D. Turnham, B. Salomé, and A. Schwarz, pp. 131-149. Paris, France: Development Centre, Organisation for Economic Co-operation and Development.

Review/ Policy analysis/ Africa

402. **King, K., and C. Abuodha. 1991.** *The Building of an Industrial Society: Change and Development in Kenya's Informal (Jua Kali) Sector, 1972-1991*. Occasional Papers, no. 30. Edinburgh, U.K.: Centre of African Studies, University of Edinburgh.

Pattern or magnitude/ Small or micro-enterprises/ Policy prescriptions/ Kenya

403. **Kitching, G. 1980.** Wage Labour and "the Informal Sector," 1952-1970. In *Class and Economic Change in Kenya: The Making of an African*

Petite Bourgeoisie, 1905-1970. G. Kitching, pp. 375- 410. New Haven, Conn.; London: Yale University Press.

Definition/ Pattern or magnitude/ Class formation/ Kenya

404. **Koll, M. 1969.** *Crafts and Cooperation in Western Nigeria: A Sociological Contribution to Indigenous Economics*. Freiburg, F.R.G.: Arnold-Bergstraesser Institut.

Handicrafts/ Social networks/ Nigeria

405. **Koo, H. 1981.** Centre-Periphery Relations and Marginalization: Empirical Analysis of the Dependency Model of Inequality in Peripheral Nations. *Development and Change* 12: 55-76.

Drawing from survey data gathered in Seoul in 1976, when the Korean export economy was at its peak and the unemployment rate at its lowest, Koo examines the applicability of the center-periphery model for interpretations of dynamic dependent nations. He finds that neither the domestic nor internationalized sector is homogeneous and that sectoral conflicts are muted by the exploitation of mostly female workers in the internationalized sector, where wages are lower than those in the domestic sector, and by the adaptability of the petty bourgeoisie whose route to upward social mobility is the informal sector. Koo concludes that class rather than sectoral relations have the greatest impact on the life chances of individuals. Without denying the dominant flow of resources from periphery to center, Koo argues that a reverse flow must be incorporated into the dependency model.

Relation to formal economy/ Differentiation/ Class processes/ Social mobility/ Korea

406. **Koo, H., and P. C. Smith. 1983.** Migration, the Urban Informal Sector, and Earnings in the Philippines. *Sociological Quarterly* 24: 219-232.

Migration/ Gender division of labor/ Philippines

407. **Koptiuch, K. 1992.** Informal Sectorization of Egyptian Petty Commodity Production. In *Anthropology and the Global Factory: Studies of the New Industrialization in the Late Twentieth Century*.

Ed. F. A. Rothstein and M. L. Blim, pp. 149-160. New York: Bergin and Garvey.

Koptiuch reviews links between economic crisis, economic liberalization, out-migration, and changing government practices regarding petty production in Egypt during the 1970s and 1980s. Mass emigration of farm laborers and skilled craftspersons through the 1970s may be seen as a response to more lucrative wages in foreign economies and to a silent protest against government development policies. As a crisis of social reproduction emerged with the continuing drain, petty production assumed an important role in keeping down the labor costs. As a consequence, the government, supported by international development institutions, redefined petty productive activities "from outmoded artisanal to the microentrepreneurial informal sector," thus "reinventing archaic productive forms" and discouraging the emergence of a unified working class.

Economic restructuring/ Petty commodity production/ State practice/ Class processes/ Migration/ Resistance/ Handicrafts/ Egypt

408. **Kowarick, L. 1979.** Capitalism and Urban Marginality in Brazil. In *Casual Work and Poverty in Third World Cities*. Ed. R. Bromley and C. Gerry, pp. 69-86. Chichester, U.K.; New York: John Wiley & Sons.

This essay examines urban marginality in light of the diversification of secondary sector activities in Brazil. Defining marginality as an atypical form of capitalist labor, Kowarick argues that these forms, which include craft production, self-employment in trade and services, and paid domestic activity, combine in a unified structure of accumulation. In the context of dependent development, marginal sectors form part of the industrial reserve army and produce value that capitalists are able to appropriate. Although the author questions the theoretical adequacy of the concept of marginality he retains the term to distinguish between wage laborers and those segments of the working class who represent a special mode of insertion into the productive structure.

Relation to formal economy/ Self-employment/ Unequal exchange/ Marginalization/ Reserve army of labor/ Brazil

409. **Kraus, W. 1991.** *Private Business in China: Revival between Ideology and Pragmatism*. Honolulu, Hawaii: University of Hawaii Press.

Small or micro-enterprises/ Pattern or magnitude/ Policy prescriptions/ China

410. **Kreckel, R. 1980.** Unequal Opportunity Structure and Labor Market Segmentation. *Sociology* 14: 525-550.

Labor market segmentation/ Industrialized economies

411. **Kundu, A., and P. N. Mathur. 1984.** Informal Sector in Cities of Different Sizes: An Explanation within the Core Theoretic Framework. *Regional Development Dialogue* 5 (2): 82-85.

This brief article defines the informal sector in terms of wage rates which fall below that of the market but are maintained by the influx of rural migrants to the city. These low wage rates allow obsolete technologies to remain profitable. The pace of technological transformation is likely to be faster in the larger cities, where the size of the informal sector is likewise likely to be large.

Dual sector or economy/ Migration/ Technological change

412. **Laguerre, M. S. 1994.** *The Informal City*. New York: St. Martin's Press.

Laguerre conceptualizes informality as hidden from yet closely linked to the activities and practices of the formal sphere. He explores the rules and structures of informal activity and informal networking to illuminate its role in the construction of life in American cities. Research was conducted in the San Francisco-Oakland Metropolitan area. Individual chapters examine processes of informal and "behind-the-scenes" maneuvering in urban spatial development, economic activity, political networking, networking in modern firms, health care services, and interethnic relations. The multivocality of the informal sphere is emphasized whereby informality serves a number of ends for different people: opportunistic politicking, economic survival and profit-making, securing needed goods and services through personal contacts, career advancement. The informal sphere is thus seen as a phenomenon that both meets basic social needs and exacerbates social inequality in democratic society.

Non-monetary exchange/ Social networks/ Self-employment/ Self-provisioning/ Spatial patterns/ Social mobility/ Racial inequality/ U.S.A.

413. **Laite, J., and P. Halfpenny. 1987.** Employment, Unemployment and the Domestic Division of Labour. In *Unemployed People: Social and Psychological Perspectives*. Ed. D. Fryer and P. Ullah, pp. 217-240. Milton Keynes, U.K.: Open University Press.

This essay explores the relationship between labor force participation and the gender and generational division of labor within the household.

Gender division of labor/ Household division of labor/ Labor processes/ Worker characteristics/ Britain

414. **Lam, T. T. F. 1982.** Food for the City: The Role of the Informal Sector Retail Marketing Network, Peninsular Malaysia. *GeoJournal* 4 (Suppl.): 49-59.

Trading/ Malaysia

415. **Landau, Z. 1987.** Selected Problems of Unofficial Economy in Poland. In *The Unofficial Economy: Consequences and Perspectives in Different Economic Systems*. Ed. S. Alessandrini and B. Dallago, pp. 175-179. Aldershot, Hants, U.K.; Brookfield, Vt.: Gower Publishing.

Landau examines the unofficial economy noting certain components common to all countries (e.g., tax evasion, smuggling), while others are system-specific. In Soviet-type economies the official economy is characterized by inappropriate legislation, planning errors in prices and quantities, market shortages, and the relationship between government and state enterprises. The unofficial economy in Poland is the result of its economic and social crisis and problems associated with economic reforms. One consequence of an expanding unofficial economy is increasing income differentiation.

Tax evasion/ Illegal activity/ Polarization/ State practice/ Poland

416. **Langfeldt, E. 1985.** Is a Growing Unobserved Sector Undermining Monetary Policy in the Federal Republic of Germany? In *The*

Economics of the Shadow Economy. Ed. W. Gaertner and A. Wenig, pp. 301-314. Berlin, F.R.G.: Springer-Verlag.

Empirical evidence suggests that the shadow economy in West Germany is growing more rapidly than the official economy. Langfeldt also argues that there is no theoretical or empirical evidence to conclude that managing the money supply is aggravated by the more intensive use of cash in the underground sector.

Pattern or magnitude/ Policy analysis/ Germany

417. **Lanzetta de Pardo, M., and G. M. Castano, with Alvaro Triana Soto. 1989.** The Articulation of Formal and Informal Sectors in the Economy of Bogota, Colombia. In *The Informal Economy: Studies in Advanced and Less Developed Countries*. Ed. A. Portes, M. Castells, and L. A. Benton, pp. 95-110. Baltimore, Md.; London: Johns Hopkins University Press.

This paper describes the informal sector in Bogota and suggests that informalization corresponds to an articulation between factors which affect both productive activities and employment as well as the reproduction of the labor force. The authors examine productive units to show how formal enterprises absorb informal labor in order to achieve higher levels of accumulation while smaller producers utilize informal labor to achieve more adequate subsistence levels. A household study to assess the impact of reproductive labor on global economic behavior indicates that informality is determined by the survival needs of working class households and by the interests of large-scale firms in decentralizing production.

Relation to formal economy/ Survival strategies/ Colombia

418. **Latouche, S. 1993.** *In the Wake of the Affluent Society: An Exploration of Post-Development*. London, U.K.; Atlantic Highlands, N.J.: Zed Books.

While modernization has extended new forms of wealth throughout the world, it also has created large numbers of people who bear most of its burdens but derive few of its benefits. Among these are the growing numbers of impoverished informal sector workers in developing countries, chronically unemployed persons in developed countries, and expropriated or otherwise socially and politically disempowered indigenous populations in both contexts. Exploring contradictions of capitalist economic development, LaTouche challenges the idea that all people can eventually be winners through the modernization process and argues for alternatives to utilitarian modes of thought. Though itself a conceptual and social fabrication of development economics, the informal sector is proposed as an area in which life-sustaining activity is often performed on the basis of non-economic principles which offer liberating possibilities for post-modern society.

Economic restructuring/ Social restructuring/ Labor relations/ Third World/ Industrialized economies

419. **Lautier, B., and C. Chevalley. 1990.** Wage Relationship, Informal Sector and Employment Policy in South America. *Journal of Development Studies* 26: 278-298.

Critique of dualism/ Labor processes/ Policy analysis/ Third World

420. **LeBrun, O., and C. Gerry. 1975.** Petty Producers and Capitalism. *Review of African Political Economy* 3 (May-October): 20- 32.

LeBrun and Gerry provide a framework for analyzing labor in urban Senegal whose key assumption is the existence of a dialectical relationship between the dominant capitalist mode and subordinate forms of production at the margins. The authors conclude that some petty producers are capitalist, while others, including artisans who retain relative control of the labor-process, are unable to accumulate capital. A contradictory process of dissolution-conservation is at work in petty production which results in either a transition to small capitalist production or to proletarianization.

Petty commodity production/ Differentiation/ Processes of accumulation/ Constraints to accumulation/ Senegal

421. **Leiter, J. 1989.** Christmas in the Summertime: Reflections on Yardsales. *Free Inquiry in Creative Sociology* 17: 25-27.

Garage sales/ U.S.A.

422. **Lem, W. 1991.** Gender, Ideology and Petty Commodity Production: Social Reproduction in Languedoc, France. In *Marxist Approaches*

in Economic Anthropology. Ed A. Littlefield and H. Gates, pp. 103-117. Lanham, Md.: University Press of America.

Lem cites the need for more rigorous examination of internal labor processes and the role of ideology and power in the labor allocation of home-based producers. In a study of family wine producers in Mediterranean France, Lem sheds new light on the Chayanovian notion of "self-exploitation" and notes that household heads mediate the pressures of the "simple reproduction squeeze" not only through the intensification of their own labor, but their command over both property and the labor of female spouses and children.

Petty commodity production/ Labor processes/ Home-based production/ Unpaid labor/ Household division of labor/ Gender ideology/ Gender relations/ Household/ Rural/ France

423. **Lemkow, L. 1987.** The Employed Unemployed: The Subterranean Economy in Spain. *Social Science and Medicine* 25: 111-113.

Home-based production/ Subcontracting/ Self-employment/ Spain

424. **Lemkow, L., and T. Torns. 1989.** Continuity and Change in the Submerged Economy. In *Unemployment, Poverty and Quality of Working Life: Some European Experiences*. Ed. B. Starrin, P. Svensson, and H. Wintersberger, pp. 277-284. Berlin, FRG: Ed. Sigma.

Pattern or magnitude/ Gender division of labor/ Spain

425. **Leonard, M. 1994.** *Informal Economic Activity in Belfast*. Aldershot, Hants, U.K.: Avebury.

Based on documentary research, interviews with key informants, and a household survey, Leonard highlights the locally and nationally constituted social and economic elements shaping informal economic activities in a working class housing estate of West Belfast. Important factors in the local pattern of informal activities include stability of residence, widespread and extended periods of unemployment, social homogeneity, and limited local access to outside resources. Informally procured goods, services, and income play an essential role in the community as a supplement to unemployment benefits. A distinction is drawn between informal activities that are relatively well integrated into the everyday economic life of the community and "shady" practices (fiddling, joy-riding, stealing) which the community may tolerate but which are often subject to sanctions by paramilitary organizations. Particularly emphasized is the importance of local kinship and friendship networks for the informal exchange of goods and services between households, as well as for linking individuals to labor markets outside the area.

Pattern or magnitude/ Social networks/ Non-monetary exchange/ Illegal activity/ Northern Ireland

426. **Lessinger, J. 1988.** Trader vs. Developer: The Market Relocation Issue in an Indian City. In *Traders versus the State: Anthropological Approaches to Unofficial Economies*. Ed. G. Clark, pp. 139-164. Boulder, Colo.; London, U.K.: Westview Press.

Lessinger draws from fieldwork on wholesale and retail produce markets in Madras to describe market spaces as contested terrains central to the city's economic growth and political development. Petty traders and wholesalers are concerned with maintaining centrally located urban markets while property-owning urban elites, endowed with financial resources, political clout, and ties to international capital have a primary interest in pursuing lucrative real estate development. A mediating role is played by elected officials in the municipal government and their parties mindful of different power bases within the city. Lessinger describes the size, structure, and function of several Madras markets to highlight important developments in municipal politics, including a review of market disputes since the 1960s.

Trading/ Political mobilization/ Spatial patterns/ Differentiation/ State practice/ India

427. **Lever, A. 1988.** Women's Employment in the Informal Sector: San Santiago, Spain. *Social Justice* 15 (3-4): 87-113.

Home-based production/ Women/ State practice/ Spain

428. **Levitan, L., and S. Feldman. 1991.** For Love or Money: Nonmonetary Economic Arrangements among Rural Households in Central New York. In *Research in Rural Sociology and Development*. Vol. 5:

Household Strategies. Ed. D. C. Clay and H. K. Schwarzweller. Greenwich, Conn.: JAI Press.

Drawing from interviews with twenty-three households in a rural country of central New York state, Levitan and Feldman examine the role of social networks in facilitating the nonmonetary exchange of goods and services. They draw from a brief theoretical review to define nonmonetary exchange as informal economic activity due to its unregulated and untaxed status as well as its importance to household reproduction. Barter (e.g. equivalent exchange of services such as child care for house repairs), noneconomistic relations between households (e.g., favors done by nearby relatives and neighbors), and use of money at below-market value (e.g., token payment by elderly neighbors for odd jobs done around their house), are found to be common forms of nonmonetary exchange in the study area. Study findings suggest the importance of these exchanges to household viability and maintaining rural household access to land, labor, and capital. While the limitations of standard economic indicators to measure regional economies are thus highlighted, study findings do not support the argument that relations of nonmonetary exchange enable liberation from market relations in the global economy.

Nonmonetary exchange/ Rural/ U.S.A.

429. **Lewin, A. C. 1985.** The Dialectic of Dominance: Petty Production and Peripheral Capitalism. In *Planning for Small Enterprises in Third World Cities*. ed. R. Bromley, pp. 107-136. Oxford, U.K.: Pergamon Press.

Review/ Petty commodity production/ Relation to formal economy/ Class processes/ Third World

430. **Light, I. H. 1972.** *Ethnic Enterprise in America: Business and Welfare among Chinese, Japanese, and Blacks*. Berkeley, Calif.: University of California Press.

Ethnicity/ Social networks/ Racial inequality/ U.S.A.

431. **Lindauer, D. 1989.** Parallel, Fragmented, or Black? Defining Market Structure in Developing Economies. *World Development* 17: 1871-1880.

Discussions of market structure and industrial organization differ in the vocabulary used to describe segmented arenas for production and distribution of goods and services. The author clarifies the significance of specific terms used for describing the existence of multiple markets for the distribution of similar goods. Definitions for parallel markets, black markets, and informal sector trade are developed, and differing policy implications denoted by each are highlighted.

Definition/ Trading/ Policy prescriptions/ Third World

432. **Lipsig-Mummé, C. 1992.** Organizing Women in the Clothing Trades: Homework and the 1983 Garment Strike in Canada. In *Feminism in Action: Studies in Political Economy*. Ed. M. P. Connelly and P. Armstrong, pp. 121-148. Toronto: Canadian Scholars' Press.

Citing the significance of a failed garment union strike in Montreal in 1983, the author examines recent changes in the organization of production and their impact on union activism. Among the features of the restructuring process in Canadian garment production since the 1980s are industrial relocation to lower cost overseas sites, drainage of runaway shops particularly to Mexico, growth of subcontracting, and the renaissance of home-based work in North American cities. Given the failure of male-dominated garment unions to address these developments, feminist organizing efforts have expanded, targeting, in particular, the industry's use of homework. New activist efforts have resulted in conflicts with union leadership that portend needed changes in union agendas and linkages with wider social movements.

Industrial restructuring/ Women/ Subcontracting/ Home-based production/ Labor movements/ Garment manufacture/ Trade unions/ Canada

433. **Lipton, M. 1984.** Family, Fungibility and Formality: Rural Advantages of Informal Non-Farm Enterprise versus the Urban-Formal State. In *Human Resources, Employment, and Development* Volume 5: *Developing Countries*. Ed. S. Amin, pp. 189-242. Proceedings of the Sixth World Congress of the International Economic Association held in Mexico City, 1980, New York: St. Martin's Press.

Survival strategies/ Rural/ Self-employment/ Migration/ State practice/ Third World

434. **Littlefield, A. 1979.** The Expansion of Capitalist Relations of Production in Mexican Crafts. *Journal of Peasant Studies* 6: 471-488.

Challenging Mexican craft production as a carryover from precapitalist Mesoamerican tradition, Littlefield emphasizes its particular place in the social division of labor shaped by the expansion of Western capitalism. Three patterns are identified: 1) simple commodity production by individual peasant artisans working without hired labor and usually selling directly to consumers; 2) production for sale, often to middlemen and wholesalers, by small-scale artisans employing several workers; and 3) production by family units using credit and/or materials provided by middlemen who supply urban wholesalers and U.S. importers with finished craft goods. Factors facilitating the growth of family production involving middlemen are the existence of a large rural semiproletariat, changing markets with the increase in tourism and exports, and the specific capital and technical requirements of particular craft goods. No evidence exists, however, of a unilinear sequence from simple commodity production to putting-out to workshop and eventual factory production as is typically cited for the case of European industrialization.

Class formation/ Petty commodity production/ Subcontracting/ Artisanal production/ Handicrafts/ Credit/ Mexico

435. **Livingstone, I. 1991.** A Reassessment of Kenya's Rural and Urban Informal Sector. *World Development* 19: 651-670.

Drawing on surveys and field studies of Kenya's informal sector, Livingstone revisits key issues raised by the seminal ILO study of 1972. Evidence reveals the sector's role in the national economy, its urban and rural characteristics, the interdependence between rural and urban activities in supporting households, and the agglomeration of informal industries in urban areas. The analysis recognizes the heterogeneity of these sectors, their provision of cheap goods and services to low-income customers, their potential for offering employment and income to poor households, and the possibility of improving systems for material supply, credit, market distribution, apprenticeship, and representation of micro- entrepreneurial interests.

Pattern or magnitude/ Survival strategies/ Social networks/ Labor market dynamics/ Spatial patterns/ Firm characteristics/ Rural/ Kenya

436. **Lloyd, P. 1976.** Marginality: Euphemism or Concept. *IDS Bulletin* 8 (2): 12-16.

Lloyd argues that in the 1950s West Africa was wedded to detribalization, a process similar to that of marginality or "cholofication" in Peru, where policies include removing marginals so that they do not disrupt city life and recognize their need for education. In contrast is a view of marginal people as highly exploited and integrated into rather than excluded from urban life. The work of Anibal Quijano, a Peruvian sociologist, is used to highlight the multilayered meanings attached to marginality.

Marginalization/ Ethnicity/ Migration/ Peru/ West Africa

437. —— **. 1979.** *Slums of Hope? Shanty Towns of the Third World.* Manchester, U.K.: Manchester University Press.

Migration/ Social networks/ Third World

438. —— **. 1982.** *A Third World Proletariat?* London: George Allen and Unwin.

Class formation/ Social networks/ Political mobilization/ Third World

439. **Logan, M. I., and G. J. Missen. 1981.** Unequal Relations and Uneven Development. In *Changing Perception of Development Problems*. Ed. R. P. Misra and M. Honjo, pp. 195-213. Regional Development Series, vol. 1. Singapore: United Nations Centre for Regional Development; Maruzen Asia.

Spatial patterns/ Relation to formal economy/ Unequal exchange/ Malaysia

440. **Lomnitz, L. A. 1978.** Mechanisms of Articulation between Shantytown Settlers and the Urban System. *Urban Anthropology* 7: 185-205.

Relation to formal economy/ Pattern or magnitude/ Urbanization/ Mexico

441. **Lomnitz, L. A. 1988.** Informal Exchange Networks in Formal Systems: A Theoretical Model. *American Anthropologist* 90: 42-55.

The malfunctioning of bureaucracies, evidenced in the rise of informal modes of exchange within the formal sector, is often viewed as the result of residual traditions that motivate against rational and efficient action. Lomnitz argues, in contrast, that informality is an intrinsic element of formality; the more a society is bureaucratically formalized without the capacity to satisfy social requirements, the more informal mechanisms tend to emerge. Attempts to clamp down on informal transactions tend only to stimulate its growth as a palliative to scarcity. Illustrating this relationship with examples from Chile, Mexico, and the Soviet Union, Lomnitz emphasizes the social embeddedness rather than simply the economic logic of informal exchange systems. Rules of sociability and different types of exchange–reciprocity, patron-client relations, or under-the-table market exchange–dominate according to the motives, goals, degree of repression, or culturally defined rules of obligation between partners.

Nonmonetary exchange/ Social networks/ Chile/ Mexico/ U.S.S.R./ Third World

442. **Long, N., 1984.** Introduction. In *Family and Work in Rural Societies: Perspectives on Non-Wage Labour*. Ed. N. Long, pp. 1-29. London: Tavistock.

Long reviews major issues in discussions of nonwage labor forms and patterns of family and household organization in industrialized Europe and the less developed world including factors that promote or inhibit the persistence of peasant forms of organization and the family farm; inter-household exchanges and community-level patterns of cooperation; and the changing roles of women in the household division of labor and in the community. Different interpretations of agrarian change suggest that landholdings and the relative weight assumed by non-agricultural activities, including wage labor, is critically important in analyses of intra-household characteristics among different social strata where nonwage labor in peasant and simple commodity forms of production is linked to unpaid domestic work. Long argues that noncapitalist forms do not lie outside the capitalist framework but rather represent the way in which local or subordinate social structures mediate the effects of capitalist penetration.

Rural/ Household division of labor/ Unpaid labor/ Household/ Social networks/ Industrialized economies/ Third World

443. **Long, N., and P. Richardson. 1978.** Informal Sector, Petty Commodity Production, and the Social Relations of Small Scale Enterprise. In *The New Economic Anthropology*. Ed. J. Clammer, pp. 176-209. New York: St. Martin's Press.

Review/ Petty commodity production/ Class formation/ Relation to formal economy/ Peru

444. **Lowenthal, M. 1975.** The Social Economy in Urban Working Class Communities. In *The Social Economy of Cities*. Ed. G. Gappert and H. M. Rose, pp. 447-489. Beverly Hills, Calif.; London: Sage Publications.

Survival strategies/ Social networks/ Non-monetary exchange/ Unpaid labor/ Industrialized economies

445. —— **. 1981.** Non-Market Transactions in an Urban Community. In *Can I Have It in Cash?: A Study of Informal Institutions and Unorthodox Ways of Doing Things*. Ed. S. Henry, pp. 90-104. New York: St. Martin's Press.

Lowenthal examines how people with inadequate incomes meet their needs and survive in the context of diminishing resources and declining real wages. Although health care and housing may remain unmet, other needs are met by peoples participation in social networks and mutual aid systems. As Lowenthal argues, economic transactions are imbedded in personal networks which structure arrangements for the provision of goods and services. These arrangements operate in a social economy through principles of reciprocity and adequacy of response where patterns of redistribution integrate groups in communities and assures the permanence of reciprocal exchange.

Survival strategies/ Social networks/ Nonmonetary exchange/ Industrialized economies/ U.S.A.

446. **Lozano, B. 1983.** Informal Sector Workers: Walking Out the System's Front Door? *International Journal of Urban and Regional Research* 7 (3): 340-362.

Lozano argues that defining the informal sector in terms of the absence of routine state regulation raises questions about what benefits are forgone or gained by operating outside the formal sector. Based on a nonrandom sample of 50 northern California flea market sellers, Lozano suggests that entry into informal work is largely involuntary, although its unregulated status allows the unemployed to convert personal resources and social networks into income-producing capital and labor. The relationship between flea market dealers and formal sector producers and distributors form a complex web of competition and interdependence which affect the structure and stability of dealers' operations. Unless we understand how informal sector workers and formal sector enterprises participate within a single economic system, policy recommendations will offer only speculative solutions to unemployment.

Trading/ Social networks/ Relation to formal economy/ Flea markets/ U.S.A.

447. **Lubell, H. 1976.** *Urban Development and Employment: The Prospects for Calcutta*. Geneva, Switzerland: International Labour Office.

Urbanization/ Under- and unemployment/ Policy prescriptions/ India

448. —— . **1977.** Urbanisation and Employment: Insights from a Series of Case Studies of Third World Metropolitan Cities. In *Studies of Urban Labour Market Behaviour in Developing Countries*. Ed. S. Kannappan, pp. 63-70. Geneva, Switzerland: International Institute for Labour Studies.

Lubell reviews four ILO studies of informal labor in Calcutta, Abidjan, Jakarta, and Bogota to examine the need to increase urban employment and to discourage urban migration. The studies reveal different patterns of labor use. In Calcutta an ethnic pattern of labor force participation has emerged; in Abidjan, unskilled jobs are filled primarily by migrants from north of the savannah and beyond the frontier; the Jakarta study emphasizes the informal sector's provision of jobs to about half of the labor force, given high rates of migration and even higher rates of rural unemployment; while the Bogota construction boom created labor shortages which were absorbed by the rural unemployed.

Labor market dynamics/ Urbanization/ Rural/ Ethnicity/ Migration/ Construction industry/ Comparative/ India/ Ivory Coast/ Indonesia/ Colombia

449. **Lutz, H. 1994.** The Tension between Ethnicity and Work: Immigrant Women in the Netherlands. In *The Dynamics of "Race" and Gender: Some Feminist Interventions*. Ed. H. Afshar and M. Maynard, pp. 182-195. London: Taylor and Francis.

In a review of policies to assimilate immigrant labor, Lutz finds that they marginalize immigrant women in the informal sector. This is revealed in the high unemployment among immigrant women, and the concentration of female immigrant workers in low-paid off-the-books, and"feminized" areas of the labor market in the garment, flower, food service, and domestic help industries. Employment statistics also reveal differences among immigrant women. Uneducated Turkish and Moroccan women are those most likely to be driven into the hidden economy or employment with family enterprises. As states reduce their involvement in economic and social policy, the new "open doors" of Europe create more "closed doors" for immigrant women.

Gender inequality/ Ethnicity/ Labor market segmentation/ Migration/ Social restructuring/ Netherlands

450. **Maasdorp, G. G., and N. Pillay. 1978.** *The Informal Sector in Clermont*. Durban, South Africa: University of Natal.

Pattern or magnitude/ South Africa

451. **Macarov, D. 1980.** *Work and Welfare: The Unholy Alliance*. Beverly Hills, Calif.: Sage.

This study critiques the concept of work, suggesting a need to reassess the conventional belief that paid employment is necessary for social life. Macarov argues that welfare policies should no longer be geared toward getting people back to work since technological development is enabling increased standards of living with reduced numbers of hours worked.

Production process/ Welfare/ Social restructuring/ State practice/ Technological change/ Industrialized economies

452. **MacGaffey, J. 1987.** *Entrepreneurs and Parasites: The Struggle for Indigenous Capitalism in Zaire*. Cambridge, U.K.: Cambridge University Press.

Indicators suggest that the second economy in Zaire expanded enormously during the 1970s and 1980s, displacing the state as the principal means of class formation. MacGaffey examines the role of capital accumulation from second economy activities in expanding production for local consumption where growing numbers of industrial and agribusiness entrepreneurs and commercial traders dominate trade in food products, and female entrepreneurs involved in various commercial activities suggest new processes of class formation. While small, this local business class distinguishes itself from the parasitic capitalism of past years by virtue of its independence from the government apparatus and systems of state patronage, and by its ability to evade government control.

Small or micro-enterprises/ Entrepreneurship/ Processes of accumulation/ Class formation/ Gender division of labor/ State practice/ Trading/ Zaire

453. **Macharia, K. 1992.** Slum Clearance and the Informal Economy in Nairobi. *Journal of Modern African Studies* 30: 221-236.

Macharia argues that the Kenyan government has yet to recognize the importance of small business activities in urban development where small-scale entrepreneurs make a significant contribution to Kenya's informal economy.

Entrepreneurship/ Small or micro-enterprises/ Kenya

454. **—— . 1993.** *The State and the Informal Sector in Nairobi, Kenya*. Nairobi, Kenya: French Institute for Research in Africa.

State practice/ Kenya

455. **Mackenzie, S. 1986.** Women's Responses to Economic Restructuring: Changing Gender, Changing Space. In *The Politics of Diversity*. Ed. R. Hamilton and M. Barrett, pp. 81-100. London: Verso.

Mackenzie examines the implications of economic restructuring for U.S. labor. The decreasing availability of employment outside the home has led to an increasing reliance on resources inside the home. In this context, changes in the use of space and changes in gender relations cannot be adequately understood as separate processes.

Economic restructuring/ Gender division of labor/ Survival strategies/ Spatial patterns/ Unpaid labor/ Women/ U.S.A.

456. **Mackintosh, M. M. 1988.** Domestic Labour and the Household. In *On Work: Historical, Comparative and Theoretical Approaches*. Ed. R. E. Pahl, pp. 392-406. Oxford, U.K.: Basil Blackwell.

Mackintosh examines weaknesses in current analyses of housework and its relationship to wage labor based on research in rural Senegal. Most analyses of household economies either overlook domestic activities as work, or assess the production of domestic goods and services solely in terms of use values. For Mackintosh the household is assumed to be constituted on the basis of the relations of subordination under which women feed and care for household members, a mediating institution between two sets of relations: the first governing domestic work and reproducing women's subordination and alienation; the second governing social labor other than domestic labor. The household thus contains both relations of domestic and social labor whose connection helps to illuminate women's subordination in processes of capitalist production.

Unpaid labor/ Household division of labor/ Double-day/ Household/ Industrialized economies/ Senegal

457. **Maliyamkono, T. L., and M. S. D. Bagachwa. 1990.** *The Second Economy in Tanzania*. London: James Currey; Athens, Ohio: Ohio University Press.

By the early 1980s, poor economic growth in Tanzania had culminated in profound economic crisis that prompted a structural adjustment and economic recovery program characterized by a broad variety of liberalization measures. The authors examine the expansion of unregulated rural and urban self-employed and illegal activities in response to acute economic pressures. The role of specific policies in accelerating growth in the second economy is analyzed, and the contradictory impact of liberalization is noted. The study concludes with broad policy recommendations, including the need to tailor policies to a more refined understanding of the second economy and to distinguish between "worthwhile (and) honest" activities and those "in which operators are in business primarily to reap rents" as smugglers, black market speculators in foreign exchange, and corrupt business persons.

Definition/ Pattern or magnitude/ Structural adjustment/ Illegal activity/ Rural/ Policy analysis/ Tanzania

458. **Marga Institute. 1979.** *The Informal Sector of Colombo City (Sri Lanka)*. Colombo, Sri Lanka: Marga Institute.

Pattern or magnitude/ Sri Lanka

459. **Mars, G., and Y. Altman. 1987a.** Case Studies in Second Economy Production and Transportation in Soviet Georgia. In *The Unofficial Economy: Consequences and Perspectives in Different Economic Systems*. Ed. S. Alessandrini and B. Dallago, pp. 197-217. Aldershot, Hants, U.K.; Brookfield, Vt,: Gower Publishing.

This paper reconstructs the second economy in Soviet Georgia in the mid-1970s based largely on fieldwork among expatriate Georgian Jews. Mars and Altman describe the organization of production and distribution of illicit goods in a biscuit factory where irregular production constituted about 40 percent of formal production. They describe how an enterprise involved in irregular production is able to (a) circumvent planned production targets, (b) obtain inputs from both the firm and those external to it, (c) obtain access to manpower and the use of machinery, and (d) avoid detection by the Soviet control system, especially with regard to unexpected audits and to the transport and distribution of illicit goods.

Transportation/ Pattern or magnitude/ Social networks/ U.S.S.R.

460. —— . **1987b.** Case Studies in Second Economy Distribution in Soviet Georgia. In *The Unofficial Economy: Consequences and Perspectives in Different Economic Systems*. Ed. S. Alessandrini and B. Dallago, pp. 218-227. Aldershot, Hants, U.K.; Brookfield, Vt.: Gower Publishing.

This article examines illicit trade in four different stores focusing on organization and staffing, profitability based on defrauding either the state or the consumer, the access to, storage and sale of goods, and how risks are avoided, especially by paying off bureaucratic superiors and the local police. The authors conclude that the second economy satisfies consumer preferences in ways unavailable to central planners, and that Georgia's informal economy rests on the degree to which social networks are institutionalized, linking individuals through trust-based commitments.

Trading/ Social networks/ U.S.S.R.

461. **Mars, G., and M. Nicod. 1981.** Hidden Rewards at Work: The Implications from a Study of British Hotels. In *Can I Have It in Cash?: A Study of Informal Institutions and Unorthodox Ways of Doing Things*. Ed. S. Henry, pp. 58-72. New York: St. Martin's Press.

Pilfering/ Britain

462. **Massey, D. 1984.** *Spatial Divisions of Labor: Social Structures and the Geography of Production*. New York: Methuen.

Industrial restructuring/ Labor market segmentation/ Spatial patterns/ Britain

463. **Matilla, J. P. 1973.** The Effects of Extending Minimum Wages to Cover Household Maids. *Journal of Human Resources* 8: 365-382.

Domestic service/ U.S.A.

464. **Mattera, P. 1985.** *Off the Books: The Rise of the Underground Economy*. New York: St. Martin's Press.

Mattera demonstrates the relations between the underground larger economy, viewing growth in the informal sector as a key element in broader processes of economic restructuring. The growing phenomenon of underground economic activity in the United States. and Britain is described from the perspective of workers cobbling together various income sources in response to the increasing insecurity of formal employment; from the perspective of employers seeking to avoid taxes, decrease overhead costs, and increase flexibility; and from that of governments who may be sympathetic to demands for unfettered capitalism but anxious about tax revenue losses. Particular attention is focused on the development of the submerged economy in Italy as the vanguard of economic transformation spreading throughout the capitalist world, on patterns of informal sector development in developing countries, and on the emergence of a second economy in the Soviet bloc since the 1950s. Mattera challenges recent arguments emphasizing the beneficial economic dynamism of informal activity, to highlight the effects of informal work as a way to reverse established workers rights and impose instead a precarious, underpaid, and unprotected status for working people.

Definition/ Pattern or magnitude/ Economic restructuring/ Social restructuring/ Labor processes/ Flexibilization/ Tax evasion/ Industrialized economies/ Centrally planned economies/ Third World/ U.S.A./ Italy

465. **Maung Maung Lwin. 1991.** *A Preliminary Study on Urban Informal Sector of Myanmar: The Case of Capital City Yangon*. International Economic Conflict Discussion Paper, no. 54. Chikusa-Ku Nagoya, Japan: Economic Research Center.

Pattern or magnitude/ Small or micro-enterprises/ Relation to formal economy/ Myanmar

466. **Mazumdar, D. 1976.** The Urban Informal Sector. *World Development* 4: 655-679.

Mazumdar profiles the informal sector labor force to suggest that (a) a disproportionate number of workers are female, outside the primary working age, and have low levels of education, (b) the sector is not a major point of entry for new rural migrants, (c) informal sector earnings are low but widely divergent, (d) only a small proportion of the urban labor force have income as low as, or lower than, the rural poor, (e) the migration function implicit in probabilistic models of job search exaggerates the volume of migration to the urban market and underplays economic performance in constraining migration, and (f) the contrast between the "vertical" development of the formal sector and the "horizontal" development of the informal sector indicate widening urban income inequality.

Pattern or magnitude/ Worker characteristics/ Dual sector or economy/ Migration/ Polarization/ Third World/ Peru/ Brazil/ Malaysia/ Korea/ India

467. —— . **1977.** Analysis of the Dual Labour Market in LDCs. In *Studies of Urban Labour Market Behaviour in Developing Countries*. Ed. S. Kannappan, pp. 13-33. Geneva, Switzerland: International Institute for Labour Studies.

Mazumdar distinguishes between the urban formal and informal labor markets to study income distribution, problems of definition, a model of earnings differentials, and the long-run growth of the dual urban labor market. He argues that unlike informal employment, formal sector work is shaped by trade unions and government as well as by the free play of market forces. The ease of entry and variable hours of informal work lead to the hypothesis that it serves as a point of transition for new migrants wishing to secure formal employment, a "job search model" which predicts levels of earnings below that in agriculture. The model predicts that informal sector growth rates in income and productivity will lag behind those of the formal sector and widen income disparities among the urban working class.

Definition/ Dual sector or economy/ Polarization/ Migration/ Polarization/ Third World

468. —— . **1991.** Import-Substituting Industrialization and Protection of the Small-Scale: The Indian Experience in the Textile Industry. *World Development* 19: 1197-1213.

Mazumdar presents a detailed review of Indian government policy to protect the household (handloom) sector. This policy benefits mainly an intermediate sector within the industry, characterized by small firms using low-grade, nonautomatic looms. At the same time, the policy severely constrained the competitiveness of the large-scale sector preventing wider takeoff of the Indian textile industry.

Small or micro-enterprises/ Artisanal production/ Policy analysis/ India

469. **McDonald, R. J. 1984.** The "Underground Economy" and BLS Statistical Data. *Monthly Labor Review* 107 (1): 4-18.

McDonald challenges the contention that the underground economy has caused an error in BLS data and argues that the BLS data are probably correct since no verifiable evidence exists to prove otherwise. While some assert that there is an underground economy, they have no evidence by which accurately to estimate its size.

Research methods/ Pattern or magnitude/ U.S.A.

470. **McGee, T. G. 1973.** Peasants in the Cities: A Paradox, a Paradox, a Most Ingenious Paradox. *Human Organization* 32: 135-142.

McGee challenges the prevailing definition of "urban peasants" who are said to retain their rural culture when they migrate to the city. He argues instead that peasants are part of a system of production based on family labor which can be found in the city as well as in the countryside. While problems arise with definitions of a peasant system of production, the concept (a) is amenable to cross-cultural measurement, (b) is not dependent on a rural-urban dichotomy, (c) does not assume preconceived peasant behaviors, and (d) provides a useful framework for analyzing urban change. Because participants in the peasant system do not fit the traditional definition of peasant, proletariat, or urban bourgeoisie, this group is better labeled the proto-proletariat.

Definition/ Migration/ Unpaid labor/ Third World/ Indonesia/ Nigeria/ Hong Kong

471. —— . **1977.** The Persistence of the Proto-Proletariat: Occupational Structures and Planning of the Future of Third World Cities. In *Third World Urbanization*. Ed. J. Abu-Lughod and R. Hay Jr., pp. 257-270. Chicago, Ill.: Maaroufa Press.

McGee describes the proto-proletariat as a fluctuating group whose delineation is complicated by conflicting concepts of class, work, and residence. Given their persistence, it is important to delineate their economic configuration. Three points are highlighted: their structural location in a dual model of the Third World city, an institutional approach to classify the peasant mode of production, and a classification based on income opportunities. Proto-proletarians are distinguished from formal sector workers based on their form of organization, as either self-employed or household-based producers; their economic activities; and their relationship to the informal and formal urban and rural sectors which can be examined in the flow of labor, money, commodities, and services.

Definition/ Pattern or magnitude/ Migration/ Class processes/ Third World/ Southeast Asia

472. —— . **1978.** An Invitation to the Ball: Dress Formal or Informal. In *Food, Shelter and Transport in Southeast Asia and the Pacific*. Ed. P. Rimmer, D. W. Drakakis-Smith and T. G. McGee, pp. 3-28. Canberra, Australia: Australian National University.

Review/ Third World

473. —— . **1979a.** Conservation and Dissolution in the Third World City: The "Shanty Town" as an Element in Conservation. *Development and Change* 10: 1-22.

Urbanization/ Relation to formal economy/ Third World

474. —— . **1979b.** The Poverty Syndrome: Making Out in the Southeast Asian City. In *Casual Work and Poverty in Third World Cities*. Ed. R. Bromley and C. Gerry, pp. 45-68. Chichester, U.K.: John Wiley & Sons.

McGee examines the survival strategies of the urban poor and their relationship to government. Their coping mechanisms include augmenting their income and resources by maximizing the number of household income-earners, engaging in diverse occupations, seeking credit from various sources as well as minimizing expenditures through underconsumption. Their lifestyles are characterized by particular attitudes toward birth control, family size, and a politics of marginality. Because governments do not understand the role and economic contribution of the urban poor they often pursue negative policy options.

Survival strategies/ State practice/ Worker characteristics/ Southeast Asia/ Indonesia

475. —— . **1982a.** Labor Markets, Urban Systems, and the Urbanization Process in Southeast Asian Countries. East-West Population Institute Paper, no. 81. Honolulu, Hawaii: East-West Population Institute.

Urbanization/ Migration/ Labor market dynamics/ Southeast Asia

476. ——. **1982b.** Labour Mobility in Fragmented Labour Markets, the Role of Circulatory Migration in Rural-Urban Relations in Asia. In *Towards a Political Economy of Urbanization in Third World Countries*. Ed. H. Safa, pp. 47-66. Delhi, India: Oxford University Press.

Labor market segmentation/ Migration/ Trading/ Social networks/ Indonesia/ Philippines/ Third World

477. —— . **1996.** On the Utility of Dualism: The Informal Sector and Mega-Urbanization in Developing Countries. *Regional Development Dialogue* 17 (1): 1-15.

McGee argues the continuing relevance of viewing informal work as an outcome of economic dualism, emphasizing the reinforcing impact of late twentieth century trends in globalization. He tracks the persistent growth of informal activities in different mega-cities and links this development with the growing interpenetration of markets and labor flows. Policy implications of these trends are highlighted.

Dual sector or economy/ Globalization/ Export production/ Urbanization/ Third World

478. **McGee, T. G., K. Salih, M. L. Young, and C. L. Heng. 1989.** Industrial Development, Ethnic Cleavages, and Employment Patterns: Penang State, Malaysia. In *The Informal Economy: Studies in Advanced and Less Developed Countries*. Ed. A. Portes, M. Castells, and L. A. Benton, pp. 265-278. Baltimore, Md.; London: Johns Hopkins University Press.

This chapter examines the informal sector when a regional economy experiences a rapid increase in gross regional product and a substantial shift in the size and composition of the labor force. Data from Penang show that a combination of capital, state, and labor processes operating at the international, national-regional, ethnic group and household levels produce a pattern of informal sector production which combines traditional practices with new informal activities. While informal enterprises offer employment opportunities for the Chinese community, they have ceased to be important for Malays or Indians. Thus, Penang represents a place where different strategies of TNCs, state policies, and ethnic divisions are juxtaposed.

Ethnicity/ Labor market segmentation/ Economic restructuring/ State practice/ Malaysia

479. **McGee, T. G., and Y. M. Yeung. 1977.** *Hawkers in Southeast Asian Cities: Planning for the Bazaar Economy*. Ottawa, Canada: International Development Research Centre.

Pattern or magnitude/ Trading/ Spatial patterns/ State practice/ Policy analysis/ Southeast Asia

480. **McKean, C. S. 1994.** Training and Technical Assistance for Small and Microenterprise: A Discussion of Their Effectiveness. In *Contrapunto: The Informal Sector Debate in Latin America*. Ed. C. A. Rakowski, pp. 199-219. Albany: State University of New York Press.

Small or micro-enterprises/ Project assistance/ Latin America

481. **McKee, K. 1989.** Microlevel Strategies for Supporting Livelihoods, Employment, and Income Generation for Women in the Third World: The Challenge of Significance. *World Development* 17: 993-1006.

McKee reviews areal, sectoral, and functional approaches that promote income generation and welfare among self-employed individuals and micro-enterprises. She also identifies criteria to measure the relative success of programs which engage these different approaches to argue that sectoral and functional strategies have the greatest potential to promote higher incomes among women.

Self-employment/ Survival strategies/ Policy prescriptions/ Project assistance/ Small or micro-enterprises/ Women/ Credit/ Third World

482. **Mead, D. C., and Christian Morrisson. 1996.** The Informal Sector Elephant. *World Development* 24 (10): 1611-1619.

Comparing 2,200 enterprises from seven countries, Mead and Morrisson examine a variety of measures of the informal sector, including its legality, size, relation to poverty, and capital intensity, to assess parallels and discontinuities in informal enterprises. They conclude that in virtually all countries in the Third World, a large number of enterprises include a small number of workers, limited participation in state activity including in terms of laws, regulation and taxation, and low levels of capitalization. Most surprising to the authors was the finding of a large degree of variability in the relationship between enterprises and questions of regulation in terms of licensing requirements, tax structures, and regulatory regimes. The informal sector, they note, should be defined within a national context given the importance of the differences noted. Such differences make cross-cultural comparisons problematic.

Pattern or magnitude/ Regulation/ State practice/ Education/ Firm characteristics/ Algeria/ Ecuador/ Jamaica/ Niger/ Swaziland/ Thailand/ Tunisia

483. **Mehta, M. 1985.** Urban Informal Sector: Concepts, Indian Evidence and Policy Implications. *Economic and Political Weekly* 20: 326-332.

Review/ Policy analysis/ India

484. **Mehta, V. 1982.** *Unemployment, Inequality, Parallel Economy: A Solution*. New Delhi: Allied Publishers.

Mehta argues that the road to India's future lies in the development and promotion of rural crafts and industries. This strategy will increase employment, production, consumption, and wealth and lead to the more even distribution of income and resources.

Rural/ Policy prescriptions/ Handicrafts/ India

485. **Meier, A. 1985.** Becaks, Bemos, Lambros and Productive Pandemonium. In *Planning for Small Enterprises in Third World Cities*. Ed. R. Bromley, pp. 27-35. Oxford, U.K.: Pergamon Press.

Meier describes the different modes of intermediate transportation in Southeast Asia to highlight the variation and efficiencies of these forms. The intermediate technology transport sector is seen as the solution to the problem of moving people and freight around a city with limited resources. The author recommends a flexible transportation policy in which competitive modes of transport are encouraged. He also argues that even though motor vehicles are more efficient, their adoption may aggravate unemployment.

Transportation/ Policy analysis/ Southeast Asia/ India

486. **Meng, N. S. 1988.** The Beginning of Small Enterprises in Laos: The Phonetong Women's Weaving Co-operative. In *Daughters in Industry: Work, Skills and Consciousness of Women Workers in Asia*. Ed. N. Heyzer, pp. 33-68. Kuala Lumpur, Malaysia: Asian and Pacific Development Centre.

Rural/ Small or micro-enterprises/ Women/ Handicrafts/ Asia/ Laos

487. **Merrick, T. W. 1976.** Employment and Earnings in the Informal Sector in Brazil: The Case of Belo Horizonte. *Journal of Developing Areas* 10: 337-354.

Pattern or magnitude/ Brazil

488. **Mesa-Lago, C. 1992.** *Social Security and the Informal Sector in Latin America: The Case of Mexico*. Informal Sector Discussion Paper, no. 2. Washington, D.C.: U.S. Department of Labor, Bureau of International Labor Affairs.

Small or micro-enterprises/ Unpaid labor/ Home-based production/ Domestic service/ State practice/ Welfare/ Mexico/ Latin America

489. **Middleton, A. 1981.** Petty Manufacturing, Capitalist Enterprises and the Process of Accumulation in Ecuador. *Development and Change* 12: 505-524.

Using data from a survey of petty manufacturers and traders in Quito, Middleton examines the linkage between petty producers and capitalist enterprises and its relevance for capital accumulation in peripheral economies. Data on backward linkages reveal that petty manufacturers buy from traders or intermediaries who trade inputs made by capitalist firms where the flow of value is from the formal to the informal sector. Thus, an important part of a petty producers reinvestment income is retained in the informal sector. Data also reveal that most small producers sell directly to consumers which generates few forward linkage to the formal sector through provision of low-priced goods and services. This finding rejects the argument that value transfer explains the poverty of petty producers.

Relation to formal economy/ Processes of accumulation/ Trading/ Ecuador

490. ——. **1985.** Class, Power and the Distribution of Credit in Ecuador. In *Planning for Small Enterprises in Third World Cities*. Ed. R. Bromley, pp. 293-308. Oxford, U.K.: Pergamon Press.

Middleton examines policy decisions which facilitate small manufacturers' access to credit. Revenues from oil exports have helped raise the value of credit to small industry but, relative to other sectors, the significance of this credit has declined. Efforts to increase capital investment limits have only succeeded in channelling credit to medium-sized, less labor-intensive enterprises, and changes to meet the needs of international finance have operated to the benefit of large scale industry. Interviews with small producers reveal a reluctance to obtain credit from state-related sources due to complicated documentation, necessary guarantees, a fear of debt, and the perceived vulnerability of small creditors. Middleton concludes that control of state financial institutions is an important element in the struggle for power in Ecuador.

State practice/ Small or micro-enterprises/ Credit/ Ecuador

491. ——. **1987.** Structural Change and the Organizational Development of Petty Manufacturers in Ecuador. *Labour, Capital and Society / Travail, Capital et Societé* 20: 34-66.

Political mobilization/ State practice/ Ecuador

492. ——. **1989.** The Changing Structure of Petty Production in Ecuador. *World Development* 17: 139-155.

Changes in petty manufacturing in Quito between 1975 and 1982 are examined to address the relationship between petty production and capitalist development. While the overall number of petty producers remained stable during this period, the structure of petty production showed some significant changes. Survey evidence suggests that while small-scale production of the means of subsistence declined, production of the means of production increased. This shift was manifested in the flourishing of informal repair shops, painters, and printers while informal shoemakers, tailors, and furniture makers became less numerous both relatively and absolutely.

Relation to capital/ Labor processes/ Petty commodity production/ Firm characteristics/ Ecuador

493. **Mies, M. 1980.** Capitalist Development and Subsistence Reproduction: Rural Women in India. *Bulletin of Concerned Asian Scholars* 12 (2): 3-14.

Women/ Household division of labor/ Home-based production/ Relation to formal economy/ Rural/ India

494. —— . **1982a.** The Dynamics of the Sexual Division of Labor and Integration of Rural Women into the World Market. In *Women and Development*. Ed. L. Benería, pp. 1-28. New York: Praeger.

Mies's study of the lace makers of Narsapur explores the changing sexual division of labor in India where changes in the lace industry are shaped by the locally constructed sexual division of labor. While women lace makers are integrated into the world economy, their relationship to global production is obscured by the social definition of women as housewives.

Gender division of labor/ Rural/ Relation to formal economy/ New international division of labor/ Home-based production/ Export production/ Gender ideology/ India

495. —— . **1982b.** *The Lace Makers of Narsapur: Indian Housewives Produce for the World Market*. London: Zed Press.

Mies examines the growth of the lace-making industry in a district of Andhra Pradesh to illuminate the process by which women's work is made invisible in the course of economic development. Drawing from fieldwork in the late 1970s, she describes the structure, production relations, and income flows to lace makers, subcontracting agents, traders, and exporters in the global market for handmade lace. Mies explores how women are recruited to the industry as housewives, a status which serves as the basis for their exploitation. Despite this, women's participation in the industry is assured since lace-making provides a stopgap livelihood strategy for pauperized rural households although it increases their poverty and undermines their social status vis à vis men.

Home-based production/ Subcontracting/ Export production/ Gender division of labor/ Relation to formal economy/ New international division of labor/ Gender ideology/ Rural/ India

496. —— . **1986.** *Patriarchy and Accumulation on a World Scale: Women in the International Division of Labor*. London: Zed Books.

New international division of labor/ Women/ Gender ideology/ Gender relations/ Subcontracting

497. **Miller, S. M. 1987.** The Pursuit of Informal Economies. *Annals of the American Academy of Political and Social Science* 493: 26-35.

Review/ Definition/ Pattern or magnitude/ Industrialized economies

498. **Mingione, E. 1978.** Capitalist Crisis, Neo-Dualism and Marginalization. *International Journal of Urban and Regional Research* 2 (2): 213-221.

In the global crises of the 1960s and 1970s, decentralization and internationalized labor processes have been the two main strategies used by firms to regain profitability. This process of recovery has generated what Mingione refers to as neo-duality whereby a shrinking unionized and protected working class exists alongside a growing mass of underemployed and unemployed workers.Two increasingly common types of conflict are linked to neodualist restructuring: the struggle of outsiders in big cities such as the actions of underemployed juveniles facing prospects of chronically unstable employment; and regional tensions between areas drained by decentralization and those where remunerative, centralized production is now concentrated.These patterns indicate the restructuring of sociopolitical activities in which the working class acts under advanced capitalism.

Social restructuring/ Labor processes/ Political mobilization/ Decentralization/ Marginalization/ Industrialized economies

499. —— . **1983.** Informalization, Restructuring and the Survival Strategies of the Working Class. *International Journal of Urban and Regional Research* 7 (3): 311-339.

Mingione theorizes the relationship between changing patterns of reproduction and capital accumulation in light of decreasing industrial employment and the diffusion of informal activities and new domestic burdens that erode the direct command of capital over social reproduction. He argues that because the socioeconomic crisis is independent from the tendency toward informalization, a mechanical coincidence of circumstances favoring informal consumption and activity is mistaken. Mingione also examines economic trends in the core, semiperiphery, and periphery to conclude that complexities of the current phase of mature capitalism do not suggest prospects for economic recovery. In fact, decentralization, informalization, and the growth of domestic work are defensive measures in a prolonged crisis where greater local and community autonomy can lead to alternative solutions to the present malaise. Extensive bibliography.

Social restructuring/ Survival strategies/ Processes of accumulation/ Decentralization/ State practice/ Italy

500. —— . **1984.** The Informal Sector and the Development of Third World Cities. *Regional Development Dialogue* 5 (2): 63-76.

In this article, Mingione examines the meaning of the informal sector in developing countries, the relationship between the informal sector and development, and the conditions needed to promote those features of the informal sector that enhance national economic growth. He argues that the term "informal sector" is useful for explaining complex transformations taking place in both developing and industrialized countries. In industrialized countries, the term refers to forms of decommodification that accompany stagnation and crisis, while in the developing world the informal sector refers to commodification and the expansion of the monetary economy. In both contexts, the term includes extra-market survival strategies as well as low and irregular monetary income but, because of its subsistence orientation, informal activities do not usually generate conditions for accumulation although accumulation is possible under conditions where an incoming surplus population is blocked and local production protected against cheap imports.

Definition/ Survival strategies/ Processes of accumulation/ Third World/ Italy

501. —— . **1985.** Social Reproduction of the Surplus Labour Force: The Case of Southern Italy. In *Beyond Employment: Household, Gender and Subsistence*. Ed. N. Redclift and E. Mingione, pp. 14-54. Oxford, U.K.: Basil Blackwell.

In this article, Mingione classifies a spectrum of human activities contributing to reproduction: formal, mixed formal/ informal, where formal work produces some informal income, purely informal activities such as employment without a contract and self-employment, illegal work, work not exchanged for income, including reciprocal and solidarity activities, work for self-consumption such as do-it-yourself projects, and domestic work to highlight relations of social survival and forms of non-monetary exchange.

Survival strategies/ Definition/ Unpaid labor/ Non-monetary exchange/ Social reproduction/ Italy

502. —— . **1988.** Work and Informal Activities in Urban Southern Italy. In *On Work: Historical, Comparative and Theoretical Approaches*. Ed. R. E. Pahl, pp. 548-578. Oxford, U.K.: Basil Blackwell.

Definition/ Pattern or magnitude/ Italy

503. —— . **1991.** *Fragmented Societies: A Sociology of Economic Life beyond the Market Paradigm*. Oxford, U.K.: Basil Blackwell.

Mingione examines current transformations in the increasingly heterogeneous world of work. These transformations are explained through a critique of the self-regulating market and a view of economic development as a process of social organization in which economic competition interacts with processes of socialization and the construction of social identity. Noting the growing heterogeneity and informalization of work in different national, sectoral, and political-economic contexts, Mingione explores the relationship between these changes, those in social reproduction, and current trends in industrial restructuring. In closing he explores linkages between the emergence of "fragmented societies," the decreasing importance of purely class-based political interaction, and the increasingly complicated nature of contestations for political power.

Review/ Definition/ Economic restructuring/ Industrial restructuring/ Social restructuring/ Survival strategies/ Class processes/ Consciousness/ Political mobilization/ Industrialized economies

504. —— . **1994.** Life Strategies and Social Economies in the Postfordist Age. *International Journal of Urban and Regional Research* 18: 24-45.

Critiquing rationalistic approaches to the study of socio-economic transitions, Mingione emphasizes the interrelationship between economic and social dimensions of change as a basis for comparing family strategies and informal relations in northern and southern Italy. In northern Italian cities, informal support systems characterize the organization of working-class households which enable resources to be channeled toward the development of family business innovations and children's education. These exchanges generate conditions for upward mobility and the region's transition out of a "black labor"-dominated economy. In contrast, southern Italy is dominated by patronage systems which tend to constrain similar transitions. The study demonstrates both the economic relevance of family strategies to long-term livelihood prospects and the importance of kinship-based social relations in the development of different systems of social integration in late 20th century capitalism.

Social networks/ Economic restructuring/ Social mobility/ Survival strategies/ Migration/ Household/ Italy

505. **Misztal, B. 1981.** The Petite Bourgeoisie in Socialist Society. In *The Petite Bourgeoisie: Comparative Studies of the Uneasy Stratum*. Ed. F. Bechhofer and B. Elliott, pp. 90-104. New York: St. Martin's Press.

Misztal argues that independent Polish businessmen occupy a position that has become increasingly marginal, with only about 1 percent of the population classifiable as petite bourgeois even though a small private sector engaging mainly family labor has survived different periods of tolerance or restriction. In the late 1940s, unsocialized trade flourished in response to problems in the distribution of essential commodities. With increased prosperity and economic differentiation in the 1970s, the state again encouraged private food shops and restaurants where the small private sector became the object of direct manipulation and intervention in the interest of state policy. The paper concludes that the petite bourgeoisie emphasis on economic self-interest, independence, and a dual standard of honesty, has penetrated the new middle class of lower-grade clerks.

Small or micro-enterprises/ Trading/ State practice/ Poland/ Centrally planned economies

506. **Mitter, S. 1986.** Industrial Restructuring and Manufacturing Homework: Immigrant Women in the UK Clothing Industry. *Capital and Class* 27: 37-80.

Industrial restructuring/ Home-based production/ Women/ Gender division of labor/ Garment manufacture/ Migration/ Ethnicity/ Britain

507. —— . **1994.** On Organising Women in Casualised Work: A Global Overview. In *Dignity and Daily Bread: New Forms of Economic Organizing among Poor Women in the Third World and the First*. Ed S. Rowbotham and S. Mitter, pp. 14-52. London: Routledge.

Given the greater flexibility of global economic restructuring during the 1980s, the use of casualized labor has become widespread, and distinctions between formal and informal economies are increasingly blurred. Mitter highlights the global rise of flexiblized production and employment emphasizing women's experience as the major source of unprotected, low-paid, and temporary workers. Implications of deregulation and casualization for labor organizing and a rethinking economic policy are explored.

Economic restructuring/ Flexibilization/ Gender division of labor/ Flexible specialization/ Home-based production/ Political mobilization/ Trade unions

508. **Mizrahi, R. 1989.** Foundations of the Urban Informal Sector. *Desarrollo Economico* 28: 601-622.

Labor market dynamics/ Migration/ Gender division of labor/ Latin America

509. **Mody, A., and D. Wheeler. 1987.** Towards a Vanishing Middle: Competition in the World Garment Industry. *World Development* 15: 1269-1284.

Industrial restructuring/ Garment manufacture/ Comparative

510. **Moghadam, V. M. 1992.** Women, Employment, and Social Change in the Middle East and North Africa. In *Women's Work & Women's Lives: The Continuing Struggle Worldwide*. Ed. H. Kahne and J. Z. Giele, pp. 87-118. Boulder, Colo.: Westview.

Valentine Moghadam examines women's work in the Middle East in the context of the austerities required by debt-servicing and structural adjustment and political repression which "have tended to delegitimize Western-style systems and raise questions of cultural identity." While the effects of this have increased or decreased is still a matter of debate, what is clear is that there has been a differential impact of these changes on women and men. The state has been a key player in these transformations in terms of defining women's legal status and in employment generation. Moghadam concludes that there is significant diversity within the region vis-à-vis women's employment which challenges notions of the homogeneity of Islam in shaping the roles of Middle Eastern women. What is clear, however, is that throughout the region there is a reservoir of underutilized female labor.

Structural adjustment/ State practice/ Policy prescriptions/ Industrial restructuring/ Gender ideology/ Gender division of labor/ Reserve army of labor/ Comparative/ Middle East

511. **Moir, H. V. J. 1978.** *The Jakarta Informal Sector.* Geneva, Switzerland: International Labour Office.

Pattern or magnitude/ Indonesia

512. **Moir, H. V. J., and C. Robinson. 1984.** Labour Market Measurement: A Review of Some Popular Labour Market Measures. In *Understanding Labour Markets in Australia.* Ed. R. Blandy and O. Covick, pp. 61-83. Winchester, Mass.: Allen and Unwin.

Research methods/ Pattern or magnitude/ Industrialized economies/ Australia

513. **Mookerjee, S. 1975.** *Under the Shadows of the Metropolis: They Are Citizens Too.* Calcutta, India: Calcutta Metropolitan Development Authority.

Pattern or magnitude/ Policy prescriptions/ India

514. **Morris, L. 1987.** Constraints on Gender: The Family Wage, Social Security and the Labour Market. *Work, Employment and Society* 1: 85-106.

Survival strategies/ Gender division of labor/ Welfare/ State practice/ Britain

515. **Moser, C. O. N. 1977.** The Dual Economy and Marginality Debate and the Contribution of Micro Analysis: Market Sellers in Bogota. *Development and Change* 8: 465-489.

Employing data from self-employed produce vendors in one of Bogota's public markets, Moser examines the survival mechanisms of urban marginal dwellers to suggest that differences in the capital resources available to individuals, rather than different views of economic rationality, account for divergent scales of operation among producers. The social characteristics and work histories of sellers indicate that age and sex determine the constraints under which sellers operate as well as their potential for upward mobility. Overall, small-scale marketing is a "refuge occupation," with only a small number able to accumulate capital.

Survival strategies/ Differentiation/ Marginalization/ Self-employment/ Trading/ Worker characteristics/ Social mobility/ Constraints to accumulation/ Colombia

516. —— . **1980.** Why the Poor Remain Poor: The Experience of Bogota Market Traders in the 1970s. *Journal of Interamerican Studies and World Affairs* 22: 365-387.

Moser examines differentiation among traders and argues that market sellers are being undermined by supermarkets. This process results in some becoming wage laborers while others continue in the trade but are becoming increasingly impoverished.

Differentiation/ Trading/ Colombia

517. —— . **1981.** Surviving in the Suburbios. *IDS Bulletin* 12 (3): 19-29.

Using data from her research in Guayaquil, Ecuador, Moser examines the function and importance of women's work in the survival strategies of low-income households where the majority of men are excluded from secure formal wage-sector employment.

Survival strategies/ Women/ Ecuador

518. —— . **1982.** A Home of One's Own: Squatter Housing Strategies in Guayaquil, Ecuador. In *Urbanization in Contemporary Latin America: Critical Approaches to the Analysis of Urban Issues*. Ed. A. Gilbert, pp. 159-190. New York: John Wiley & Sons.

Housing/ Survival strategies/ Ecuador

519. —— . **1989.** The Impact of Recession and Structural Adjustment Policies at the Micro-Level: Low Income Women and Their Households in Guayaquil, Ecuador. In *Invisible Adjustment: Poor Women and the Economic Crisis*. UNICEF, Regional Office for the Americas and the Caribbean, Regional Programme on Women in Development.

Structural adjustment/ Survival strategies/ Women/ Household division of labor/ Policy analysis/ Project assistance/ Ecuador

520. —— . **1994.** The Informal Sector Debate, Part 1: 1970-1983. In *Contrapunto: The Informal Sector Debate in Latin America*. Ed C. A. Rakowski, pp. 31-50. Albany: State University of New York Press.

In a revised and abridged version of a 1984 article [see separate citation], Moser highlights key debates following the early ILO studies on informal economic activities in developing economies. Major conclusions of early debates are noted, including the need to recognize informal activity as an important component of developing economies, the reemergence of small-scale production with competitive economic pressures, and the need to clarify specific social relations embodied in informal work to understand its variable implications for labor exploitation as well as city, regional, national, and international development.

Review/ Pattern or magnitude/ Gender division of labor/ Firm characteristics/ Labor relations/ Third World

521. **Moser, C. O. N., and K. Young. 1978.** Informal Sector or Petty Commodity Production: Dualism or Dependence in Urban Development? *World Development* 6: 1041-1064.

Moser and Young review recent studies of Third World poverty and unemployment to identify problems of definition in the informal sector debate. Recognizing the essentially dependent and involutionary character of the informal sector, she proposes a model based on petty commodity production and its subordinate relationship to the capitalist sector.

Review/ Definition/ Critique of dualism/ Petty commodity production/ Third World/ Colombia/ Sri Lanka/ Kenya

522. —— . **1981.** Women of the Working Poor. *IDS Bulletin* 12 (3): 54-61.

Skeptical of the rigid conceptual distinction between formal and informal sectors, the authors question whether the wages offered by capitalist enterprises have a direct economic relation to informal sector wages and women's housework. The factors they identify within capitalism to explain unpaid or marginalized work include the privatization of women's work which alters and makes invisible particular forms of economic participation and recruitment (e.g. domestic outwork and employment access through kin networks), and the definition of women as subsidiary or secondary workers, economically limited by an ideology of gender-based labor market segregation. Gender differential access to the labor market makes it possible for capital to engage production within the family unit. The authors conclude that women are often victims of capitalist accumulation because policy makers fail to recognize class and gender differences in the access people have to resources and power.

Review/ Gender inequality/ Labor market segmentation/ Unpaid labor/ Home-based production/ Subcontracting/ Social networks/ Third World

523. —— . **1984.** The Informal Sector Reworked: Viability and Vulnerability in Urban Development. *Regional Development Dialogue* 5 (2): 135-178.

Moser identifies reasons for the persistence of the informal sector and highlights its capacity to generate growth and employment. Following a review of development agency concerns she explores the assumptions underlying the use of the informal sector concept, the limits of global generalizations, and the importance of a refined methodology for data collection. She then examines the size and sectoral breakdown of the sector as well as with the particular characteristics of diverse small-scale enterprises to distinguish between urban spatial studies and those focused on productive units, and between cross-sectional surveys and in-depth anthropological studies. She notes that distinguishing between productive enterprises and those in the distributive service sector are critical in determining the growth potential of informal enterprises.

Review/ Research methods/ Pattern or magnitude/ Gender division of labor/ Firm characteristics/ Processes of accumulation/ Third World

524. **Mosley, P. 1978.** Implicit Models and Policy Recommendations: Policy towards the "Informal Sector" in Kenya. *IDS Bulletin* 9 (3): 3-10.

Mosley argues that the ILO model of the informal sector is inadequate as a basis for policy reform because of its assumption that informal incomes are lower, labor intensity higher, and products less dependent on imports and more attuned to the needs of low income consumers than the formal sector. Four definitions of informal economic activity are discussed which focus on accounting, firm size, patterns of industrial relations, and relations between the enterprise and the state. The latter is a preferred basis for definition because it differentiates the effects of state policy on different product-groups. Evidence supports redefining the "informal sector" to include a low-income goods sector as a refuge in times of hardship but with little dynamic potential, and a high-income goods and services sector with the potential for growth but without possibilities for redistribution.

Definition/ Differentiation/ Policy analysis/ Kenya

525. **Murphy, A. D. 1991.** City in Crisis. *Urban Anthropology* 20: 1-13.

Survival strategies/ Industrial restructuring/ Mexico

526. **Murphy, M. 1978.** The Value of Non-Market Household Production: Opportunity Cost versus Market Cost Estimates. *Review of Income and Wealth* (3): 243-255.

Murphy examines the issues involved in valuing time allocated to nonmarket production. In determining an appropriate valuation, he concludes that when interest is primarily in the product generated by the household, market cost is a suitable approach and a method consistent with the use of GNP as a measure of production. In contrast, as a total measure of welfare, it is appropriate to add a measure of nonmarket production to GNP.

Unpaid labor/ Research methods

527. **Murray, F. 1983.** The Decentralization of Production--the Decline of the Mass Collective Worker. *Capital and Class* 19: 74-99.

Decentralization/ Gender division of labor/ Class processes/ Subcontracting/ Production process/ Italy

528. **Nash, J. 1988.** The Mobilization of Women in the Bolivian Debt Crisis. *Women and Work* 3: 67-86.

Survival strategies/ Social networks/ Political mobilization/ Gender division of labor/ Structural adjustment/ Women

529. **Nash, J., and M. P. Fernández-Kelly, eds. 1983.** *Women, Men and the International Division of Labor*. Albany: State University of New York Press.

A collection of 18 papers focuses on labor force inequalities and the process by which these are shaped by the changing international division of labor. Growing fluidity in capital investments and the increasingly global integration of industrial production are sharpening inequalities between women and men, minorities and dominant racial and ethnic groups, rural and urban localities. Exploring links between patterns of female employment and gender roles and ideology, the collection also focuses on changes in the garment, textile, and electronics industries, as well as on changes in services-related work with the relocation of production to new overseas and rural North American sites. The changing international division of labor signifies loss of employment in old sites of production in the industrial core, while new multinational investments in receiving countries and geographical spaces of the periphery are involving women in work characterized by extremely low pay, hazardous conditions, and repressive labor relations.

New international division of labor/ Gender ideology/ Gender division of labor/ Ethnicity/ Racial inequality/ Export production/ Export processing zones/ Garment manufacture/ Electronics manufacture/ Services/ Subcontracting/ Migration/ State practice/

Rural/ U.S.A/ Brazil/ Jamaica/ Mexico/ Venezuela/ Curaçao/ Taiwan/ Malaysia/ Philippines/ Asia

530. **Nattrass, N. J. 1987.** Street Trading in Transkei--A Struggle Against Poverty, Persecution, and Prosecution. *World Development* 15: 861-875.

Nattrass examines both the socioeconomic position of hawkers in Transkei, and the relationship between hawkers, big business, and the state in Umtata. The study combines theories of marginality and petty commodity production to examine the industrial reserve army, the marginal pole, the formal sector, and the location of the informal sector. This approach highlights the heterogeneity of and income differentiation among informal sector participants. Characteristics of informal enterprises include the small scale of their operation, the absence of official recognition and regulation, and the labor intensity of work. Transkei hawkers, most of whom are female, fit within the marginal pole as they are generally unskilled, denied access to migrant contracts, and discriminated against in the internal labor market. These hawkers vend as a last resort since hawking is the object of police oppression and is symptomatic of struggles between small wholesalers who supply both hawkers and supermarkets.

Marginalization/ Petty commodity production/ Reserve army of labor/ State practice/ Trading/ Differentiation/ Firm characteristics/ South Africa

531. **Neck, P. A., and R. E. Nelson, eds. 1987.** *Small Enterprise Development: Policies and Programmes.* 2d ed., Management Development Series, no. 14. Geneva, Switzerland: International Labour Office.

Small or micro-enterprises/ Policy analysis/ Third World/ Industrialized economies/ Centrally planned economies

532. **Nelson, M. K. 1988.** Providing Family Day Care: An Analysis of Home-based Work. *Social Problems* 35: 78-94.

Home-based production/ Unpaid labor/ U.S.A.

533. **Nelson, N. 1979.** How Women and Men Get By: The Sexual Division of Labour in the Informal Sector of a Nairobi Squatter Settlement.

In *Casual Work and Poverty in Third World Cities*. Ed. R. Bromley and C. G. Gerry, pp. 283-304. New York: John Wiley & Sons.

Pattern or magnitude/ Gender division of labor/ Survival strategies/ Kenya

534. **New York State Department of Labor. 1982a.** *Report to the Governor and the Legislature on the Garment Manufacturing Industry and Industrial Homework*. Albany, N.Y.: State of New York.

Pattern or magnitude/ Garment manufacture/ Home-based production/ Subcontracting/ U.S.A.

535. — . **1982b.** Study of State-Federal Employment Standards for Industrial Homeworkers in New York City. Albany, N.Y.: Division of Labor Standards.

State practice/ Regulation/ Home-based production/ Subcontracting/ U.S.A.

536. **Nihan, G., E. Demol, and C. Jondoh. 1979.** The Modern Informal Sector in Lome. *International Labour Review* 118: 631-644.

Pattern or magnitude/ Togo

537. **Nihan, G., and R. Jourdain. 1978.** The Modern Informal Sector in Nouakchott. *International Labour Review* 117: 709-720.

Pattern or magnitude/ Mauritania

538. **Noe, S. V. 1991.** Public and Private Responses to Hypergrowth in Third World Metropolitan Areas: Two Case Studies. *Third World Planning Review* 13: 217-235.

Urbanization/ Policy analysis/ Turkey/ Indonesia

539. **North, D. S., and M. F. Houston. 1976.** *The Characteristics and Role of Illegal Aliens in the U.S. Labor Market: An Exploratory Study*. Washington, D.C.: Linton.

Migration/ Labor market dynamics/ Ethnicity/ Worker characteristics/ U.S.A.

540. **O'Higgins, M. 1985.** The Relationship between the Formal and Hidden Economies: An Exploratory Analysis for Four Countries. In *The Economics of the Shadow Economy*. Ed. W. Gaertner and A. Wenig, pp. 127-143. Berlin, F.R.G.: Springer-Verlag.

The hidden economy literature suggests an inverse relationship between the health of the formal and hidden economies—a suggestion with important implications for both economics and politics. This paper examines this relationship in a number of Western European countries and the United States. to highlight the complexity of this relation: the size of the hidden economy is positively related to the size of the measured economy and to inflation, while unemployment is shown to have no clear effect. He concludes that structural rather than cyclical phenomena explain the growth of the hidden economy.

Pattern or magnitude/ Dual sector or economy/ U.S.A./ Britain/ Canada/ Germany

541. **O'Neill, D. M. 1983.** *Growth of the Underground Economy, 1950-1981: Some Evidence from the Current Population Survey: A Study Prepared for the Use of the Joint Economic Commission, Congress*. Washington, D.C.: G.P.O.

O'Neill reviews existing information on the size and character of the U.S. underground economy and notes that available evidence is indirect and tenuous. Estimates of the size of the underground economy in relation to the GNP vary from less than 5 percent to 20 percent. This discrepancy is due to the different measures and definitions used. Drawing on data from the Current Population Survey he concludes that the underground economy may not be as large as is often expected, possibly constituting only 7.5 percent of total U.S. GNP.

Pattern or magnitude/ Research methods/ U.S.A.

542. **O. S., Maria, ed. 1990.** *The Second Economy in Marxist States*. New York: St. Martin's Press.

This book examines the relationship between the informal and the formal sector in socialist economies.

Relation to formal economy/ Pattern or magnitude/ State practice/ Comparative/ Centrally planned economies/ U.S.S.R./ Poland/

Hungary/ Romania/ Yugoslavia/ Cuba/ Nicaragua/ China/ Angola/ Tanzania

543. **Ofer, G., and J. Pickersgill. 1980.** Soviet Household Saving: Study of Soviet Emigrant Families. *Quarterly Journal of Economics* 95: 121-143.

Ofer and Pickersgill document patterns of savings among Soviet families in the USSR to estimate the proportion of income saved from the public and private sector.

Pattern or magnitude/ Research methods/ U.S.S.R.

544. **Ofer, G., and A. Vinokur. 1983.** The Labor-Force Participation of Married Women in the Soviet Union: A Household Cross-Section Analysis. *Journal of Comparative Economics* 7: 158-176.

Gender division of labor/ Worker characteristics/ U.S.S.R.

545. **Offe, C., and R. G. Heinze, with U. Götting, K. Hinrichs and R. Vlek. 1992.** *Beyond Employment: Time, Work and the Informal Economy*. Trans. Alan Braley. Philadelphia, Pa.: Temple University Press.

Advanced industrialized countries are plagued by a pattern of growing unemployment and an increasing colonization of the lifeworld by the market. This results in increasing numbers of households left without the necessary means for social reproduction which raises the question; Can useful human activity and the distribution of its results be organized differently than in a market economy without diminished efficiency, loss of rationality, or the need for increased state bureaucracy? Offe and Heinze address this question by examining the "grey area" in industrialized economies where regular activity is performed neither as a function of formal employment nor as household reproduction. Their analysis describes cooperative exchange systems where useful activities are organized according to formal, though not money-based rules. Despite constraints associated with nonmonetary exchange the authors propose the value and viability of cooperative exchange systems as a means to address immediate individual and social needs as well as to facilitate reforms such as a shorter work week and basic income rights.

Social reproduction/ Social restructuring/ Nonmonetary exchange/ Social networks/ Policy prescriptions/ Industrialized economies/ Canada/ Netherlands/ Germany/ U.S.A.

546. **Okojie, C. E. E. 1984.** Female Migrants in the Urban Labour Market: Benin City, Nigeria. *Canadian Journal of African Studies / Revue Canadienne des Études Africaines* 18: 547-562.

Migration/ Women/ Nigeria

547. **Organisation for Economic Co-operation and Development. 1993.** *New Directions in Donor Assistance to Microenterprises*. Paris: OECD.

Small or micro-enterprises/ Credit/ Policy analysis/ Project assistance/ Niger/ Swaziland/ Senegal/ Third World

548. **Osirim, M. J. 1992.** The State of Women in the Third World: The Informal Sector and Development in Africa and the Caribbean. *Social Development Issues* 14 (2-3): 74-87.

Women/ Gender ideology/ Gender division of labor/ Economic restructuring/ Policy analysis/ Africa/ Caribbean

549. **Otero, M. 1994.** The Role of Governments and Private Institutions in Addressing the Informal Sector in Latin America. In *Contrapunto: The Informal Sector Debate in Latin America*. Ed. C. A. Rakowski, pp. 177-198. Albany: State University of New York Press.

State practice/ Project assistance/ Latin America

550. **Otsuka, K., M. Kikuchi, and Y. Hayami. 1986.** Community and Market in Contract Choice: The Jeepney in the Philippines. *Economic Development and Cultural Change* 34: 279-298.

Social networks/ Spatial patterns/ Rural/ Transportation/ State practice/ Philippines

551. **Oyeneye, O. Y. 1980.** The Nature and Process of Human Resource Development in Nigeria's Informal Sector. *Labour and Society* 5: 373-384.

Pattern or magnitude/ Nigeria

552. **Pahl, R. E. 1980.** Employment, Work and the Domestic Division of Labor. *International Journal of Urban and Regional Research* 4 (1): 1-20.

Pahl highlights the consequences of the shift from employment to work, the latter including productive activities generally hidden in national accounts to explore the shift within local labor markets as they interact with the household economy. Hé argues that increasing levels of unemployment are unlikely to produce low priced formal services but do generate conditions which expand informal production. Informal work also may be more satisfying and rewarding, provide reskilling, and offer greater choice and control over one's labor than formal employment. An examination of a single labor market suggests that those strata which resist incorporation into the dominant values of industrial capitalism and develop informal support systems find it easier to survive the problems imposed by declining formal employment. Patterns of "getting by" indicate the weaving of formal, informal, and domestic work among different household members which reconstitute strategies of survival as well as the domestic division of labor.

Economic restructuring/ Social restructuring/ Social networks/ Survival strategies/ Household division of labor/ Household/ Industrialized economies/ Britain

553. —— . **1984.** *Divisions of Labour*. Oxford, U.K.; New York: Blackwell.

Pahl offers an historical and ethnographic study of "what ordinary people do" to cope with changing economic circumstances on the Isle of Sheppey, challenging the distinction between work and employment. Focusing on household work strategies in a changing political economy he argues that while the total amount of work done is more likely to increase rather than decline for most households, new divisions of labor are emerging which increasing polarization among households. Under economic crises, household members rely on illegal work or proto-industrial patterns of domestic labor. He also explores the privatization of the public sector, the growth of self-provisioning, cultural values, and the role of women in cultural and social reproduction.

Labor processes/ Household/ Household division of labor/ Survival strategies/ Gender division of labor/ Polarization/ Rural/ Economic restructuring/ Research methods/ Social reproduction/ Self-provisioning/ England

554. —— . **1987a.** A Comparative Approach to the Study of the Informal Economy. Paper presented at the American Sociological Association Annual Convention, 17-22 August 1987, Chicago, Ill.

Pahl argues that literature on the informal sector suffers from conceptual and definitional confusion, is ahistorical, and lacks a comparative framework. He identifies five critical issues: (1) state regulation or deregulation of the formal economy creates the conditions for the existence of the informal economy, (2) comparative statistics may conceal more than they reveal since responses to global change is context-specific, (3) descriptions of multiple economies within a social formation lead to questionable conclusions, (4) reference to all work outside formal employment as constituting the informal economy is deceptive, and (5) the concept of the informal economy has been variously defined, each with its own literature and internal debates. To move beyond formal taxonomies, Pahl suggests that the concept of work be based on the actor's subjective definition of the situation and on the social relations in which a given task or activity is embedded, a suggestion which assumes that global processes of restructuring and patterns of state regulation and deregulation underpin comparative analysis.

Review/ Economic restructuring/ Social restructuring/ State practice/ Comparative

555. —— . **1987b.** Does Jobless Mean Workless? Unemployment and Informal Work. *The Annals of the American Academy of Political and Social Science* 493: 36-46.

Definition/ Survival strategies/ Britain

556. —— . **ed. 1988a.** *On Work: Historical, Comparative and Theoretical Approaches*. Oxford: Basil Blackwell.

This rich edited volume brings together historical and comparative studies of work and employment. Divided into six sections, the volume combines historical analyses of work, employment, unemployment and the sexual division of labor; employers' and workers' strategies in the workplace; a reconceptualization of home-based activities, household labor and homework; and analyses of "new world factories," including studies of the electronics and high-tech industries, subcontracting work and women employed in strawberry export agribusiness. This volume offers a sophisticated theoretical contribution to many of the current debates in the field. Many of the chapters are from work available elsewhere.

Pattern or magnitude/ Gender division of labor/ Home-based production/ Industrial restructuring/ Labor market segmentation/ Subcontracting/ Class processes/ Labor processes/ Rural/ Social networks/ Household division of labor/ Household/ Garment manufacture/ Electronics manufacture/ Comparative/ Britain/ U.S.A./ Hungary/ Italy/ Canada/ Germany/ Mexico/ Israel

557. ——. **1988b.** Some Remarks on Informal Work, Social Polarization and the Social Structure. *International Journal of Urban and Regional Research* 12: 247-267.

Labor processes/ Industrial restructuring/ Labor market segmentation/ Polarization/ State practice/ Britain

558. **Pahl, R. E., and C. Wallace. 1985.** Household Work Strategies in Economic Recession. In *Beyond Employment: Household, Gender and Subsistence*. Ed. N. Redclift and E. Mingione, pp. 189-227. Oxford, U.K.: Basil Blackwell.

Pahl and Wallace disaggregate household provisioning work to describe three kinds of informal work: the production of goods and services for household consumption, working for cash for others on one's own account, and unpaid informal or communal work outside the household. The authors link the incidence of unemployment to the increase in self-provisioning and privatization and show that there is growing polarization between busy, highly work-motivated,and well-off households and those at the other end of the scale. This suggests a form of dependent domesticity which belies the optimistic scenarios offered by Bell and Gershuny.

Survival strategies/ Unpaid labor/ Polarization/ Self-provisioning/ Subsistence production/ Britain

559. **Panos Staff, E. Marquez-Gonzalez, O. Ogunseitan, and E. Bolido. 1989.** Focus: The Other Economy. *Panoscope* 13 (July): 2- 11.

This volume examines various aspects of informal sector work to highlight both the dynamic potential of the informal sector as well as the difficulties encountered by those involved in its least remunerative activities. The opening article reviews research by De Soto and subsequent articles examine different aspects of the informal work experience: dependence on street selling in Bogota, Colombia (Marquez-Gonzalez); survival strategies by informal workers in the face of economic restructuring in Nigeria (Ogunseitan); the role of the informal sector in economic development in the Philippines (Erlinda Bolido); and an interview with Maria Otero of Accion International about their programs to assist poor, informal workers.

Project assistance/ Survival strategies/ Trading/ Credit/ Nigeria/ Philippines/ Colombia/ Latin America/ Third World

560. **Papola, T. S. 1980.** Informal Sector: Concept and Policy. *Economic and Political Weekly* 15: 817-824.

Definition/ Review/ Policy analysis/ Third World

561. —— . **1981.** *Urban Informal Sector in a Developing Economy*. New Delhi, India: Vikas Publishing House.

Pattern or magnitude/ Dual sector or economy/ Migration/ India

562. **Pearson, R. 1986.** Female Workers in the First and Third Worlds: The "Greening" of Women's Labour. In *The Changing Experience of Employment: Restructuring and Recession*. Ed. K. Purcell, S. Wood, A. Waton, and S. Allen, pp. 75-94. London: Macmillan Press. Also published in R.E. Pahl, ed., *On Work: Historical, Comparative & Theoretical Approaches*, pp. 449-466. New York: Basil Blackwell.

Pearson examines the role of the state in making available a cheap labor force for hire by multinational companies. This process of constructing a labor force allows one to examine capitalist restructuring at the global level and move beyond a myopic focus on the Third World. It also offers a non-deterministic account of labor market dynamics.

Gender division of labor/ Globalization/ Labor processes/ State practice/ Comparative

563. **Peattie, L. 1975.** Tertiarization, Marginality and Urban Poverty in Latin America. *Latin American Urban Research* 5: 109-124.

Pattern or magnitude/ Survival strategies/ Marginalization/ Differentiation/ Latin America

564. —— . **1980.** Anthropological Perspectives on the Concepts of Dualism, the Informal Sector and Marginality in Developing Urban Economies. *International Regional Science Review* 5 (1): 1- 31.

Peattie's seminal paper critically analyzes the concepts of economic dualism, urban marginality, and the informal sector. Illustrated with data from Bogota, she argues that the concepts of marginality and the informal sector direct attention to phenomena ordinarily ignored by economists; the spectrum of activity which seems to proliferate "on its own," the lack of protection for small entrepreneurs and casual laborers, and the institutional aspects of urban economic activity. As guides to policy these dualist conceptions are misleading because they divert attention from the diversity and complexity of such enterprises, their varying attractiveness to participants, their specific linkages to the rest of the economy, and the institutional arrangements and market structures which set their context.

Review/ Critique of dualism/ Marginalization/ State practice/ Relation to formal economy/ Colombia

565. —— . **1982.** What Is to Be Done with the "Informal Sector"? A Case Study of Shoe Manufacturers in Colombia. In *Towards a Political Economy of Urbanization in Third World Countries*. Ed. H. Safa, pp. 209-232. Delhi: Oxford University Press.

Interviews with owners of shoemaking firms, ranging in size from one-person enterprises to plants employing over one hundred workers, identify the salient features of the Colombian industry. Peattie finds an expanding but sharply segmented domestic market in which new firms come into existence and flourish with differing strategies of mechanization and standardization. Though small firms have some advantages where markets are segmented, processes of growth depend on the availability of capital, skilled labor and raw materials. Peattie argues that success and failure relate not only to a firm's efficiency but to their capacity to acquire the resources necessary for production and to control their economic environment, both of which characterize larger, well-established firms. In this context, a small-industry loan program is analyzed and found to be inimical to small producers. To help the very smallest firms, direct government control of the leather supply is recommended.

Differentiation/ Polarization/ Credit/ Artisanal production/ Processes of accumulation/ Small or micro-enterprises/ Constraints to accumulation/ Project assistance/ Credit/ Shoe production/ Colombia

566. —— . **1987.** An Idea in Good Currency and How It Grew: The Informal Sector. *World Development* 15: 851-860.

Reviewing the concept of the informal sector, Peattie links its appeal to the way it has bridged, though not integrated, the traditions of economic dualism and economic accounting. Peattie suggests that by adopting Hart's terminology, the ILO has changed the concept from a description of the range of subsistence activities among the urban poor to a focus on the structural features of the economy as a whole. While the concept has been widely used, it is factually incorrect and politically obfuscating since the informal sector is not equivalent to the poor, and poverty also exists among modern enterprise workers. These problems are traced to a gap between macro-analytical categories and institutional relations of the economy.

Review/ Definition/ Relation to formal economy

567. **Peattie, L. 1996.** The Informal Sector in Latin America. *Regional Development Dialogue* 17 (1): 58-65.

Review/ Latin America

568. **Peker, M. 1996.** Internal Migration and the Marginal Sector. In *Work and Occupation in Modern Turkey*. Ed. E. Kahveci, N. Sugur, and T. Nichols, pp. 7-37. London: Mansell Publishing.

Peker examines patterns of migration between 1950 and 1990 in Turkey to illuminate trends in urban growth and the expansion of the "marginal sector," defined as unregulated, untaxed, and poorly remunerated economic activity such as fruit and vegetable trading. Demographic data is presented along with results of interviews with four informal sector workers.

Migration/ Marginalization/ Urbanization/ Turkey

569. **Perera, L. A. S. R., and A. T. M. N. Amin. 1996.** Accommodating the Informal Sector: A Strategy for Urban Environmental Management. *Journal of Environmental Management* 46 (1): 3-15.

Urban poor livelihood strategies are examined to challenge the view of informal sector workers as "eye-sores" who must be removed from their street location because of increased public concern for cleanliness. The authors conclude that the provision of appropriate entrepreneurial values and secure tenure create a sense of belonging fostering environmental management. Accommodating informal workers into the urban built environment is assumed to be an effective strategy for environmental management.

Policy analysis/ Recycling/ Urbanization/ Sri Lanka

570. **Pérez-López, J. F. 1995.** *Cuba's Second Economy: From behind the Scenes to Center Stage*. New Brunswick, N.J.: Transaction Publishers.

Favoring the concept of the "second" rather than "informal" economy, Pérez-López argues that the growing unregulated sector in Cuba will aid the transition to a market economy. The book's main purpose is to describe the present scope and pattern of the Cuban second economy and trace its evolution over time. Examination of emergent unregulated activity during the 1980s is followed by a discussion of the growing prominence of the second economy with the economic crisis of the 1990s. Data are drawn from available secondary literature on the Cuban economy and Cuban economic policy.

Definition/ Pattern or magnitude/ Centrally planned economies/ Cuba

571. **Pestieau, P. 1985.** Belgium's Irregular Economy. In *The Economics of the Shadow Economy*. Ed. W. Gaertner and A. Wenig, pp. 144-160. Berlin, F.R.G.: Springer-Verlag.

Pestieau estimates the size and nature of irregular activities in Belgium from both a demand and a supply side. He distinguishes between off-the-books activities of the self-employed and black labor representing the salaried or unemployed to suggest that labor is supplied by low-income groups such as pensioners, the unemployed, and blue-collar workers to cater to the relatively rich.
Pattern or magnitude/ Self-employment/ Belgium

572. **Petersen, H. 1982.** Size of the Public Sector, Economic Growth and the Informal Economy. *Review of Income and Wealth* 28: 191-215.

The hidden economy in West Germany includes activities ranging from illegal to domestic, do-it-yourself and volunteer work. Most of these are not represented in national accounts but do contribute to social welfare. If the size of the hidden economy remains proportional to GNP then total welfare can still be measured by GNP. Petersen notes that the size of the hidden sector tends to increase as the tax burden increases, but this is often countered by increased regulations as politicians believe that illicit work is bad for the state. An alternative position is that "the official economy has certain imperfections which . . . might be reduced by the informal economy [which] . . . produces without distortions resulting from taxes and contributions as well as excessive regulations."

Pattern or magnitude/ Illegal activity/ Volunteer work/ Unpaid labor/ Self-provisioning/ Policy analysis/ Tax evasion/ Germany

573. **Phillips, A. 1983.** *Hidden Hands: Women and Economic Policies*. London: Pluto Press.

Gender division of labor/ New International Division of Labor/ State practice/ Trade unions/ Policy prescriptions/ Britain

574. **Pineda-Ofreneo, R. 1982.** Philippine Domestic Outwork: Subcontracting for Export-Oriented Industries. *Journal of Contemporary Asia* 12: 281-293.

With the emerging new international division of labor, the Philippines is increasingly oriented toward production for export. This involves the proliferation of various joint venture and international subcontracting arrangements which indirectly link small enterprises and home-based producers to foreign firms. By this process a growing, poorly paid, often home-based, rural and urban female labor force is engaged in production for the international market. Case studies of complex subcontracting arrangements in the garment and handicraft industries are presented to highlight extremely exploitative conditions of work for home-based producers.

New international division of labor/ Processes of accumulation/ Export production/ Subcontracting/ Home-based production/ Gender division of labor/ Garment manufacture/ Handicrafts/ Philippines

575. **Ping-Yu, S. 1984.** The Impact of the Informal Sector on Urban and Rural Socioeconomic Development in China. *Regional Development Dialogue* 5 (2): 105-120.

Ping-Yu describes the impact of the informal agriculture sector on urban and rural development which, in China, consists of private crops, poultry, livestock breeding, fisheries, and handicrafts. These activities revitalized the rural economy, enhance production, and rapidly increase peasant incomes. They also facilitate urban-rural commodity flows to subsidize state-owned commercial networks as well as changed the rural labor structure and reduced the pressure of rural people moving into the cities. In many cases, rural markets have developed as prototypes of new towns.

Rural/ Handicrafts/ Migration/ Relation to formal economy/ China

576. **Pinnarò, G., and E. Pugliese. 1985.** Informalization and Social Resistance: The Case of Naples. In *Beyond Employment: Household, Gender and Subsistence*. Ed. N. Redclift and E. Mingione, pp. 228-247. Oxford, U.K.: Basil Blackwell.

Reviewing the industrial history of Naples, the authors challenge the view that informal work represents a liberating option for workers to escape commodification on the factory floor. Evidence suggests that the old "street corner economy" characterized by a variety of subsistence-level artisanal and other self-employed activites is in decline, while formal industry has grown slowly, accompanied by new state services and rising open unemployment. Women and children dominate the workforce in the lingering informal/black economy. Resistance to informal work includes registering with the unemployment office despite informal employment and persistent efforts to attain formal employment. Thus, informalization is an imposed rather than chosen process, linked to the "industrial socialization" characterizing the city of Naples and is shaped by local social and economic conditions as well as state policy.

Resistance/ State practice/ Pattern or magnitude/ Gender division of labor/ Child labor/ Italy

577. **Piore, M. 1979.** *Birds of Passage: Migrant Labor and Industrial Societies*. Cambridge, U.K.: Cambridge University Press.
Migration/ Labor market dynamics/ Industrialized economies

578. **Piore, M. J., and C. F. Sabel. 1984.** *The Second Industrial Divide: Possibilities for Prosperity*. New York: Basic Books.

Piore and Sabel highlight contrasting regimes of mass versus craft-based production in advanced capitalist countries of North America, Europe and Asia (Japan). Mass production regimes—the first industrial divide—are characterized by the dominance of large manufacturing plants, assembly line production using deskilled labor, large volume manufacture of standardized goods, multinational firms, and Keynesian macroregulation. This is contrasted with the economic history of different regions in France, Germany, Italy and Japan, where principles of craft production are characterized by the employment of skilled labor, the use of all-purpose equipment to produce specialized goods, close subcontracting networks, and micro-regulation of production and labor management practices through local government and inter-firm dynamics. In contrast to the resilience of "flexible specialisation," mass production is poorly suited to cope with market shrinkage, volatility, and niche-based growth characterizing the global economy of the last two decades. Facing a second industrial divide, advanced capitalist economies choose either of two strategies to regain prosperity and arrest alarming trends in growing income disparity: Promotion of "multinational Keynesianism" to refurbish and extend the principles of institutional organization embodied in mass production or the spread of flexible specialization, involving a shift of technology and the development of new regulatory systems to ensure nonexploitative labor practices and the adequate distribution of wealth.

Economic restructuring/ Industrial restructuring/ Production process/ State practice/ Artisanal production/ Flexible specialization/ Technological change/ Industrialized economies

579. **Portes, A. 1978.** The Informal Sector and the World Economy: Notes on the Structure of Subsidised Labour. *IDS Bulletin* 9 (4): 35-40.

Portes defends the concept of the informal sector as fundamental to understanding the operations of capitalism as a world phenomenon and as constituting a missing element in world-system formulations of core-periphery relations. He argues that direct subsidies to consumption provided by informal workers offer indirect subsidies to core-nation workers which, as a mechanism of cooptation, increase their purchasing power to avert crises of overproduction and maintain rates of profit. Within the periphery, interests focus on production for export at minimum labor costs. Downward pressure on wages is attained by manipulating a reserve army of labor and cheapening workers' consumption by transferring reproduction costs to rural cultivators and cheap urban informal sector producers. This is explained by the labor intensity of small-scale enterprises and the absence of state supervision and regulation. Thus, the informal sector is not interstitial, transitional, or dependent on the formal sector, but is a survival strategy among the poor that is functional to the global capitalist economy and processes of accumulation.

Subsidy to capital/ Relation to formal economy/ Survival strategies/ Reserve army of labor/ Latin America

580. —— . **1979.** Illegal Immigration and the International System: Lesson from Recent Legal Mexican Immigrants to the United States. *Social Problems* 26: 425-38.

Migration/ Relation to capital/ Ethnicity/ U.S.A.

581. —— . **1983.** The Informal Sector: Definition, Controversy, and Relation to National Development. *Review* 7 (1): 151-74.

Definition/ Migration/ Third World/ Industrialized economies

582. —— . **1994.** When More Can Be Less: Labor Standards, Development, and the Informal Economy. In *Contrapunto: The Informal Sector Debate in Latin America*. Ed. C. A. Rakowski, pp. 113-130. Albany: State University of New York Press.

Portes examines available evidence from the Third World to address two broad issues: 1) consequences of high labor protection standards in labor-surplus economies; and 2) characteristics and potential of economic activities occuring beyond state regulation. The application of strong standards of protective legislation in Third World countries has resulted in a process of informalization whereby small unregulated enterprises thrive and to which formal firms channel the production and distribution of goods in various direct and indirect ways. This has largely adverse consequences for workers as well as governments. In outlining alternative policy frameworks, Portes stresses that promoting "grassroots" enterprises does not involve simply removing the state from the economy but depends on formulating "new and unorthodox" forms of state involvement to ensure worker survival as well as the opportunity for creative and flexible production.

Labor relations/ Legislation/ Policy analysis/ Economic restructuring/ Small or micro-enterprises/ Relation to capital/ Flexible specialization/ Third World

583. **Portes, A., and L. A. Benton. 1984.** Industrial Development and Labor Absorption: A Reinterpretation. *Population and Development Review* 10: 589-611.

Labor market dynamics/ Migration/ Third World

584. **Portes, A., S. Blitzer, and J. Curtis. 1986.** The Urban Informal Sector in Uruguay: Its Internal Structure, Characteristics and Effects. *World Development* 14: 727-741.

Pattern or magnitude/ Survival strategies/ Relation to formal economy/ Worker characteristics/ Uruguay

585. **Portes, A., M. Castells, and L. A. Benton. 1989.** Conclusion: The Policy Implications of Informality. In *The Informal Economy: Studies in Advanced and Less Developed Countries*. Ed. A. Portes, M. Castells, and L. A. Benton, pp. 298- 311. Baltimore, Md.; London: Johns Hopkins University Press.

Review/ Policy prescriptions/ Economic restructuring/ Industrial restructuring/ Third World/ Industrialized economies

586. **Portes, A., and J. M. Clark. 1987.** Mariel Refugees: Six Years After. *Migration World Magazine* 15 (5): 14-18.

Refugees/ Ethnicity/ Migration/ U.S.A.

587. **Portes, A., and S. Sassen-Koob. 1987.** Making It Underground: Comparative Material on the Informal Sector in Western Market Economies. *American Journal of Sociology* 93: 30-61.

This paper examines the informal economy and its relationship to both orthodox and Marxist theories of industrial development which assume that it is transitory and bound to disappear with the advance of modern, industrial growth; a refuge from destitution; and primarily a feature of peripheral economies. Evidence shows that these assumptions are mistaken since informal employment has neither declined with industrialization nor serves as an alternative of last resort, since it attracts the voluntary shift of formal workers because of its high earnings, especially among entrepreneurs. The authors argue that the reappearance of informality in the West is due to Third World immigration, the growth of union power, and competition posed by Third World exports. They also argue that domestic circumstances shape the informal economy, but that the rise of informalization in the mid-1970s is rooted in a process of global economic re-adjustment.

Relation to capital/ State practice/ Economic restructuring/ Survival strategies/ Migration/ Flexibilization/ Comparative/ Industrialized economies/ Latin America/ U.S.A./ Italy

588. **Portes, A., and A. Stepick. 1985.** Unwelcome Immigrants: The Labor Market Experiences of 1980 (Mariel) Cuban and Haitian Refugees in South Florida. *American Sociological Review* 50: 493-514.

Refugees/ Migration/ Ethnicity/ Labor market segmentation/ U.S.A.

589. **Portes, A., and J. Walton. 1981.** Unequal Exchange and the Urban Informal Sector. In *Labor, Class, and the International System*. Ed. A. Portes and J. Walton, pp. 67-106. New York, London: Academic Press.

Portes and Walton critique the literature on economic dependency and unequal exchange to argue that return migration and declining subsistence production are mechanisms for the cheap reproduction of the peripheral labor force. Examples of income-producing strategies among urban working-class households outside the formal economy are examined, including subsistence and networking activities, petty commodity production and trade, and informal land occupation. Firms reduce labor costs by directly using informal labor to facilitate production and circulation. The authors conclude that: the informal sector subsidizes the labor costs of formal capitalist enterprises, thereby increasing the rate of surplus value extraction; informal sector work is not a vestige of precapitalism, but a modern and integral component of peripheral capitalism; and the informal sector will not disappear through gradual involution but will continue to exist and expand given contemporary conditions in the world-system.

Relation to formal economy/ Migration/ Survival strategies/ Unequal exchange/ Relation to capital/ Self-provisioning/ Subsistence production/ Latin America/ Third World

590. **Pradhan, R. K. 1989.** On Helping Small Enterprises in Developing Countries. *World Development* 17: 157-159.

Small or micro-enterprises/ Credit/ Project assistance/ Third World

591. **Pradilla, E., and C. Jimenez. 1985.** Architecture, Urbanism and Neocolonial Dependence. In *Planning for Small Enterprises in Third World Cities*. Ed. R. Bromley, pp. 191-202. Oxford, U.K.: Pergamon Press.

Under neocolonial dependency, production in the construction sector lags behind social production, employing petty manufacturing on a large scale and placing construction workers as proletarian-artisans in an ambiguous position vis-à-vis industrial sector workers. In this context, the builder-architect is an exploiter of wage labor who reproduces bourgeois ideology and the relationship between designer and capitalist producer generates a "vulgar" urban and architectural ideology skillfully manipulated by the sellers of housing.

State practice/ Housing/ Construction industry/ Disguised wage labor/ Colombia/ Third World

592. **Quijano Obregon, A. 1974.** The Marginal Pole of the Economy and the Marginalised Labor Force. *Economy and Society* 3: 393-428.

Pattern or magnitude/ Marginalization/ Relation to formal economy/ Latin America

593. **Racelis, M. 1986.** Metropolitan Growth: Poverty Eradication through Popular Participation. *Habitat International* 10 (1-2): 167-179.

Empowerment/ Project assistance/ Asia

594. **Rainnie, A. F. 1984.** Combined and Uneven Development in the Clothing Industry: The Effects of Competition on Accumulation. *Capital and Class* 22: 141-156.

Rainnie examines the clothing industry to understand its dominance by small, technologically backward firms. Using the example of the

British firm Marks and Spencer, the author argues that the drive to accumulate has underestimated the role of competition by focusing almost exclusively on the extraction of surplus value. The paper critiques the labor process debate and the arguments put forward by Braverman.

Industrial restructuring/ Labor processes/ Subcontracting/ Garment manufacture/ Britain

595. ——. **1985.** Small Firms, Big Problems: The Political Economy of Small Businesses. *Capital and Class* 25: 140-168.

Rainnie examines the role and importance of small businesses in advanced capitalism. Contrary to conventional myth, the author claims that small enterprises should not be viewed as anachronistic survivors of a bygone age destined for destruction. Rather, small businesses are an integral part of Thatcher's Britain.

Industrial restructuring/ Subcontracting/ Small or micro- enterprises/ Britain

596. **Raj, M., and P. Nientied, eds. 1990.** *Housing and Income in Third World Urban Development.* New Delhi, India: Oxford and IBH Publishing Co.

Housing/ Construction industry/ Tunisia/ India/ Ghana/ Colombia/ Nigeria/ Philippines

597. **Rakodi, C. 1991.** Women's Work or Household Strategies? *Environment and Urbanization* 3 (2): 39-45.

Household division of labor/ Survival strategies/ Unpaid labor/ Home-based production/ Social networks/ Third World

598. **Rakowski, C. A., ed. 1994a.** *Contrapunto: The Informal Sector Debate in Latin America.* Albany: State University of New York Press.

Debates over the informal sector have commonly been characterized by disagreement over the role of the informal sector in economic development and over the role of the state in organizing, managing, or repressing informal activities. The papers clarify and compare the outcomes of different policy strategies on the informal sector, explore the implications of competing paradigms influencing policy development, and reconcile the diverse roles of informal activities in development and of the state. The volume is divided into five sections: 1) overviews of the informal sector debate and insights offered by labor market research over the past five decades; 2) macro-level policy issues; 3) micro-level intervention issues; 4) critical examination of links between poverty and informality, and their implications for appropriate development planning; 5) summary and policy review.

Review/ Small or micro-enterprises/ State practice/ Policy analysis/ Project assistance/ Latin America

599. —— . **1994b.** The Informal Sector Debate, Part 2: 1984-1993. In *Contrapunto: The Informal Sector Debate in Latin America*. Ed C. A. Rakowski, pp. 31-51. Albany: State University of New York Press.

During the 1980s, discussions of the informal sector became increasingly popular, extending beyond the field of development economics and other social sciences to involve nongovernmental organizations, business organizations, legislators, and other interest groups across the world. Rakowski outlines broad analytical and policy approaches that have characterized yet not yet been integrated into discussions in Latin America. These include the structuralist, the underground economy, the legalist or de Soto, and the microenterpise development approaches. While a growing orientation toward less academic and more applicable analysis is evident, disagreement persists over the degree of state intervention needed to facilitate genuine development among informal firms and over the appropriateness of promoting small business. Also noted are ongoing ideological differences over posing the question of informal sector development as one of redistributing scarce resources versus improving human productivity.

Review/ Policy analysis/ Latin America

600. **Ranney, S. I. 1985.** The Labour Market in a Dual Economy: Another Look at Colonial Rhodesia. *Journal of Development Studies* 21: 505-524.

Dual sector or economy/ Labor market dynamics/ Zimbabwe

601. **Ratner, S., and P. Ide. 1985.** Strategies for Community Economic Development through Natural Resource Use in Northern New York. Department of Agricultural Economics, AE Res. 85-10. Ithaca, N.Y.: Cornell University, Dept. of Agricultural Economics.

Ratner and Ide examine the potential of small-scale enterprises to utilize natural resources and fill the gap between household-level informal activities and large commercial activities. Using community economic development theory, the authors suggest three approaches to stimulate growth, provide long-term stability, and integrate regional economies: basic needs, small business development, and sectoral intervention.

Rural/ Survival strategies/ Small or micro-enterprises/ Policy prescriptions/ U.S.A.

602. **Redclift, N. 1985.** The Contested Domain: Gender, Accumulation and the Labour Process. In *Beyond Employment: Household, Gender and Subsistence*. Ed. N. Redclift and E. Mingione, pp. 92-125. Oxford, U.K.: Basil Blackwell.
Also published in R. E. Pahl, ed. 1988. *On Work: Historical, Comparative & Theoretical Approaches*, pp. 428-448. New York: Basil Blackwell.

Redclift identifies the misleading conflation of the informal sector, the household economy, subsistence production, and the domestic domain to outline the conceptual and methodological issues in analyses of the relationship between gender and work, the role of noncapitalist forms of accumulation, the connections between the international and the sexual division of labor, and reproduction. She argues that a number of separate debates on urban informal economies, agrarian subsistence, and the contribution of domestic labor to capitalism could be seen as different facets of the same problematic, viz., the connections between seemingly separate spheres of social and economic life.

Review/ Relation to capital/ Household division of labor/ Gender division of labor/ Unpaid labor/ Rural/ Gender relations/ Household/ Processes of accumulation

603. **Redclift, N., and E. Mingione, eds. 1985.** *Beyond Employment: Household, Gender and Subsistence*. Oxford, U.K.: Basil Blackwell.

Ten essays investigate links between developments of advanced capitalism and household- and community-level struggles over livelihood and social reproduction. Emphasized are the impacts of postindustrial economic and technological change. Changing politics of state intervention in economic activity, including the informal sector, also are explored. Drawing from feminist critique of social and labor theory, the authors highlight the need for reconceptualizing categories of work and economic activity. Individual essays focus on developments in Italy, Mexico, and Britain.

Economic restructuring/ Social restructuring/ Gender relations/ Subcontracting/ State practice/ Class processes/ Resistance/ Small or micro-enterprises/ Italy/ Mexico/ Britain

604. **Rempel, H. 1996.** Rural-to-Urban Migration and Urban Informal Activities. *Regional Development Dialogue* 17 (1): 37-51.

Migration/ Labor market dynamics/ Urbanization/ Third World

605. **Remy, D. 1982.** Formal and Informal Sectors of the Zaria, Nigeria Economy: An Analytical Framework with Empirical Content. In *Towards a Political Economy of Urbanization in Third World Countries*. Ed. H. Safa, pp. 253-246. Delhi, India: Oxford University Press.

Relation to formal economy/ State practice/ Nigeria

606. **Reubens, E. P. 1978.** Aliens, Jobs, and Immigration Policy. *Public Interest* 51: 113-134.

Migration/ Ethnicity/ Labor market dynamics/ State practice/ Policy prescriptions/ U.S.A.

607. **Reza, S. 1989.** The Black Economy in Bangladesh: Some Preliminary Observations. *Savings and Development* 1: 23-43.

Pattern or magnitude/ Bangladesh

608. **Richardson, H. 1984.** The Role of the Urban Informal Sector: An Overview. *Regional Development Dialogue* 5 (1): 3-40.

Richardson argues that the informal sector contributes to labor absorption with informal employment in services and manufacturing growing faster than formal employment. He suggests: (1) the heterogeniety of the sector makes generalization suspect, (2) the performance of the sector depends on changes in the formal sector and the economy at large, (3) the informal sector enhances labor absorption, price reductions, capital savings and skills training, (4) income and earnings curves of the formal and informal sectors overlap, debunking the idea that the informal sector is uniformly low-income and the job supplier of last resort, (5) while the informal sector is important in the economic structure of primary cities, its contribution to that of secondary cities is probably even greater, and (6) while government policies can aid the informal sector, its expansion is the product of a competitive environment which flourishes best when unhampered by government regulation.

Review/ Relation to formal economy/ Labor market dynamics/ Third World

609. **Riedel, J., and H. Schmitz. 1989.** *Grass-Roots Industrialization in a Ghanaian Town*. Munich, Cologne, F.R.G.; London, U.K.: Weltforum Verlag.

Small or micro-enterprises/ Industrial restructuring/ Ethnicity/ Policy prescriptions/ Ghana

610. **Rivera, R. L. K. 1985.** Children at Work: The Labor Scene through the Eyes of Filipino Children. *Philippine Sociological Review* 33 (1-2): 11-17.

Child labor/ Philippines

611. **Roberts, B. R. 1978.** *Cities of Peasants: The Political Economy of Urbanization in the Third World*. London: Edward Arnold.

Urbanization/ Migration/ Pattern or magnitude/ Differentiation/ Third World

612. —— **. 1989.** Employment Structure, Life Cycle, and Life Chances: Formal and Informal Sectors in Guadalajara. In *The Informal Economy: Studies in Advanced and Less Developed Countries*. Ed. A. Portes, M. Castells, and L. A. Benton, pp. 41- 59. Baltimore, Md.; London: Johns Hopkins University Press.

Roberts examines the significance of informal activities in the fragmented labor market of Guadalajara, Mexico. Variations in labor markets, both those internal and external to a particular firm, explain workers, and salary characteristics. Guadalajara's dual labor market means that most firms operate both formally and informally with contradictory implications for the quality of urban life. While kinship and neighborhood ties are strengthened as they become essential supports for economic survival, pressures on household relationships, particularly on women, are increased.

Labor market segmentation/ Survival strategies/ Social networks/ Gender division of labor/ Worker characteristics/ Double-day/ Women/ Unpaid labor/ Mexico

613. —— . **1991.** The Changing Nature of Informal Employment: The Case of Mexico. In *Towards Social Adjustment: Labour Market Issues in Structural Adjustment*. Ed. G. Standing and V. E. Tokman. Geneva: International Labour Office.

Roberts examines the heterogeneity of informal enterprises; factors behind the growth of informal employment; the role played by the strategies of entrepreneurs and workers in the creation of informal work; and the changing significance of informal employment since the 1960s when Mexico enjoyed high rates of economic growth. Roberts argues that contrary to assessments about the positive role of informal sector informality makes almost no independent contribution to employment generation as informal employment represents less a boon to economic development than a poor replacement for effective state welfare policies. Processes of economic restructuring since the 1980s, moreover, further depress incomes in both the formal and informal sectors. A new emphasis on government action rather than further deregulation is needed to redress the situation.

Pattern or magnitude/ Economic restructuring/ Relation to formal economy/Welfare/ Structural adjustment/ State practice/ Policy prescriptions/ Mexico

614. —— . **1992.** *The Dynamics of Informal Employment in Mexico*. Informal Sector Discussion Papers, no. 3. Washington, D.C.: U.S. Department of Labor, Bureau of International Labor Affairs.

Pattern or magnitude/ Child labor/ Gender division of labor/ Mexico

615. —— . **1994.** Informal Economy and Family Strategies. *International Journal of Urban and Regional Research* 18: 6-23.
Special issue: Informal Economy and Family Strategies.

Informalization has emerged as a key issue in debates on industrial andeconomic restructuring and flexibilization. Noting that the basis for noncontractual relationships characterizing informal production is often found in kin and neighborhood networks, Roberts reviews recent perspectives on family strategies and the informal economy to emphasize the need for contextual analysis given the local understandings, practices, and relationships in which both informal economic activity and family strategies are embedded.

Social networks/ Survival strategies/ Economic restructuring/ U.S.A./ Britain/ Spain/ Italy/ Hungary/ Mexico

616. **Roberts, J. T. 1995.** Trickling Down and Scrambling Up: The Informal Sector, Food Provisioning and Local Benefits of the Carajas Mining "Growth Pole" in the Brazilian Amazon. *World Development* 23 (3): 385-400.

This project evaluation of a World Bank-funded mining scheme examines the benefits and traces the origins of food consumed at Carajas. The author concludes that ranchers and middlemen receive the greatest share of benefits that result from the project, while small farmers receive very few of them. Roberts examines four kinds of food vendors and places them on a continuum of formal to informal, depending on their levels of capital investment, relations to the state and productive relations. Beginning with the most formal are capitalized supermarkets, permanent open air vendors, corner stores that pay minimal fees to local administrators, stands and street vendors who pay no taxes, have no permanent location, and little capital, and individual farmers who sell their own produce. Supermarkets control 85 percent of the retail food sales and sell primarily imported goods. By contrast, 80 percent of the goods sold by street vendors is produced locally. Timmons concludes that the viability of local producers requires linking local government and small scale producers. However, such a linking is unstable since it is forged in the context of struggles with local elites who control a vast majority of the population.

Trading/ Project assistance/ Brazil

617. **Rogerson, C. M. 1986.** Johannesburg's Informal Sector: Historical Continuity and Change. *African Urban Quarterly* 1: 139- 151.

Pattern or magnitude/ Labor market dynamics/ South Africa

618. **Rogerson, C. M., and K. S. O. Beavon. 1980.** The Awakening of "Informal Sector" Studies in Southern Africa. *South African Geographical Journal / Suid-Afrikaanse Geografiese Tydskrif* 62: 175-190.

The authors attribute the increased interest in the southern African informal sector to three factors: (a) the restructuring process within Southern African studies as a whole, where a new Marxist school favoring "popular" history has generated historical work related to the informal sector, (b) recognition of the chronic problems of structural unemployment, and the search for solutions through the informal sector, and (c) the matching of the concept's associated policy implications with the reformist strategies of capitalist development in the region. On the whole, the literature displays a marked trend towards addressing empirical rather than substantive theoretical issues, and towards urban- rather than rural-focused research.

Review/ Policy analysis/ South Africa

619. —— . **1982.** Getting by in the "Informal Sector" of Soweto. *Tijdschrift voor Econ. en Soc.Geografie* 73 (4): 250-265.

Trading/ Relation to formal economy/ Survival strategies/ South Africa

620. —— . **1985.** A Tradition of Repression: The Street Traders of Johannesburg. In *Planning for Small Enterprises in Third World Cities*. Ed. R. Bromley, pp. 233-246. Oxford, U.K.: Pergamon Press.

This paper examines changes in street trading in Johannesburg highlighting the attitudes and policies of the local municipality and the national state toward Black and Indian traders. The anti-hawker policies pursued are shown to be interwoven with the pursuit of a pure white city. Nevertheless, mechanisms of control such as licensing requirements and police raids, as well as official attitudes against hawkers, who are viewed as an eyesore, a traffic nuisance, and a public health hazard, find their parallels in many urban areas of the Third World where such policies have limited success given inadequate alternative employment opportunities. Thus, hawking remains a survival strategy among the urban poor.

Trading/ State practice/ Survival strategies/ Racial inequality/ South Africa

621. **Rogerson, C. M., and D. M. Hart. 1989.** The Struggle for the Streets: Deregulation and Hawking in South Africa's Major Urban Centers. *Social Dynamics* 15 (1): 29-45.

Trading/ State practice/ Policy analysis/ South Africa

622. **Roldán, M. 1985.** Industrial Outworking, Struggles for the Reproduction of Working-Class Families and Gender Subordination. In *Beyond Employment: Household, Gender and Subsistence*. Ed. N. Redclift and E. Mingione, pp. 248-285. Oxford, U.K.: Basil Blackwell.

Roldán criticizes Marxist analyses which treat the sexual division of labor as a secondary issue, prioritizing instead global aspects of the dissolution-conservation process of petty commodity production and the weak structural position of all sections of the marginal masses. This omission constitutes a theoretical and practical weakness of an approach that underestimates the role of family relations in the reproduction of small enterprises or home-based, industrial outworking activity using unpaid family labor. To redress this gap, Roldán highlights the significance of hierarchical relations other than class--gender, ethnicity, and race--in processes of proletarianization. Data indicate that women form a quasi- proletarianized, isolated and, therefore, fragmented labor force earning wages well below the value they generate.

Globalization/ Social reproduction/ Gender division of labor/ Ethnicity/ Racial inequality/ Class processes/ Gender relations/ Subcontracting/ Home-based production/ Survival strategies/ Mexico

623. **Romanos, M., and C. Chifos. 1996.** Contributions of the Urban Informal Sector to Environmental Management. *Regional Development Dialogue* 17 (1): 122-155.

Recycling/ Trading/ Third World

624. **Romatet, E. 1983.** Calcutta's Informal Sector: Theory and Reality. *Economic and Political Weekly* 18 (50): 2115-2128.

Romatet argues that the informal sector is neither transitory nor will it evolve into the formal sector, but it will continue to provide jobs to Calcutta's poor. Since the informal-formal dichotomy applies to firms rather than to individuals, households, or economic activities, Romatet suggests replacing this dichotomy with an economic continuum which ranges from self-employed artisans to large public or private sector workers. He shows that the survival, development, and capacity of the sector to provide employment is explained by its low wages, deplorable working conditions, and prices which are set by the market since competition between units inhibits their ability to exert control over the market. Moreover, production units depend on the formal sector for raw materials and thus lack the same ability to negotiate lower input prices.

Constraints to accumulation/ Continuum debate/ India

625. **Rose, K. 1992.** *Where Women Are Leaders: The SEWA Movement in India*. London: Zed Books.

Rose examines the emergence of the Self-Employed Women's Association (SEWA) in Ahmedabad. Founded in 1972, SEWA forged a model of trade unionism involving women engaged in a diverse range of activities as home-based producers, street vendors, agricultural workers, and rural artisans. Their role and struggles as workers have been largely ignored by policy makers and mainstream industrial unions. Among their aims is to organize effective strategies for resisting the poverty, financial exploitation, physical abuse, and social harassment regularly faced by the self-employed by virtue of their isolated and vulnerable position as informal workers.

Self-employment/ Women/ Political mobilization/ Trade unions/ Empowerment/ Project assistance/ Home-based production/ Rural/ Artisanal production/ Trading/ India

626. **Roseberry, W. 1986.** The Ideology of Domestic Production. *Labour, Capital and Society* 19: 70-93.
Special Issue: Rethinking Petty Commodity Production.

Unpaid labor/ Petty commodity production/ Nonmonetary exchange/ Household division of labor/ Household/ Gender ideology

627. **Ross, I. 1978.** Why the Underground Economy Is Booming. *Fortune* 98 (October 9): 92-98.

Pattern or magnitude/ U.S.A.

628. **Rothstein, F. A., and M. L. Blim, eds. 1992.** *Anthropology and the Global Factory: Studies of the New Industrialization in the Late Twentieth Century*. New York: Bergin & Garvey.

Major features of late 20th century capitalism include the expansion of industrial production to most regions of the world as well as growing numbers of workers engaged in formal as well as informal labor processes oriented to the world marketplace. Fifteen papers examine this pattern in different national and industrial contexts as well as from the perspective of gender-based divisions of labor. Building upon various streams of social science theory that view local phenomenon in a global framework, the essays incorporate anthropology's emphasis on an insider point of view specific to the locality being studied. A common theme is the prominence of high capital mobility, small-scale production, and kinship and other informal networks in current patterns of industrialization.

Globalization/ Industrial restructuring/ Labor processes/ Subcontracting/ Home-based production/ Small or micro-enterprises/ Gender division of labor/ Social networks/ Political mobilization/ Survival strategies/ Rural/ Relation to capital/ China/ Latin America/ India/ Italy/ Spain/ Wales/ Egypt/ U.S.A./ Puerto Rico/ South Korea/ Hong Kong/ Britain/ South Africa

629. **Rowbotham, S., and S. Mitter, eds. 1994.** *Dignity and Daily Bread: New Forms of Economic Organising among Poor Women in the Third World and the First*. London: Routledge.

Nine papers are presented placing women's experience of insecure, low-paid, and poorly protected employment in both historical and global perspectives. Following a global overview by Mitter [see separate citation], individual papers describe both the the history of women's employment in various contexts and the strategies taken against exploitative conditions of casualized work. Specific case studies examine Indian textile production, Southeast Asian Free Trade Zones, the Mexican garment industry, self-employment in India and Tanzania, sweatshop production, and homeworking in

Britain. A concluding chapter by Rowbotham and Mitter emphasizes the emergent patterns of resistance and organized struggle among women highlighted by the case studies.

Home-based production/ Subcontracting/ Resistance/ Political mobilization/ Trade unions/ Empowerment/ Self-employment/ Garment manufacture/ Export processing zones/ Women/ India/ Malaysia/ Philippines/ Sri Lanka/ Mexico/ Tanzania/ Britain

630. **Rubery, J. 1988.** Women and Recession: A Comparative Perspective. In *Women and Recession*. Ed. J. Rubery, pp. 253-286. London: Routledge & Kegan Paul.

Examining women's changing social positions and economic experiences in four industrialized countries, Rubery highlights differences in women's economic roles, links these variations to country-specific social and economic patterns, and illuminates the differences as well as similarities in the specific responses to recessionary trends. Expanded female participation in permanent formal employment and persistent differentiation between male and female labor is a pattern across the four countries. Women's labor market position continues to be disadvantaged, and the extent to which this is ultimately modified will likely depend on the ability to resist pressures to restructure labor market regulation arising with recessionary conditions.

Labor market segmentation/ Gender division of labor/ Economic restructuring/ State practice/ Women/ Comparative/ Britain/ France/ Italy/ U.S.A.

631. **Rubery, J., and F. Wilkinson. 1981.** Outwork and Segmented Labour Markets. In *The Dynamics of Labour Market Segmentation*. Ed. F. Wilkinson, pp. 115-132. London: Academic Press.

The authors argue that firms use outwork to meet peaks in demand, to increase the range of skills, services or products available to the firm, or to provide component parts or services for factorized production. This production strategy increases firm flexibility, shifts risk, minimizes cost, and provides a means to mobilize a latent reserve supply of labor. The authors stress that the use of outwork varies by industry and country, as well as over time, and is unlikely to disappear in the future.

Reserve army of labor/ Home-based production/ Subcontracting/ Flexibilization/ Britain

632. **Ruggeri, F. 1987.** Unofficial Economy and the Meaning of Labour: Toward a Theoretical Hypothesis. In *The Unofficial Economy: Consequences and Perspectives in Different Economic Systems*. Ed. S. Alessandrini and B. Dallago, pp. 107-124. Aldershot, Hants, U.K.; Brookfield, Vt.: Gower Publishing.

Ruggeri argues that the unofficial economy has modified the meaning of work in contemporary society. While the centrality of labor still holds, it is now based on the connection between various forms of work and the reproduction of their diverse social relations. Thus, it is important to examine the relationship between the official and unofficial economies, assuming that certain concrete forms of activity will disappear and others will come into existence.

Labor processes/ Relation to formal economy/ Industrialized economies

633. **Ruggiero, V. 1985.** The Encounter between Big Business and Organised Crime. *Capital and Class* 26: 93-104.

The author argues that distinctions between "criminal" and "clean" business are becoming increasingly blurred as characteristics of mafia enterprises are features of all enterprises. Moreover, relations between criminal and healthy businesses are increasingly collaborative and mutually enabling since the institutions of law, administration, and finance have adapted their traditionally repressive functions to the vital, cohesive role of providing the instruments and framework of economic regulation.

Illegal activity/ Relation to formal economy/ State practice/ Italy

634. **Ruiz-Perez, S. 1979.** Begging as an Occupation in San Cristobal las Casas, Mexico. In *Casual Work and Poverty in Third World Cities*. Ed. R. Bromley and C. Gerry, pp. 251-266. New York: John Wiley & Sons.

Pattern or magnitude/ Mexico

635. **Rusque-Alcaino, J., and R. Bromley. 1979.** The Bottle Buyer: An Occupational Autobiography. In *Casual Work and Poverty in Third*

World Cities. Ed. R. Bromley, and C. Gerry, pp. 185-216. New York: John Wiley & Sons.

Recycling/ Research methods/ Colombia

636. **Sabel, C. F. 1982.** *Work and Politics: The Division of Labor in Industry*. New York: Cambridge University Press.

Assessing trends in work organization under advanced capitalism, Sabel synthesizes research on industrial technology, factory workers, industrial organization, and labor movements. In his discussion of economic dualism accompanying the rise of Fordist production, he explores the persistence of small-scale production units serving inherently unstable market sectors to highlight the role of unskilled factory and skilled craft labor in both stable and unstable economic sectors. Comparative case histories challenge the primacy of class as a means of defining the life aspirations, political position and labor struggles assumed by different individuals. Proposed instead is the concept of "work groups" bound by shared social and historical experiences. Contemplating the end of Fordism, he identifies the need to experiment with new forms of production for advanced industrialized countries within the global economy such as those innovations in Italian industry which give rise to the possibility of distinct national systems of industrial organization that defy old ideas of viable industrial development. But such possibilities will depend on the political struggles that take place in different local and national contexts.

Dual sector or economy/ Industrial restructuring/ Production process/ Class processes/ Labor movements/ Artisanal production/ Technological change/ Industrialized economies

637. **Safa, H. I., ed. 1982.** *Towards a Political Economy of Urbanization in Third World Countries*. Delhi, India: Oxford University Press.

Thirteen papers relate processes of urbanization in Latin America, Africa, and Asia to dependent capitalist development. Four foci frame the papers: the nature of dependent capitalism in urban contexts; the historical changes in city structures with the switch from precapitalist to capitalist modes of production; the class structure of cities; and the role of the state in strengthening urban elites at the expense of the poor through fiscal, monetary, and infrastructure policies. Attention is given to the role of informal economic activities both to support the urban poor and subsidize the formal economy. Individual analyses highlight different features of the informal economy—its relationship to the peasant economy, articulation with the formal economy, role as a means for subsistence or upward mobility, and the possibilities of collective protest.

Urbanization/ Relation to capital/ Relation to formal economy/ Migration/ Political mobilization/ State practice/ Survival strategies/ Social mobility/ Mexico/ Colombia/ Chile/ Peru/ Brazil/ Nigeria/ Sudan/ West Africa/ Indonesia/ India/ Lebanon/ Third World

638. —— . **1986.** Urbanization, the Informal Economy and State Policy in Latin America. *Urban Anthropology* 15: 135-163.

Urbanization/ Gender division of labor/ Migration/ State practice/ Latin America

639. —— . **1992.** Development and Changing Gender Roles in Latin America and the Caribbean. In *Women's Work & Women's Lives: The Continuing Struggle Worldwide*. Ed. H. Kahne and J. Z. Giele, pp. 69-86. Boulder, Colo.: Westview.

Gender relations/ Labor market dynamics/ Flexibilization/ Survival strategies/ Resistance/ Latin America/ Caribbean

640. **Salahuddin, K., and I. Shamin. 1992.** *Women in Urban Informal Sector: Employment Pattern Activity Types and Problems*. Dhaka, Bangladesh: Women for Women.

Salahuddin and Shamin describe aspects of women's informal work experience, including their role as wage or self- employed workers and unpaid family labor. They identify the specific characteristics of the female informal labor force and the relationship between these activities and levels of income to reveal that women are concentrated in the lowest paid and most menial of informal sector work (i.e., domestic work and minor manufactured products). Self-employed women such as ash sellers, brick gatherers, and fish and other types of food vendors have a higher income than wage workers, but represent only 14 percent of the survey sample. They conclude that women perform both productive and reproductive roles yet remain largely unrecognized, undervalued, exploited, and unprotected.

Women/ Gender inequality/ Worker characteristics/ Self-employment/ Double-day/ Domestic service/ Trading/ Policy prescriptions/ Pattern or magnitude/ Social reproduction/ Bangladesh

641. **Sampson, S. 1985.** The Informal Sector in Eastern Europe. *Telos* 66 (Winter): 44-66.

Social networks/ Pattern or magnitude/ Eastern Europe

642. —— . **1987.** The Second Economy of the Soviet Union and Eastern Europe. *Annals of the American Academy of Political and Social Science* 493: 120-136.

Pattern or magnitude/ Home-based production/ Rural/ Trading/ Social networks/ Centrally planned economies/ U.S.S.R.

643. **Sanyal, B. 1988.** The Urban Informal Sector Revisited: Some Notes on the Relevance of the Concept in the 1980s. *Third World Planning Review* 10 (1): 65-83.

Sanyal reviews research and policies geared toward the informal sector in the developing world to assess possibilities for growth, identify the heterogeneity of its activities, highlight its lack of autonomy vis à vis the formal sector, and explore the impact of global capitalist crises in which decentralization has emerged as an important means to regain growth and profitability. Policies which support the informal sector aim to increase either their productivity or the demand for informal sector goods and services. In the face of harsh economic realities, the sector is likely to absorb an increasing share of the labor force, even as returns from most informal enterprises are likely to decrease. While possibilities for demand-stimulating policies are weak in an age of austerity, questions remain about the effectiveness of supply-side assistance.

Review/ Industrial restructuring/ Policy analysis/ Third World

644. —— . **1996.** Intention and Outcome: Formalization and Its Consequences. *Regional Development Dialogue* 17 (1): 161-178.

Policy analysis/ Policy prescriptions/ Housing/ Third World

645. **Sarin, M. 1979.** Urban Planning, Petty Trading, and Squatter Settlements in Chandigarh, India. In *Casual Work and Poverty in*

Third World Cities. Ed. R. Bromley and C. Gerry, pp. 133-160. New York: John Wiley & Sons.

Trading/ Housing/ State practice/ Pattern or magnitude/ India

646. **Sassen-Koob, S. 1989.** New York City's Informal Economy. In *The Informal Economy: Studies in Advanced and Less Developed Countries*. Ed. A. Portes, M. Castells, and L. A. Benton, pp. 60-77. Baltimore, Md.; London: Johns Hopkins University Press.

Sasson-Koob examines whether the formation and expansion of the informal sector in advanced industrialized countries results from conditions created by advanced capitalism or is fostered by immigration. Surveys of the informal sector in New York City suggest that it meets the demands of the larger economy and of particular communities confronted by processes of restructuring. The heterogeneity of informal sector activities must be taken into account in the formulation of policy.

Pattern or magnitude/ Migration/ Relation to formal economy/ Industrial restructuring/ Ethnicity/ U.S.A.

647. **Sastrosasmita, S., and A. T. M. N. Amin. 1990.** Housing Needs of Informal Sector Workers: The Case of Yogyakarta, Indonesia. *Habitat International* 14 (4): 75-88.

Housing/ State practice/ Policy prescriptions/ Social networks/ Indonesia

648. **Savara, M. 1981.** Organizing the Annapurna. *IDS Bulletin* 12 (3): 48-53.

Savara describes how a scattered group of women in Bombay, who cook for male migrant workers in their own homes, organized to improve their working conditions. Although isolated from each other and with interests in conflict with those of their worker customers, they have succeeded in freeing themselves from reliance on moneylenders and winning recognition of their rights as workers.

Women/ Home-based production/ Empowerment/ Trade unions/ Political mobilization/ India

649. **Scase, R. 1982.** The Petit Bourgeoisie and Modern Capitalism. In *Social Class and the Division of Labour*. Ed. A. Giddens and G. Mackenzie, pp. 148-161. Cambridge, U.K.: Cambridge University Press.

Class processes/ Small or micro-enterprises

650. **Schildkrout, E. 1980.** Children's Work Reconsidered. *International Social Science Journal* 32: 479-489.

Child labor/ Gender division of labor/ Nigeria

651. **Schmitz, H. 1982a.** Growth Constraints on Small-scale Manufacturing in Developing Countries: A Critical Review. *World Development* 10: 429-450.

Review/ Small or micro-enterprises/ Constraints to accumulation/ Third World

652. —— . **1982b.** *Manufacturing in the Backyard: Case Studies on Accumulation and Employment in Small-Scale Brazilian Industry*. Totowa, N.J.: Allenheld, Osmun.

Small or micro-enterprises/ Home-based production/ Constraints to accumulation/ Labor market segmentation/ Unpaid labor/ Brazil

653. **Scott, A. J. 1983a.** Industrial Organization and the Logic of Intra-metropolitan Location, I: Theoretical Considerations. *Economic Geography* 59: 233-250.

Production process/ Subcontracting/ Spatial patterns/ Labor market dynamics/ Industrial restructuring

654. ——. **1983b.** Industrial Organization and the Logic of Intra-metropolitan Location, II: A Case Study of the Printed Circuits Industry in the Greater Los Angeles Region. *Economic Geography* 59: 343-367.

Production process/ Subcontracting/ Spatial patterns/ Labor market dynamics/ Industrial restructuring/ Electronics manufacture/ U.S.A.

655. ——. **1983c.** Industrial Organization and the Logic of Intra-metropolitan Location, III: A Case Study of the Women's Dress Industry in the Greater Los Angeles Area. *Economic Geography* 60: 3-27.

Production process/ Subcontracting/ Spatial patterns/ Labor market dynamics/ Industrial restructuring/ Garment manufacture/ U.S.A.

656. **Scott, A. M. 1974.** Differentiation among the Urban Poor: An Argentine Study. In *Sociology and Development*. Ed. E. De Kadt and G. Williams, pp. 197-226. London: Tavistock.

Survival strategies/ Differentiation/ Pattern or magnitude/ Argentina

657. —— . **1979.** Who Are the Self-Employed? In *Casual Work and Poverty in Third World Cities*. Ed. R. Bromley and C. Gerry, pp. 105-132. Chichester, U.K.: John Wiley & Sons.

A number of intermediate forms of employment exist between the self-employed and the wage laborer but they remain largely undetected by official census categories which individualize production relations and utilize inconsistent criteria to define types of employment. In Lima, forms of production exist along a continuum in terms of the autonomy enjoyed by individual producers and the extent of their subordination to capital. The persistence of petty production is explained by the specific features of Peruvian capitalist development including: a large peasant sector with ancillary forms of production that provide the capital and labor power for large-scale capital, the dominance of merchant capital which delays industrial development, and the lack of homogeneous production relations based on wage labor, even in areas where industrial capital is well established.

Relation to capital/ Self-employment/ Class processes/ Continuum debate/ Peru/ Third World

658. —— . **1986a.** Introduction: Why Rethink Petty Commodity Production? *Social Analysis* 20 (December): 3-10.

MacEwen introduces a collection of papers addressing problems in earlier discussions of petty commodity production (PCP) which were flawed by ahistoricism, teleology, and functionalism. In recent years, due both to the need for effective analyses of small-scale production within capitalism and to new insights contributed by recent theorists of simple commodity production working outside the British structural marxist framework, PCP has become the object of renewed interest. This work highlights PCP's compatibility with advanced capitalism, its articulation with wider capitalist society, and the diversity of its forms. However, areas of ambiguity and contention remain, most notably with regard to the relationship between PCP and the social formation providing the conditions for its existence, the relationship between economic structures of PCP, politics, and ideology, the internal labor processes within PCP, and possibilities PCP offers for change.

Review/ Petty commodity production/ Labor processes/ Class processes/ Differentiation

659. —— . **1986B.** Towards a Rethinking of Petty Commodity Production. *Social Analysis* 20 (December): 93-105.

This summary essay reaffirms MacEwen's remarks on the continued importance of petty commodity production for understanding production relations under conditions of advanced capitalism.

Petty commodity production/ Class processes

660. —— . **1986c.** Women and Industrialisation: Examining the "Female Marginalisation" Thesis. *Journal of Development Studies* 22: 649-680.

Women are incorporated into the labor market in a number of different ways, not simply as a source of cheap labor but as a particular type of laborer. MacEwen challenges the feminist marginalization thesis by showing women's increased employment in manufacturing, especially during the 1980s.

Gender division of labor/ Marginalization/ Peru/ Brazil

661. —— . **1991.** Informal Sector or Female Sector: Gender Bias in Urban Labour Market Models. In *Male Bias in the Development Process*. Ed. D. Elson, pp. 105-132. U.K.: Manchester University Press.

Gender division of labor/ Gender ideology/ Class processes/ Social restructuring/ Economic restructuring/ Latin America

662. —— . **1994.** *Divisions and Solidarities: Gender, Class and Employment in Latin America*. London: Routledge.

Scott develops a theoretical framework for understanding class and gender as interlinked systems of inequality involving structures of inequality, subjective experience and consciousness, and political action. Analyzing the labouring class in Peru during the 1960s and 1970s, she draws from secondary data, survey results, and interviews to argue the inadequacy of an exclusive focus on shop floor relations emphasizing instead the need to incorporate consumption-based issues (e.g., household reproduction and survival, housing, health, and education) in the concept of class. While the experience of inequality at home and beyond signifies structural conflicts of interest between women and men, survival and upward mobility is made possible through household strategies for generating income (including informal work), obtaining goods and services to meet daily needs, and organizing at the community level to gain access to key resources for longer term improvements in the quality of life. These experiences of struggle and upward mobility at the household and community levels mediate gender divisions, support latent solidarity at the workplace, and engender class solidarity among Peru's *clase trabajadore*. The lack of a politically active labor movement can thus be traced to the structure of the Peruvian political system dominated by political elites rather than to the lack of class solidarity.

Economic restructuring/ Class processes/ Consciousness/ Gender relations/ Household/ Resistance/ Social networks/ Social mobility/ Social reproduction/ Migration/ Peru

663. **Scott, E. P. 1985.** Lusaka's Informal Sector in National Economic Development. *Journal of Developing Areas* 20: 71-99.

Trading/ State practice/ Policy analysis/ Zambia

664. **Scoville, J. 1977.** Sectoral Interdependence in Urban Labour Markets and Variations in the Social and Economic Environment. In *Studies of Urban Labour Market Behaviour in Developing Countries*. Ed. S. Kannappan, pp. 71-84. Geneva, Switzerland: International Institute for Labour Studies.

Scoville argues that models of urban labor markets must incorporate the internal diversity of traditional sector activities, the income opportunities offered by traditional industry, and the workings of internal labor markets which account for the training, discipline and stability of the modern sector labor force. He offers a model of modern and traditional labor market interdependence which suggests that attractive opportunities in traditional skills may raise the modern sector wage structure. The "ambitious proliferation" of sectors amplifies wage differentials and patterns of labor mobility.

Labor market dynamics/ Dual sector or economy/ Afghanistan/ Third World

665. **Senghaas-Knobloch, E. 1977.** Informal Sector and Peripheral Capitalism: A Critique of a Prevailing Concept of Development. *Manpower and Unemployment Research* 10 (2): 3-24.

Review/ Critique of dualism/ Third World

666. **Sethuraman, S. V. 1976.** The Urban Informal Sector: Concept, Measurement and Policy. *International Labour Review* 114: 69-81.

Review/ Definition/ Pattern or magnitude/ Research methods/ Third World

667. —— . **1977a.** Migration, the Informal Sector and the Urban Labour Market: The Case of Jakarta. In *Studies of Urban Labour Market Behaviour in Developing Areas*. Ed. S. Kannappan, pp. 181- 189. Geneva, Switzerland: International Institute for Labour Studies.

Sethuraman reviews patterns of migration to Jakarta in response to the capitalization of agriculture. The availability of formal sector employment has responded to shifts in the supply of labor. However, since the late 1960s, there has been a growing dependence on the informal sector even though mobility between sectors has been constrained by the requirement of residence and work permits. Despite constraints to advancement, there is mobility within the informal sector where working conditions are poor and wages are low.

Migration/ Labor market dynamics/ Indonesia

668. —— . **1977b.** Urban Poverty and the Role of the Informal Sector in Creating Employment. In *Equality of Opportunity Within and Among Nations*. Ed. K. Haq, pp. 73-80. New York: Praeger.

Pattern or magnitude/ Policy analysis/ Third World

669. ___**, ed. 1981.** *The Urban Informal Sector: Employment, Poverty and Environment*. Geneva, Switzerland: International Labour Office.

Pattern or magnitude/ Policy analysis/ Sierra Leone/ Nigeria/ Ghana/ Sri Lanka/ Indonesia/ Philippines/ Argentina/ Brazil

670. **Shaheed, F., and K. Mumtaz. 1983.** *Invisible Workers: Piecework Labour amongst Women in Lahore*. Islamabad, Pakistan: Women's Division, Government of Pakistan.

Home-based production/ Subcontracting/ Household division of labor/ Unpaid labor/ Gender ideology/ Policy prescriptions/ Piecework/ Women/ Pakistan

671. **Shankland, G., with Roy Turner. 1988.** *Wonted Work: A Guide to the Informal Economy*. New York: Bootstrap Press.

Review/ Pattern or magnitude/ Gender division of labor/ Comparative/ Industrialized economies/ Britain

672. **Sharpe, B. 1988.** Informal Work and Development in the West. *Progress in Human Geography* 12: 315-336.

Unpaid labor/ Labor processes/ Review/ Industrialized economies

673. **Sharpston, M. 1975.** International Subcontracting. *Oxford Economic Papers* 27: 94-135.

Subcontracting/ State practice

674. **Shaw, A. 1984.** Wage Labour in Slum Households of Calcutta. *Labour, Capital and Society* 17: 26-42.

The noncapitalist mode of production is said to service capital through unequal exchange and by maintaining and reproducing labor power to allow for capitalist accumulation. Unequal exchange also operates between the informal and formal economy as the capitalist sector benefits from petty production that maintains low levels of subsistence and the low cost of reproducing labor. Shaw finds a clear gender division of wage labor: men participate in unstable wage employment in capitalist firms while women participate in more stable but lower paying wage work, especially domestic work, in the noncapitalist sector. This division, based on the duration, time cycles, and geographic proximity of work, ensures the household as a viable economic unit. Moreover, female wage and domestic labour can be regarded as the pivot around which the peripheral capitalist economy has developed an efficient system of lowering the costs of its own reproduction.

Gender division of labor/ Relation to capital/ Unequal exchange/ Domestic service/ Social reproduction/ India

675. —— . **1985.** The Informal Sector in a Third World Urban Economy: A Case Study of Calcutta, India. *Bulletin of Concerned Asian Scholars* 17 (1): 42-53.

Shaw asserts the interdependence between the informal and formal sectors and argues that a net transfer of value from the informal to formal sector is an untested conjecture. To what extent does the informal sector serve as a source of undervalued goods and services for the formal sector and by what specific mechanism is this value transferred? As Shaw argues, cheap labor in the informal sector subsidizes wages when cheap goods and services can be bought by workers in the formal sector. While lowering the cost of living for the urban working class, this unequal exchange of goods for money does not result in lower prices to the consumer and thus must be distinguished from unequal trade across sectors. She also argues that labor relations in informal manufacturing, where over 55 percent of workers produce nonwage goods that enter the formal sector, results in unequal trade and the transfer of surplus to the formal sector.

Relation to formal economy/ Subsidy to capital/ Unequal exchange/ India

676. **Shifflett, P. A., and M. W. Hoskins. 1985.** Household Processing: Women's Contribution to Family Income. In *The Rural Work Force: Nonagricultural Occupations in America*. Ed. C. D. Bryant, D. J. Shoemaker, J. K. Skipper Jr., and W. E. Snizek, pp. 241-253. South Hadley, Mass.: Bergin and Garvey.

This study explores women's perceptions of supports and constraints affecting household processing of natural resources and crafts for household survival. The authors note that women perceive their income from household production as necessary, identify their desire to limit the size of the operation, are embarrassed at selling to neighbors, and view child care needs and policy regulations as constraints to enterprise development. Thus the authors conclude that one needs to recognize women's home-based processing as a viable means to supplement family income and to create policy mechanisms in support of these efforts.

Home-based production/ Household division of labor/ Survival strategies/ Rural/ Women/ Handicrafts/ Double-day/ U.S.A.

677. **Sicular, D. T. 1991.** Pockets of Peasants in Indonesian Cities: The Case of Scavengers. *World Development* 19: 137-161.

Class processes/ Scavenging/ Spatial patterns/ Indonesia

678. **Sik, E. 1994.** From the Multicoloured to the Black and White Economy: The Hungarian Second Economy and the Transformation. *International Journal of Urban and Regional Research* 18: 46-70.

While beset by the economic problems associated with the shift from a centrally planned to a market economy, Hungary has enjoyed a relatively nonviolent political and social transition. Behind this success has been the second economy which flourished during the last decades of centralized planning. Sik describes the dense personal networks for household survival in the transition to capitalism, the investments made by households in these networks, the increasing incidence of full-time employment in informal activity, and the growing links between informal activity and smuggling, black currency markets, and illegal migration. He concludes that current indicators suggest the growing resemblance of Hungary's informal economy to dualistic patterns in the Third World.

Social networks/ Economic restructuring/ Survival strategies/ Illegal activity/ Dual sector or economy/ Centrally planned economies/ Hungary

679. **Silverio, S. Jr. 1982.** The Neighborhood Sari-Sari Store. In *The Philippine Poor I: Two Monographs*. Ed. M. S. Fernandez, pp. 59-134. Quezon City, Philippines: Institute of Philippine Culture, Ateneo de Manila University.

Social networks/ Pattern or magnitude/ Trading/ Philippines

680. **Simis, K. M. 1982.** *USSR–the Corrupt Society: The Secret World of Soviet Capitalism*. New York: Simon & Schuster.

Pattern or magnitude/ U.S.S.R.

681. **Simon, C. P., and A. D. Witte. 1982.** *Beating the System: The Underground Economy*. Boston, Mass.: Auburn House Publishing.

The authors examine transactions that involve money or similar goods that are not recorded in official economic statistics such as taxable income or unemployment figures. A sectoral approach is used to examine the structure, size, and growth of the underground economy in the United States.

Pattern or magnitude/ Research methods/ U.S.A.

682. **Simon, D. 1984.** Urban Poverty, Informal Sector Activity and Intersectoral Linkages: Evidence from Windhoek, Namibia. *Development and Change* 15: 551-576.

Data from 217 Namibian formal sector workers show widespread wage discrimination by race and sex under conditions of increased urban migration, the result of the 1977 abolition of influx controls, and the escalation of the guerilla war. Simon argues that the informal sector is a survival mechanism where women, despite earning irregular income, must fight against police harassment. Data from 25 informal enterprises show tenuous intersectoral linkages (except for procurement of goods for sale), and competition among traders.

Labor market segmentation/ Gender inequality/ Survival strategies/ Dual sector or economy/ State practice/ Racial inequality/ Namibia

683. **Sinay-Aguilar, V. 1983.** Domestic Outwork Arrangement in the Footwear and Garments Industries. *Philippine Journal of Industrial Relations* 5 (1-2): 44-57.

Home-based production/ Subcontracting/ Shoe production/ Garment manufacture/ Philippines

684. **Sinclair, S. 1976a.** Informal Economic Activity in African Cities: Proposals for Research. *Journal of Modern African Studies* 14: 696-699.

Dual sector or economy/ Africa

685. —— **. 1976b.** The "Intermediate" Sector in the Economy. *Manpower and Unemployment Research* 9 (2): 55-60.

Dual sector or economy/ Africa/ Third World

686. —— . **1977.** Ease of Entry into Small-Scale Trading in African Cities: Some Case Studies from Lagos. *Manpower and Unemployment Research* 10 (1): 79-90.

Research methods/ Pattern or magnitude/ Trading/ Dual sector or economy/ Nigeria

687. —— . **1978.** *Urbanisation and Labour Markets in Developing Countries.* London: Croom Helm.

Review/ Urbanization/ Labor market dynamics/ Third World

688. **Singer, H. 1970.** Dualism Revisited: A New Approach to the Problems of the Dual Society in the Developing Countries. *Journal of Development Studies* 7: 60-75.

Dual sector or economy/ Third World

689. **Singh, A. M., and A. Kelles-Viitanen, eds. 1987.** *Invisible Hands: Women in Home-Based Production.* New Delhi, India: Sage Publications.

A conference collection on women and the household questions the household as an undifferentiated unit to explore the centrality of the household in the production and reproduction of material life. Each entry explores different forms and relations of home-based work: a discussion of SEWA and the call for a workers' protection bill, the configuration of home-based, self-employed or own-account workers, piece rate workers including those engaged in garment manufacture, households whose members engage in agricultural production including livestock rearing, and beedi production, as well as those securing income through handicrafts production. The studies address program evaluation and development policy concerns as well as historical reviews of changes in traditional handicrafts production through government and NGO efforts to capitalize production and increase domestic and export consumption.

Gender inequality/ Gender division of labor/ Home-based production/ Subcontracting/ Piecework/ Relation to formal economy/ Handicrafts/ Women/ Trading/ Rural/ Garment manufacture/ Labor movements/ Trade unions/ Empowerment/ Rural/ Project assistance/ Policy prescriptions/ India

690. **Singh, M. 1990.** *The Political Economy of Unorganised Industry: A Study of the Labour Process*. New Delhi, India: Sage Publications.

Labor processes/ Class processes/ Unpaid labor/ Gender division of labor/ Domestic service/ India

691. **Sison, R. G. 1990.** *A Review of Institutional Linkages for Assistance to the Urban Informal Sector*. New Delhi, India: UNDP; ILO, Asian Regional Team for Employment Promotion.

Project assistance/ Policy analysis/ Philippines

692. **Skolka, J. V. 1976A.** Long-Term Effects of Unbalanced Productivity Growth: On the Way to a Self-Service Society. In *Private and Enlarged Consumption: Essays in Methodology and Empirical Analysis*. Ed. L. Solari and J. N. Pasquier, pp. 279-301. Amsterdam, Netherlands: North-Holland Publishing.

Research methods/ Self-provisioning/ Unpaid labor/ Industrialized economies

693. —— **. 1976B.** The Substitution of Self-Service Activities for Marketed Services. *Review of Income and Wealth* 22: 297-304.

Self-service activities are defined as those activities which are carried on outside the market and which challenge the division of time into work for market and for leisure. This definition could be refined by distinguishing between market, subsistence household, and self-service activities where the latter includes the use of private cars for transportation, self-service supermarkets, renting holiday apartments and camping, do-it-yourself repairs, and the use of radio and television rather than concert attendence. Consumer preferences for self-service results from high taxes, high real wages, and an equal distribution of personal income. The recording of self-service activities has consequences for how we measure national welfare.

Self-provisioning/ Unpaid labor/ Research methods/ Industrialized economies

694. —— **. 1987.** A Few Facts about the Hidden Economy. In *The Unofficial Economy: Consequences and Perspectives in Different Economic Systems*. Ed. S. Alessandrini and B. Dallago, pp. 35-60. Aldershot, Hants, U.K.; Brookfield, Vt.: Gower Publishing.

This paper reviews the literature on the hidden economy in Western countries and criticizes exaggerated estimates of its size. The author argues that technical feasibility and productivity determine which activities are performed in a hidden way.

Review/ Pattern or magnitude/ Industrialized economies

695. **Smart, A. 1988.** The Informal Regulation of Illegal Economic Activities: Comparisons Between the Squatter Property Market and Organized Crime. *International Journal of the Sociology of Law* 16 (1): 91-101.

Illegal activity/ Social networks/ Hong Kong

696. **Smith, C. A. 1984.** Labor and International Capital in the Making of a Peripheral Social Formation: Economic Transformations in Guatemala, 1850-1980. In *Labor in the Capitalist World-Economy*. Ed. C. Bergquist, pp. 135-156. Beverly Hills, Calif.: Sage Publications.

Petty commodity production/ Relation to capital/ Class processes/ State practice/ Rural/ Guatemala

697. —— **. 1986a.** The Petty Bourgeoisie as a "Fundamental" Revolutionary Class in Nicaragua. *Labour, Capital and Society* 19: 8-35.

Smith analyzes the dominant role which the petty bourgeoisie played in the Nicaraguan revolution to show that petty commodity producers (PCP) are growing rather than disappearing as a social class in the Third World and their relation to proletarian and "traditional" bourgeois classes is changing. She argues that the state facilitates the emergence of this class who are only partially proletarianized; i.e., they do not completely depend on wages for their livelihood nor do they extract surplus value from other waged workers. The deepening of capitalism in Nicaragua challenges large petty bourgeois interests that depend on communal or borrowed forms of property rather than on individual, competitive forms of ownership for their reproduction.

Petty commodity production/ Class processes/ Political mobilization/ Nicaragua

698. —— **. 1986b.** Reconstructing the Elements of Petty Commodity Production. *Social Analysis* 20 (December): 29-46.

Petty commodity production/ Review/ Relation to capital/ Class processes/State practice

699. **Smith, G. 1994.** Towards an Ethnography of Idiosyncratic Forms of Livelihood. *International Journal of Urban and Regional Research* 18: 71-87.

Smith highlights the incongruity between conventional sociological research methods relying on mass survey techniques and the dynamics of highly heterogenous and dispersed livelihoods increasingly characteristic of capitalist development today. Citing ethnographic data from southern Valencia, the author suggests the need for new categories to study the process of social labor. She argues for a new framework to synthesize cultural production into the concept of social labor, allowing a better understanding of the dynamics of regulation and the process by which an ideology of shared identity is constructed outside fixed institutional spaces.

Research methods/ Social networks/ Economic restructuring/ Class processes/ Spain

700. **Smith, J. D. 1985.** Market Motives in the Informal Economy. In *The Economics of the Shadow Economy*. Ed. W. Gaertner and A. Wenig, pp. 161-177. Berlin, F.R.G.: Springer-Verlag.

Smith estimates the size of the U.S. informal economy and examines what motivates people to deal in informal exchange. The research used survey techniques to measure the value of goods and services purchased from informal vendors over a one-year period.

Pattern or magnitude/ Trading/ U.S.A.

701. **—— . 1987.** Measuring the Informal Economy. *Annals of the American Academy of Political and Social Science* 493: 83-99.

Research methods/ Pattern or magnitude/ U.S.A.

702. **Smith, J., I. Wallerstein, and H. Evers, eds. 1984.** *Households and the World Economy*. Beverly Hills, Calif.: Sage.
Exploring households as basic units of an emerging world- system, the papers in this volume examine processes of reproduction of labor power and intra-household labor dynamics. Part I of the volume asks: What is the relationship between processes of commodification,

crisis, and the formation of households. The two remaining sections focus on the relationship between households and the state on the one hand, and intra-household dynamics on the other hand. The various contributions address patriarchal relations, non-wage labor and subsistence production, the peasant-proletarianization debate, as well as household savings and income-pooling among household members. Most of the articles employ a world systems framework and the individual papers examine household formation in South Africa, intra-household conflict in West Africa, the contribution of public goods to household reproduction in Brazil, and processes of accumulation in China, as well as historical studies of the working class in the United States and England.

Household/ Unpaid labor/ Home-based production/ Household division of labor/ Gender ideology/ Gender division of labor/ Relation to capital/ Processes of accumulation/ Social reproduction/ Subsistence production/ West Africa/ South Africa/ Brazil/ China/ Britain/ Industrialized economies

703. **Smith, M. 1973.** Domestic Servants as a Channel of Upward Mobility for the Lower Class Woman: The Lima Case. In *Female and Male in Latin America: Essays*. Ed. A. Pescatella, pp. 191-207. Pittsburgh, Penn.: University of Pittsburgh Press.

Migration/ Gender division of labor/ Domestic service/ Social mobility/ Peru

704. **Smith, M. E. 1988.** Overview: The Informal Economy and the State. In *Traders versus the State: Anthropological Approaches to Unofficial Economies*. Ed. G. Clark, pp. 189-199. Boulder, Colo.: Westview Press.

Smith sketches problems in defining informal activities and the state's contradictory relationship to the informal sector. While the trend towards privatization encourages private entrepreneurism, it also enables the state to monitor and control informal activities. She concludes that anthropological contributions illuminate problems of informal activities "from the perspective of those at the bottom looking up."

State practice/ Research methods/ Definition

705. **Smith, M. E. et al., eds. 1990.** *Perspectives on the Informal Economy.* Monographs in Economic Anthropology, no. 8. Lanham, Md.: University Press of America; Society for Economic Anthropology.

Discussions that introduced the concept of the informal sector in the early 1970s suggested a paradigmatic shift in how problems of underdevelopment were perceived, exploring productive systems that existed outside the control of the state. Other discussions stressed the social costs of the growing informal economy in the form of reduced state resources. The fifteen papers focus on different countries and activities to illuminate debates on the informal sector, particularly those shaped by recent discussions of economic restructuring and the role of the state in defining and shaping informality.

Comparative/ Pattern or magnitude/ State practice/ Economic restructuring/ Survival strategies/ Social networks/ Trading/ Housing/ Critique of dualism/ Relation to formal economy/ Class processes/ Ethnicity/ Welfare/ Resistance/ Brazil/ U.S.A./ Mexico/ Spain/ Denmark/ Norway/ Sweden/ Hong Kong/ Myanmar/ Dominican Republic/ India/ Tanzania

706. **Smith, S. 1986.** *Britain's Shadow Economy.* Oxford, U.K.: Clarendon Press.

Review/ Pattern or magnitude/ Britain

707. **Smith, S., and S. Wied-Nebbeling. 1986.** *The Shadow Economy in Britain and Germany.* London: Anglo-German Foundation for the Study of Industrial Society.

The shadow economy includes all illegal activity as well as productive, nonformal and nonmarket activities by households and voluntary organizations. It is associated with increasing tax evasion and abuse of the social security system when there are increases in the costs of public expenditure. Focused on the size and economic implications of these activities for policy in Germany and Britain, this collection makes available German studies likely to be inaccessible to English-speaking audiences.

Pattern or magnitude/ Unpaid labor/ Volunteer work/ Social networks/ Illegal activity/ Policy analysis/ Tax evasion/ Germany/ Britain

708. **Smithies, E. 1984.** *The Black Economy in England since 1914*. Atlantic Heights, N.J.: Humanities Press.

Pattern or magnitude/ Britain

709. **Soiffer, S. M., and G. M. Herrman. 1987.** The Underground Economy. *Choice* July/August: 1658-1667.

Review/ Pattern or magnitude/ Industrialized economies

710. **Solinas, G. 1982.** Labour Market Segmentation and Workers' Careers: The Case of the Italian Knitwear Industry. *Cambridge Journal of Economics* 6: 331-352.

Labor market segmentation/ Industrial restructuring/ Home-based production/ Garment manufacture/ Italy

711. **Souza, P., and V. Tokman. 1976.** The Informal Sector in Latin America. *International Labour Review* 114: 355-365.

Souza and Tokman examine the origins of the informal sector in Latin America, describe its characteristics and its labor force, and identify issues for policy. The sector consists of the surplus labor force that could not be absorbed into the limited formal productive sector and is defined in terms of income earned below the legal minimum wage. Data for the 1960/70 period suggest that the sector's share of urban employment has grown and that it employs mostly young and/or female heads of families and migrants. Policy proposals center on measures to increase the sector's productivity and total income, while maximizing employment opportunities.

Dual sector or economy/ Definition/ Pattern or magnitude/ Policy prescriptions/ Worker characteristics/ Latin America

712. **Späth, B., ed. 1993.** *Small Firms and Development in Latin America: The Role of the Institutional Environment, Human Resources, and Industrial Relations*. Geneva, Switzerland: ILO.

Small or micro-enterprises/ Industrial restructuring/ Policy analysis/ Brazil/ Colombia/ Peru/ Latin America/ Third World

713. **Srivastava, R. S. 1997.** "Informalisation" of the Workforce. *Economic and Political Weekly Reviews* February 1: 210- 212.

This review of Jan Breman's new book, *Footloose Labour: Working in India's Informal Sector*, highlights the significance of discussions of poverty in the nonagrarian economy of south Gujarat and challenges notions of informal workers as self- employed to show that wage laborers, including those working under the putting out system, are twice as dominant in the sector as self-employed workers. The importance of Srivastava's review is its clear outline of the salience of discussions of informalization in India today.

Self-employment/ Rural/ Disguised wage labor/ Labor processes/ Migration/ Technological constraints/ Relation to formal economy/ Mobility/ India

714. **Stack, C. 1974.** *All Our Kin: Strategies for Survival in a Black Community*. New York: Harper and Row.

Survival strategies/ Social networks/ Racial inequality/ U.S.A.

715. **Stack, O. 1982.** On Modelling the Informal Sector. *World Development* 10: 413-416.

Labor market dynamics/ Migration/ Third World

716. **Standing, G. 1977.** Urban Workers and Patterns of Employment. In *Studies of Urban Labour Market Behaviour in Developing Countries*. Ed. S. Kannappan, pp. 35-48. Geneva, Switzerland: International Institute for Labour Studies.

Standing proposes an urban sector schema which includes a formal sector divided into a core and periphery, an informal sector, and an irregular stagnant sector composed of criminal as well as legal fringe activities such as begging and casual labor. The formal sector core is characterized by standardized wage employment of skilled, highly paid secure workers, and a periphery shaped by subcontracting arrangements where jobs are erratic but "progressive" in that workers can increase skills, productivity, and responsibility as they gain experience. The wage structure of the core and periphery are linked by institutional factors rather than competitive markets. Informal work, in contrast, is neither paid nor regulated by capital, and the allocation of individual or family labor time is discretionary. Both rural and urban workers and households combine multiple activities or occupations in different sectors as a way to minimize risk.

Pattern or magnitude/ Survival strategies/ Multiple jobs/ Flexibilization/Jamaica/ Third World

717. —— . **1986.** Meshing Labour Flexibility with Security: An Answer to British Unemployment? *International Labour Review* 125: 87-106.

Flexibilization/ Social restructuring/ Welfare/ State practice/ Britain

718. —— . **1989a.** The "British Experiment": Structural Adjustment or Accelerated Decline? In *The Informal Economy: Studies in Advanced and Less Developed Countries*. Ed. A. Portes, M. Castells, and L. A. Benton, pp. 279-297. Baltimore, Md.; London: Johns Hopkins University Press.

Standing describes the implications of the breakdown of social consensus about the commitment to full employment. Deindustrialization, inflation, technological change, low industrial investment, and the state's fiscal crisis mark the inapplicability of "the halcyon days of Keynesian orthodoxy" which was a response to supply-side economics to restore market capitalism and reverse institutional trends toward welfare capitalism. The result has been the fragmentation of labor markets and an enormous loss of jobs which Standing examines through its effects on labor, the move from wage to self-employment, and the growing dependence on state transfers.

Economic restructuring/ Social restructuring/ State practice/ Structural adjustment/ Welfare/ Under- and unemployment/ Technological change/ Britain

719. —— . **1989b.** Global Feminization through Flexible Labor. *World Development* 7: 1077-1095.

Industrial restructuring/ Gender division of labor/ Export processing zones/ Labor market segmentation/ Flexibilization/ Third World/ Industrialized economies

720. **Stark, D. 1986.** Rethinking Internal Labor Markets: New Insights from a Comparative Perspective. *American Sociological Review* 51: 492-504.

Labor market dynamics/ Subcontracting/ Hungary/ Comparative/ Industrialized economies/ Centrally planned economies

721. ——. **1989.** Bending the Bars of the Iron Cage: Bureaucratization and Informalization in Capitalism and Socialism. *Sociological Forum* 4: 637-664.

State practice/ Comparative/ Centrally planned economies/ Industrialized economies

722. **Stark, O. 1982.** On Modeling the Informal Sector. *World Development* 10: 413-416.

Labor market dynamics/ Migration/ Third World

723. **Stearns, K., and M. Otero, eds. 1990.** *The Critical Connection: Governments, Private Institutions, and the Informal Sector in Latin America*. Washington, D.C.: Accion International.

Project assistance/ Policy analysis/ Colombia/ Ecuador/ Guatemala/ Mexico/ Paraguay/ Peru/ Latin America

724. **Steel, W. F. 1976.** Empirical Measurement of the Relative Size and Productivity of Intermediate Sector Employment: Some Estimates from Ghana. *Manpower and Unemployment Research* 9 (1): 23-32.

Dual sector or economy/ Pattern or magnitude/ Ghana

725. ——. **1977.** *Small-Scale Employment and Production in Developing Countries: Evidence from Ghana*. New York: Praeger.

Small or micro-enterprises/ Labor market dynamics/ Research methods/ Ghana

726. **Steel, W. F., and Y. Takagi. 1983.** Small Enterprise Development and the Employment Output Trade-Off. *Oxford Economic Papers* 35: 423-446.

Small or micro-enterprises/ Policy prescriptions

727. **Steele, D. 1975.** The Theory of the Dual Economy and African Entrepreneurship in Kenya. *Journal of Development Studies* 12: 18-38.

Steele identifies the need to recognize an intermediate sector between traditional agricultural and modern sectors. The expansion of this third sector is characterized by the growth of high income small farms, the increased concentration of people in towns and periurban areas, and the growth of unplanned urban settlements providing housing, services, and manufactured goods for lower middle class modern sector workers as well as those in the third sector.

Dual sector or economy/ Urbanization/ Kenya

728. **Stein, B. 1985.** Subterranean Labor Markets: A Conceptual Analysis. In *The Economics of the Shadow Economy*. Ed. W. Gaertner and A. Wenig, pp. 37-44. Berlin, F.R.G.; New York: Springer-Verlag.

Stein develops a taxonomy in which underground markets are divided into two categories: one for illegal goods and services and another where the transaction rather than the object traded is illegal or constrained. Focusing on the latter, Stein notes that since market information is available to transactors, it must be available to law enforcers. The persistence of underground markets suggests an optimal tolerance between the shadow and sunlight sectors.

Pattern or magnitude/ Illegal activity/ Industrialized economies

729. **Stein, H., and E. W. Nafziger. 1991.** Structural Adjustment, Human Needs and the World Bank Agenda. *Journal of Modern African Studies* 29: 173-189.

Structural adjustment/ State practice/ Policy analysis/ Tanzania

730. **Stepick, A. 1989.** Miami's Two Informal Sectors. In *The Informal Economy: Studies in Advanced and Less Developed Countries*. Ed. A. Portes, M. Castells, and L. A. Benton, pp. 111-134. Baltimore, Md.; London: Johns Hopkins University Press.

Stepick compares Miami's Cuban immigrant community and their links to the broader economy, with the more isolated Haitian community of informal sector workers. Cubans participate as both owners and workers in the garment industry, restaurants and construction and have altered Miami's integrated informal sector to include a co-ethnic alliance between capital and labor in which workers voluntarily submit to high levels of exploitation in return for assistance in subsequently establishing and maintaining their own business. These alliances impede the exploitation of labor as they deter the incorporation of new sources of labor, such as Haitian refugees, who may be cheaper and more pliable than Cuban workers.

Haitian activities, in contrast, are mainly confined to their own ethnic community.

Pattern or magnitude/ Migration/ Ethnicity/ Racial inequality/ Refugees/ Social networks/ Construction industry/ Garment manufacture/ U.S.A.

731. —— . **1991.** The Haitian Informal Sector in Miami. *City and Society* 5: 10-22.

Migration/ Ethnicity/ Racial inequality/ State practice/ U.S.A.

732. **Stichter, S. 1990.** Women, Employment and the Family: Current Debates. In *Women, Employment and the Family in the International Division of Labour*. Ed. S. Stichter and J. L. Parpart, pp. 11-71. London: Macmillan.

Indicators suggest a global trend toward increased female labor force participation as well as the incorporation of growing numbers of women in export-oriented industries. However, marked variations in female employment exist between different countries and industrial sectors. What are the factors behind these variations? To what extent are they shaped by the gender division of reproductive and productive labor in the household? Stichter stresses the inadequacy of discussions focused solely on market conditions or sectoral and technical changes in the organization of production to explain patterns of female employment and emphasizes the importance of women's age, marital and household socialization patterns in shaping both the supply of and demand for female labor. Examining different conceptions of the household, she notes that although productive and reproductive relations shape women's lives, units of co-residence, consumption, production, and reproduction vary across contexts.

Gender division of labor/ Worker characteristics/ Economic restructuring/ Social reproduction/ Gender relations/ Export processing zones/ Household/ Social reproduction/ Household/ Household division of labor

733. **Strassman, W. P. 1987.** Home-Based Enterprises in Cities of Developing Countries. *Economic Development and Cultural Change* 36: 121-144.

Home-based production/ Peru/ Sri Lanka/ Zambia

734. **Straussman, J. D. 1977.** The Reserve Army of Unemployed Revisited. *Society* 14 (3): 40-45.

Reserve army of labor/ Labor processes/ U.S.A.

735. **Streefland, P. 1977.** The Absorptive Capacity of the Urban Tertiary Sector in Third World Countries. *Development and Change* 8: 293-305.

Labor market dynamics/ Pakistan

736. **Stretton, A. 1979.** Instability of Employment among Building Industry Labourers in Manila. In *Casual Work and Poverty in Third World Cities*. Ed. R. Bromley and C. Gerry, pp. 267-282. New York: John Wiley & Sons.

Under- and unemployment/ Construction industry/ Philippines

737. **Suarez-Berenguela, R. 1987.** *Informal Sector, Labor Markets, and Returns to Education in Peru*. Living Standards Measurement Study (LSMS) Working Paper, no. 32. Washington, D.C.: World Bank, Development Research Department.

Review/ Pattern or magnitude/ Dual sector or economy/ Labor market dynamics/ Education/ Peru

738. **Sullivan, T. A. 1978.** *Marginal Workers, Marginal Jobs: The Underutilization of American Workers*. Austin, Texas: University of Texas Press.

Labor market dynamics/ U.S.A.

739. **Sundar, P. 1983.** Women's Employment and Organization Modes. *Economic and Political Weekly* 18 (48): M171-176.

Sundar explores the advantages and disadvantages of home-based self-employment by questioning its potential to maximize output and income and to improve women's economic and social status. She finds that home-based self-employment reinforces women's lower status and suggests that collective production may enable women to control the means of production and decision-making. She also proposes an organizational strategy likely to enhance women's status.

Home-based production/ Self-employment/ Women/ Empowerment/ Social networks/ India

740. **Swaminathan, M. 1991.** *Understanding the "Informal Sector": A Survey*. WIDER Working Papers, WP 95. Helsinki, Finland: World Institute for Development Economics Research.

Review/ Definition/ Pattern or magnitude/ Relation to formal economy/ State practice/ Economic restructuring/ Third World/ Industrialized economies

741. **Swantz, M. L. 1992.** Patterns of Empowerment: Cultural Identity and Global Integration. *Development* 3: 46-49.

Social restructuring/ Survival strategies/ Consciousness/ Empowerment

742. **Swetnam, J. 1980.** Disguised Employment and Development Policy. *Human Organization* 39: 32-39.

Petty commodity production/ Survival strategies/ Disguised wage labor/ Guatemala

743. **Szelenyi, I. 1981.** Structural Changes of and Alternatives to Capitalist Development in the Contemporary Urban and Regional System. *International Journal of Urban and Regional Research* 5 (1): 1-14.

Szelenyi argues for a shift from the Althusserian understanding of capitalism as a set of structural relationships to an analysis of capitalism as process. He identifies three areas of theoretical and policy concern: (1) the restructuring of capital and labor, given the transfer of capital into capital intensive sectors nationally and into free trade zones internationally; (2) the identification of forces within advanced capitalism which could serve as alternatives to it and be used for a democratic socialist transformation; and (3) a historical and comparative analysis of the relationship between socialism and socialist industrialization and urbanization. Possible alternatives to capitalist development include strengthening the domestic sphere or informal economy which responds to feminist critiques of economics and sociology and makes "decommodification" permanent. It also includes developing a counterhegemony to support alternative forms of social mobilization.

Relation to formal economy/ State practice/ Economic restructuring/ Labor processes/ Export processing zones/ Comparative/ Industrialized economies

744. **Szita, E. 1987.** New Types of Entrepreneurial and Organizational Forms in the Hungarian Economy. In *The Unofficial Economy: Consequences and Perspectives in Different Economic Systems*. Ed. S. Alessandrini and B. Dallago, pp. 181-193. Aldershot, Hants, U.K.; Brookfield, Vt,: Gower Publishing.

Since 1982 Hungary has adopted a policy to stimulate the "auxiliary economy" by bringing previously independent activities and incomes under state control. Policies to establish new entrepreneurial and organizational forms were conceived by the government as strategies to fill production gaps, mitigate shortages, improve services, and create new employment opportunities. Szita shows how new organizational forms have contributed to inflation and fostered an expanding second economy. She argues that these policies have failed to integrate the second economy and instead represent elements of restructuring within the "socialist sector."

State practice/ Industrial restructuring/ Centrally planned economies/ Hungary

745. **Tangri, S. 1982.** Family Structure and Industrial Entrepreneurship in Urban India: The Evolution of a Field Study. In *Towards a Political Economy of Urbanization in Third World Countries*. Ed. H. Safa, pp. 188-207. Delhi, India: Oxford University Press.

Household division of labor/ Self-employment/ Home-based production/ India

746. **Tanzi, V., ed. 1982.** *The Underground Economy in the United States and Abroad*. Lexington, Mass.: Lexington Books.

Pattern or magnitude/ Research methods/ U.S.A./ Britain/ Italy/ Norway/ Sweden/ U.S.S.R./ Canada/ Colombia/ Australia/ Israel

747. —— . **1983.** The Underground Economy in the United States: Annual Estimates, 1930-1980. *IMF Staff Papers* 30 (2): 283-305.

Pattern or magnitude/ U.S.A.

748. **Taylor, M. J., and N. J. Thrift. 1982.** Industrial Linkage and the Segmented Economy: I. Some Theoretical Proposals. *Environmental Planning A* 14 (12): 1601-13.

Labor market segmentation/ Industrial restructuring/ Industrialized economies

749. **Teilhet-Waldorf, S., and W. H. Waldorf. 1983.** Earnings of the Self-Employed in an Informal Sector: A Case Study of Bangkok. *Economic Development and Cultural Change* 31: 587-608.

The authors compare informal sector and formal sector earnings and argue that self-employed entrepreneurs earn more than workers in the formal sector. They also question the usefulness of the concept of dualistic urban labor market.

Pattern or magnitude/ Self-employment/ Critique of dualism/ Thailand

750. **Telles, E. E. 1992.** Who Gets Formal Sector Jobs? Determinants of Formal-Informal Participation in Brazilian Metropolitan Areas. *Work and Occupations* 19 (2): 108-127.

Labor market segmentation/ Gender division of labor/ Brazil

751. **—— . 1993.** Urban Labor Market Segmentation and Income in Brazil. *Economic Development and Cultural Change* 41: 231-249.

Labor market segmentation/ Gender division of labor/ Self-employment/ Polarization/ Brazil

752. **Terrell, K. 1989.** An Analysis of the Wage Structure in Guatemala City. *Journal of Developing Areas* 23: 405-42.

Labor market segmentation/ Gender division of labor/ Trading/ Polarization/ Guatemala

753. **Thomas, J. J. 1992.** *Informal Economic Activity*. Ann Arbor, Mich.: University of Michigan Press.

Defining informal work as unreported productive activity, Thomas classified work into four types: 1) the household sector, involving goods and services produced within the household for home consumption; 2) the informal sector of small-scale, self-employed entrepreneurs producing for the market; 3) the irregular sector characterized by the evasion of taxes, regulations and social security payments; and 4) the criminal sector, composed of all activities producing illegal products or services (drug production and trade, prostitution, theft, smuggling). The extent and nature of each economic type and formulations of appropriate policy are noted.

Definition/ Pattern or magnitude/ Unpaid labor/ Small or micro-enterprises/ Pilfering/ Tax evasion/ Illegal activity/ Housing/ Urbanization/ Industrialized economies/ Third World

754. —— . **1995.** *Surviving in the City: The Urban Informal Sector in Latin America*. London: Pluto Press.

Failed ISI policies followed by debt, economic crisis, and structural adjustment contributed to the stagnant and declining capacity of the formal labor market to absorb the growing numbers of Latin America's urban migrants. Some theorists emphasize the poverty and dead-end prospects of informal employment, while others view informality as a dynamic channel for entrepreneurship. Following a broad overview of contending definitions and interpretations, Thomas compares the pattern and structure of informal employment in Latin American cities, noting common characteristics among workers while highlighting differences between countries. Particular problems of the informal economy are discussed, including high rates of poverty, discriminatory gender ideology undergirding labor market segmentation, destitution among female-headed households dependent on informal incomes, and unprotected child laborers and street children. Possibilities for extending protection to informal workers and addressing problems of inadequate housing are highlighted. Thomas also notes trends in demographics and economic policy that make a continuing prominence of informal work likely. Data suggest that for many urban residents, particularly poor women and children, informal employment will continue to be a means for day-to-day survival rather than upward mobility.

Definition/ Pattern or magnitude/ Economic restructuring/ Labor market dynamics/ Labor market segmentation/ Gender inequality/ Child labor/ Housing/ Comparative/ Latin America

755. **Thorbeck, S. 1988.** Women and Urbanisation. *Acta Sociologica* 31: 283-301.

Urbanization/ Gender division of labor/ Gender ideology/ Women/ Sri Lanka/ Thailand

756. **Tilly, L. A. 1979a.** The Family Wage Economy of a French Textile City: Roubaaix, 1872-1906. *Journal of Family History* 4: 381-394.

Household/ Home-based production/ Labor processes/ France

757. **—— . 1979b.** Individual Lives and Family Strategies within the French Proletariat. *Journal of Family History* 4: 137-152.

Survival strategies/ Unpaid labor/ Home-based production/ Household division of labor/ Labor processes/ France

758. **Tinker, I. 1987.** Street Foods: Testing Assumptions about Informal Sector Activity by Women and Men. *Current Sociology* 35 (3): 1-110.

Women/ Trading/ Gender inequality/ Survival strategies/ Rural/ Philippines/ Indonesia/ Bangladesh/ Senegal/ Nigeria/ Egypt/ Thailand

759. **Todd, D. M., and C. Shaw. 1980.** The Informal Sector and Zambia's Employment Crisis. *Journal of Modern African Studies* 18: 411-425.

Pattern or magnitude/ Zambia

760. **Tokman, V. E. 1978a.** Competition Between the Informal and Formal Sectors in Retailing: The Case of Santiago. *World Development* 6: 1187-1198.

Using survey data collected in Santiago in 1976, Tokman shows that informal grocers are able to compete successfully with modern supermarkets. Although small retail shops may sell their products at rates 7 to 10 percent higher than formal outlets, the informal sector retains demand because imperfections in the product and factor markets create demand segmentation. He suggests that this activity represents an efficient use of resources given the overall framework of modern sector job scarcity, the low purchasing power of the population, and the organization of informal production units whose ability to compete ensures their survival.

Pattern or magnitude/ Relation to formal economy/ Trading/ Chile

761. —— . **1978b.** An Exploration into the Nature of Informal-Formal Sector Relationships. *World Development* 6: 1065-1075.

Tokman explores two prevailing approaches to the debate on the informal sector: one framed in terms of its benign relationship to the formal sector and the second in terms of its subordination. Challenging both, Tokman presents a model of "heterogeneous subordination" which, he argues, allows the informal sector to be seen neither as a completely integrated nor as an autonomous sector, but rather as one linked to the broader economy, while enjoying considerable self-containment. He concludes that in terms of balance of payments a declining trend in the informal sector's terms of trade should be expected.

Review/ Relation to formal economy/ Critique of dualism/ Third World

762. —— . **1989.** Policies for a Heterogeneous Informal Sector in Latin America. *World Development* 17: 1067-1076.

Following a brief overview of the economic, cultural, and political factors behind the growing interest in the informal sector Tokman highlights the heterogeneity of informal enterprises and the growing feminization of informal employment in many Latin American countries. He identifies forms of productive assistance to informal producers, measures to ensure the welfare of the poor, and legal reforms for both improving protection for as well as removing undue burdens on informal producers. The need for local-level, grassroots strategies are also highlighted.

Pattern or magnitude/ Gender division of labor/ State practice/ Welfare/ Policy analysis/ Legislation/ Project assistance/ Latin America

763. —— . **1990.** The Informal Sector in Latin America: Fifteen Years Later. In *The Informal Sector Revisited*. Ed. D. Turnham, B. Salomé, and A. Schwarz, pp. 93-110. Paris, France: Development Centre, Organisation for Economic Co-operation and Development.

Review/ Latin America

764. ___, **ed. 1992a.** *Beyond Regulation: The Informal Economy in Latin America*. Boulder: Lynne Rienner Publishers.

Nine papers summarize the results of an international study of the informal sector in Latin America focusing on the administrative and legal rules shaping the operation of informal enterprises. Separate chapters are devoted to broad descriptions of informal activities in Bolivia, Brazil, Mexico, Venezuela; informal taxi services in Chile and Peru, barriers to legality and their costs for informal firms, and the question of ensuring social security for informal sector workers. The editor summarizes the study findings and major policy recommendations in an introductory chapter [see separate abstract].

Transportation/ State Practice/ Policy analysis/ Regulation/ Welfare/ Comparative/ Bolivia/ Brazil/ Colombia/ Chile/ Dominican Republic/ Ecuador/ El Salvador/ Guatemala/ Honduras/ Mexico/ Panama/ Peru/ Uruguay/ Venezuela

765. ——. **1992b.** The Informal Sector in Latin America: From Underground to Legality. In *Beyond Regulation: The Informal Economy in Latin America*. Ed V. E. Tokman, pp. 3-22. Boulder: Lynne Rienner Publishers.

Tokman summarizes data collected for a comparative study of the informal sector in fourteen countries to highlight the degree of illegality characterizing informal sector enterprises in Latin America, major factors contributing to this pattern, and policy alternatives. Results show that the majority of firms operate in a gray area between illegal and legal status, often having at least part of their business legally registered yet evading extant legislation in matters ranging from taxes to minimum wage levels or non-wage benefits. Time and money are the main barriers discouraging firms from full regulation compliance. Though regulations are critical to protect public interests, room for reform does exist in the promotion of laws and tax structures. Measures also are needed to improve regulation efficiency and to increase the likelihood of systemic enforcement.

State practice/ Policy prescriptions/ Regulation/ Tax evasion/ Welfare/ Comparative/ Bolivia/ Brazil/ Colombia/ Chile/ Ecuador/ El Salvador/ Guatemala/ Honduras/ Mexico/ Panama/ Peru/ Dominican Republic/ Uruguay/Venezuela

766. **Trager, L. 1984.** Family Strategies and the Migration of Women: Migrants to Dagupan City, Philippines. *International Migration Review* 18: 1264-1277.

Migration/ Survival strategies/ Gender division of labor/ Women/ Philippines

767. —— . **1987.** A Re-Examination of the Urban Informal Sector in West Africa. *Canadian Journal of African Studies / Revue Canadienne des Études Africaines* 21: 238-255.

Review/ Relation to formal economy/ Rural/ Policy analysis/ West Africa

768. **Tripp, A. M. 1990.** The Informal Economy and the State in Tanzania. In *Perspectives on the Informal Economy*. Ed M. E. Smith et al., Monographs in Economic Anthropology, no. 8. Lanham, Md.: University Press of America; Society for Economic Anthropology.

Based on fieldwork completed in 1987-1988, Tripp finds informal economic activities to be ubiquitous, lucrative, and critical to the survival of most households in Dar es Salaam. Under conditions of economic crisis, a contradictory relationship obtains between the state and the informal economy whereby despite the latter's importance to the national economy various government policies have attempted to control "unproductive" activities in the interests of national self-reliance. Informant interviews demonstrate that engagement in informal activity in face of such policies reflect resistance maneuvers by so-called marginal workers, forming a proactive, collective attempt to promote new policy directions.

State practice/ Resistance/ Economic restructuring/ Survival strategies/ Tanzania

769. —— . **1997.** *Changing the Rules: The Politics of Liberalization and the Urban Informal Economy in Tanzania*. Berkeley, Calif.: University of California Press.

Tripp examines the proliferation of informal enterprises in wake of economic crisis in Tanzania, arguing that the burgeoning informal sector has formed a far-reaching challenge to the country's existing political and economic order. With this challenge, "the rules of the game" for doing business and securing livelihoods have changed fundamentally, as informal activities have become the source of new economic and institutional resources. Following theorization of the informal economy as "a manifestation of societal noncompliance" and "a tool for institutional change," Tripp traces the Tanzanian economic crisis of the 1980s, outlines the shift in the boundaries of state control over the national economy with the onset of structural adjustment, discusses the political alliances emergent from and shaping the reform process, and describes informal strategies for survival which became the mainstay of the majority of Tanzanian households. She highlights the renewed centrality of women's work to the viability of the household, local community, and national economy, identifying its for household dependencies and gender relations. She also explores the impact that everyday forms of resistance embodied in the informal economy have had on economic policy, intra-ruling elite conflicts, and ideology, and analyzes the implications of institutional conflicts for the growth of the informal economy and for "understanding state-society relations and problems of local governance."

Economic restructuring/ Social restructuring/ State practice/ Resistance/ Survival strategies/ Gender relations/ Tanzania

770. **Truelove, C. 1990.** Disguised Industrial Proletarians in Rural Latin America: Women's Informal-Sector Factory Work and the Social Reproduction of Coffee Farm Labor in Columbia. In *Women Workers and Global Restructuring*. Ed K. Ward, pp. 48-63. Ithaca, N.Y.: ILR Press, School of Industrial and Labor Relations, Cornell University.

Disguised wage labor/ Social reproduction/ Gender division of labor/ Rural/ Social restructuring/ Subcontracting/ Piecework/ Export production/ Colombia

771. **Turnham, D., B. Salomé, and A. Schwarz, eds. 1990.** *The Informal Sector Revisited*. Paris: Development Centre, Organisation for Economic Co-operation and Development.

Definition/ Pattern or magnitude/ Small or micro-enterprises/ Labor market dynamics/ Policy analysis/ Africa/ Latin America/ Third World

772. **Ungerson, C. 1985.** *Policy Is Personal: Sex, Gender, and Informal Care*. London: Tavistock.

Unpaid labor/ Gender division of labor/ Britain

773. **United Nations, Department of International Economic and Social Affairs, Statistical Office, and International Research and Training Institute for the Advancement of Women. 1990.** *Methods of Measuring Women's Participation and Production in the Informal Sector*. Studies in Methods. Series F, no. 46. New York: United Nations.

Research methods/ Women/ Gender division of labor

774. **United States Department of Labor, and Mexican Secretariat of Labor and Social Welfare. 1992.** *The Informal Sector in Mexico*. Occasional Paper Series on the Informal Sector, no. 1. Washington, D.C.: U.S. Department of Labor, Bureau of International Labor Affairs.

Pattern or magnitude/ Small or micro-enterprises/ Labor market dynamics/ Mexico

775. **Uppal, J. S. 1987.** Unemployment in Indonesia. *Journal of Developing Societies* 3: 92-99.

Pattern or magnitude/ Under- and unemployment/ State practice/ Rural/ Indonesia

776. **—— . 1989.** Informal Sector in Third World Countries. *Journal of Developing Societies* 5: 42-57.

Pattern or magnitude/ Migration/ Third World

777. **Uribe Echevarria, F. 1983.** *The Informal Sector and the Development of Small and Intermediate Cities: An Approach to a Research Strategy*. The Hague, Netherlands: Institute of Social Studies.

Urbanization/ Migration/ Third World

778. **Uzzell, D. J. 1980.** Mixed Strategies and the Informal Sector: Three Faces of Reserve Labor. *Human Organization* 39: 40-49.

Uzzell argues that informal sector workers serve as a pool of reserve labor given an inadequate institutional structure and poverty. While some members of the informal sector choose to participate because it offers a more remunerative livelihood than formal wage employment, for others there is little choice but to secure work in the informal sector. Workers in the informal sector are then available to the formal sector as reserve labor pool.

Reserve army of labor/ Survival strategies/ Mexico/ Peru/ U.S.A.

779. **Vale Souza, A. d., L. Guimares Neto, and T. P. De Araujo. 1988.** Employment Implications of Informal Sector Policies: A Case Study of Greater Recife. *International Labour Review* 127: 243-258.

Policy analysis/ Brazil

780. **Valentine, B. 1978.** *Hustling and Other Hard Work: Life Styles in the Ghetto*. New York: Free Press.

Valentine offers an ethnography of a low-income African American community and characterizes hustling as both a form of livelihood and as a survival strategy.

Survival strategies/ Social networks/ Illegal activity/ U.S.A.

781. **Van Eck, R., and B. Kazemier. 1988.** Features of the Hidden Economy in the Netherlands. *Review of Income and Wealth* 34: 251-273.

Van Eck and Kazemier argue that there is no uniform framework for scheduling that part of productive activity not in the formal economy and suggest that income is its key distinguishing feature. They also argue that the structure of the hidden economy involves those with high wage rates and limited working hours, as well as those who are poorly paid and have trouble finding employment. Income from the hidden economy is at least 1 percent of national income and is shared by more than one million participants. There is no evidence that the hidden labor market, which excludes do-it-yourself, household and volunteer forms of work as part of a parallel economy, compensates those who are worse off in the formal economy.

Definition/ Pattern or magnitude/ Differentiation/ Volunteer work/ Netherlands

782. **Vandemoortele, J. 1991.** Labour Market Informalisation in Sub-Saharan Africa. In *Towards Social Adjustment: Labour Market Issues in Structural Adustment*. Ed. G. Standing and V. E. Tockman, pp. 81-114. Geneva: International Labour Office.

Vandemoortele argues that informalization is a consequence of structural adjustment in sub-Saharan Africa. Four major labor market adjustments characterize African economic development, namely: 1) erosion and compression of wages; 2) stagnation in modern sector wage employment; 3) mounting unemployment; and 4) saturation of informal and agricultural labor markets. Given falling educational levels and a steady erosion of living standards, current trends do not represent a basis for sustained growth. Such failures make evident the inappropriateness of structural adjustment policies aimed simply at correcting short-term imbalances that are attributed to government overinvolvement in economic processes, yet that originate in deeply rooted economic inequalities. Recommended instead is a policy of "directive" adjustment in which governments make selective interventions to steer a process of structural change.

Structural adjustment/ Under- and unemployment/ Policy analysis/ Africa

783. **Vashishtha, P. S. 1990.** Urban Informal Sector: A Profile of Marginalised Irregulars. *Social Action* 40: 126-145.

Marginalization/ Pattern or magnitude/ India

784. **Vereda del Abril, A. 1988.** *Desafio de la Economia Informal.* San Isiro, Peru: Imprenta para American Latina S. A. (IPALSA).

Pattern or magnitude/ Labor market dynamics/ Welfare/ Policy analysis/ Peru

785. **Vijverberg, W. P. M. 1990.** Nonfarm Self-Employment and the Informal Sector in Cotê d'Ivoire: A Test of Categorical Identity. *Journal of Developing Areas* 24: 523-542.

Pattern or magnitude/ Self-employment/ Rural/ Ivory Coast

786. **Vinay, P. 1985.** Family Life Cycle and the Informal Economy in Central Italy. *International Journal of Urban and Regional Research* 9 (1): 82-98.

Unpaid labor/ Household division of labor/ Survival strategies/ Italy

787. **von Werlhof, C. 1988.** The Proletarian Is Dead: Long Live the Housewife! In *Women: The Last Colony*. Ed. M. Mies, V.

Bennholdt-Thomsen, and C. von Werlhof, pp. 168-181. London: Zed Books.

Citing a crisis in the global economy marked by an inexorable rise in unemployment in the West, von Werlhof suggests the imminent disappearance of the proletarian from advanced industrialized society. As production relocates to the developing world to take advantage of coercive labor conditions, there is an expansion of informal work among housewives, petty traders, scavengers, artisans, and craftspeople leading to the "housewifization" of the economy. As the exploitation embodied in the gender division of labor becomes the norm, employers benefit whereas workers, work situations, and the quality of life continues to erode. Only effective struggle to recapture ownership over knowledge, creativity, women's bodies, land, houses, and the fruits of labor can alter these declines

Social restructuring/ Labor processes/ Gender division of labor/ Gender relations/ Industrialized economies

788. **Voydanoff, P. 1984.** Economic Distress and Families: Policy Issues. *Journal of Family Issues* 5: 273-288.

Survival strategies/ Policy prescriptions/ U.S.A.

789. **Wachter, M. L. 1974.** Primary and Secondary Labor Markets: A Critique of the Dual Approach. *Brookings Papers on Economic Activity* 3: 637-681.

Labor market dynamics/ Critique of dualism/ Industrialized economies

790. **Waldinger, R., and M. Lap. 1993.** Back to the Sweatshop or Ahead to the Informal Sector? *International Journal of Urban and Regional Research* 17 (1): 6-29.

Labor processes/ Economic restructuring/ Industrial restructuring/ Migration/ Industrialized economies/ U.S.A.

791. **Walker, A. et al. 1988.** Survival Strategies in the Popular Sectors of Managua. *Critical Sociology* 15 (1): 5-32.

Survival strategies/ Gender ideology/ State practice/ Nicaragua

792. **Wallace, T. 1973.** Working in Rural Buganda: A Study of the Occupational Activities of Young People in Rural Villages. *African Review* 3 (1): 133-178.

Wallace argues that the distinction between the formal and informal sectors is based neither on urban-rural differences nor on the activity itself, but rather on the structure within which people operate. The formal sector is enumerated, supervised and often protected from competition by government, employees are entitled to minimum wages, hold work contracts, may grieve to the labor office, and are granted access on the basis of sex, age, and formal education. By contrast, the informal sector is open, unenumerated, and unregulated and entrée is determined by the opportunities and market demands and by the holding of informally acquired skills. In this sector, financial returns are low due to the lack of capital and technical skills which require young people to hold multiple jobs.

Pattern or magnitude/ Dual sector or economy/ Rural/ Multiple jobs/ Worker characteristics/ Buganda

793. **Ward, K., ed. 1990.** *Women Workers and Global Restructuring*. Ithaca, N.Y.: ILR Press.

Following an overview of the field, Ward brings together a number of important studies on the interconnections between formal and informal work, forms of resistance, and the role of state policy in processes of economic restructuring. Studies range from the linking of women's labor in Java to processes of globalization, disguised urban proletarians in Columbia's coffee sector, and garment manufacturing workers in Greece. Others explore contradictions of race, class and sex among workers in Silicon Valley to complement chapters on workers in Western Europe, Latin America, and Asia.

Economic restructuring/ New international division of labor/ Disguised wage labor/ Social reproduction/ Under- and unemployment/ Consciousness/ Rural/ State practice/ Empowerment/ Resistance/ Export production/ Gender ideology/ Gender division of labor/ Racial inequality/ Garment manufacture/ Indonesia/ Colombia/ Greece/ Ireland/ Japan/ U.S.A./ Taiwan/ Mexico

794. **Watanabe, S. 1971.** Subcontracting, Industrialisation and Employment Creation. *International Labour Review* 104: 51-76.

Subcontracting/ Under- and unemployment/ Policy prescriptions/ Japan

795. —— . **1978.** *Technical Linkages between Formal and Informal Manufacturing Industries*. Geneva, Switzerland: International Labour Office.

Relation to formal economy/ Dual sector or economy/ Policy analysis

796. ___, **ed. 1979.** *Technology, Marketing, and Industrialization: Linkages between Large and Small Enterprises*. Delhi, India: Macmillan.

Relation to formal economy/ Dual sector or economy/ Small or micro-enterprises/ Subcontracting/ Technological change/ Japan/ Ghana/ Egypt/ Philippines/ India/ Mexico/ China

797. **Webb, R. 1974.** *Income and Employment in the Urban and Traditional Sectors of Peru*. Washington, D.C.: World Bank.

Dual sector or economy/ Peru

798. **Weck-Hannemann, H., and B. Ferry. 1985.** Measuring the Shadow Economy: The Case of Switzerland. In *The Economics of the Shadow Economy*. Ed. W. Gaertner and A. Wenig, pp. 76-104. Berlin: Springer-Verlag.

The structure, size, and development of the shadow economy in Switzerland is analyzed using different methods of estimation: a survey among experts, the discrepancy between different income measures, the participation rate and money approaches, and structural and causal methods. Evidence suggests that the Swiss shadow economy has grown between the end of the 1950s and 1980 with an estimated size in the range of 3 to 4 percent of GNP in 1975.

Pattern or magnitude/ Research methods/ Switzerland

799. **Weeks, J. 1973.** Uneven Sectoral Development and the Role of the State. *IDS Bulletin* 5 (2/3): 76-82.

Weeks argues that the state and its planning process play a major role in fostering industrial dualism through mechanisms that restrict access to resources and profit-making opportunities. For Weeks, the essence of the formal/informal distinction is their respective relationship to the state which counters the view that economic duality in poor, non-socialist countries results from inherent sectoral characteristics. Under ISI international firms are induced to set up operations in poor countries through a system which "formalizes" their role in the economy. Thus, the formal sector develops in a protected, noncompetitive environment while the informal sector remains competitive given the absence of state intervention.

Review/ Dual sector or economy/ State practice/ Relation to capital/ Kenya/ Japan/ U.S.A.

800. ——. **1975.** Policies for Expanding Employment in the Informal Urban Sector of Developing Economies. *International Labour Review* 111: 1-13.

Weeks analyzes the determinants of growing output and employment in the urban unenumerated sector of less developed countries. His distinction between the formal and informal sectors is based on the organizational characteristics of exchange relations and the relationship between economic activities and the state. A model of the determinants of sector growth highlights four critical factors: changes in aggregate income, relative price levels, technical change, and consumer tastes. The model's implications for policies to stimulate growth include improving income distribution, government purchase of goods and services, smallholder agricultural development, and the elimination of formal sector subsidies.

Pattern or magnitude/ State practice/ Policy analysis/ Third World

801. **Weeks, S. 1973.** Where Are All the Jobs? The Informal Sector in Bugisu, Uganda. *African Review* 3 (1): 111-132.

Weeks describes the range of informal occupations among a sample of rural youth in a village cluster in Eastern Uganda. With generally high levels of productivity and agricultural incomes, 85 percent of the employed youths have found informal work in agriculture, cottage industry and trade. Despite low returns, these youths maximize their opportunities and increase their total incomes through occupational pluralism as more than 60 percent have more than one job. The data also suggest that those in formal jobs are more likely to be male, older, urban-based, better educated, and have fathers with more land than those in informal occupations. However, while formal sector workers may be relatively better off, there is a comparative advantage to staying in the rural informal sector.

Pattern or magnitude/ Multiple jobs/ Trading/ Rural/ Worker characteristics/ Uganda

802. **Weil, G. 1992.** Caught in the Crisis: Women in the Economies of Sub-Saharan Africa. In *Women's Work & Women's Lives: The Continuing Struggle Worldwide*. Ed. H. Kahne and J. Z. Giele, pp. 47-68. Boulder, Colo.: Westview.

Declines in agricultural and industrial production coupled with a contraction of international trade have shaped the large proportion of women in the labor market. This change has not been mediated by the introduction of solar cooking stoves which have failed to reduce the demands on women's labor. Moreover, the introduction of cash crops and new technologies have also led to an increase in women's work loads. In other instances, agricultural intensification has displaced women from their central role in production. As a result, women are forced into informal sector work such as selling prepared foods, handicrafts, or services, generally work long hours with little capital, enjoy little security or status, and earn very little income.

Rural/ Structural adjustment/ Gender relations/ Social reproduction/ Ghana/ Nigeria/ Mali/ Zambia/ Sub-Saharan Africa

803. **Weintraub, S., and S. R. Ross. 1980.** *The Illegal Alien from Mexico: Policy Choices for an Intractable Issue*. Austin, Tx.: University of Texas Press.

Migration/ Ethnicity/ Policy analysis/ U.S.A.

804. **——. 1982.** *"Temporary" Alien Workers in the United States: Designing Policy from Fact and Opinion*. Boulder, Colo.: Westview Press.

Migration/ Ethnicity/ Policy analysis/ State practice/ U.S.A.

805. **Weiss, L. 1987.** Explaining the Underground Economy: State and Social Structure. *British Journal of Sociology* 38: 216-234.

Industrial restructuring/ State practice/ Social networks/ Italy

806. **Weiss, P. 1990.** An Evolutionary Approach to the Informal Sector in Third World Metropolitan Areas. *Socio-Economic Planning Sciences* 24: 97-105.

Urbanization/ Policy prescriptions/ Thailand/ Third World

807. **Wellings, P., and M. Sutcliffe. 1984.** "Developing" the Urban Informal Sector in South Africa: The Reformist Paradigm and Its Fallacies. *Development and Change* 15: 517-550.

Critique of dualism/ State practice/ South Africa

808. **Wellman, B. 1979.** The Community Question: The Intimate Network of East Yorkers. *American Journal of Sociology* 84: 1201- 1231.

Social networks/ Nonmonetary exchange/ Canada

809. **Werlin, H. W. 1974.** The Informal Sector: The Implications of the ILO's Study of Kenya. *African Studies Review* 17: 205-212.

Review/ Pattern or magnitude/ Trading/ State practice/ Kenya

810. **White, L. T., III. 1978.** Low Power: Small Enterprises in Shanghai, 1949-67. *China Quarterly* 73: 45-76.

Small or micro-enterprises/ State practice/ China

811. **Wiles, P. 1987.** The Second Economy, Its Definitional Problems. In *The Unofficial Economy: Consequences and Perspectives in Different Economic Systems*. Ed. S. Alessandrini and B. Dallago, pp. 21-33. Aldershot, Hants, U.K.; Brookfield, Vt.: Gower Publishing.

Wiles equates the second economy with illegitimacy and focuses on the consequences of these activities on national income accounts, doubting whether the second economy is ever a net economic advantage. He highlights the motives for such activities including tax evasion, theft of labor time or wages, evasion of Soviet-type output plans, and shortages, to suggest different approaches to measuring the second economy; e.g., monetary, consumption-income gap, and survey. These different approaches makes international comparisons extremely difficult.

Definition/ Pattern or magnitude/ Tax evasion/ Research methods/ Centrally planned economies/ Industrialized economies

812. **Wilkinson, P., and D. Webster. 1982.** Living in the Interstices of Capitalism: Towards a Reformulation of the "Informal Sector" Concept. *Social Dynamics* 8 (2): 1-10.

Previous approaches to the informal sector emphasize the economic content of such activity using the enterprise as a unit of analysis. This paper delineates a broader conceptual framework showing that informal sector activity is articulated with the trajectory of capital accumulation and social reproduction and provides a mechanism by which the working class as a whole sustains its physical existence and its social coherence. The authors argue that understanding the matrix of social relations and cultural practices within which informal activity is embedded is necessary for developing an adequate analysis of the processes of class formation among informal operators and the urban proletariat.

Review/ Definition/ Social networks/ Class formation/ Third World/ South Africa

813. **Williams, C. C., and J. Windebank. 1994.** Spatial Variations in the Informal Sector: A Review of Evidence from the European Union. *Regional Studies* 28 (8): 819-825.

Spatial patterns/ Europe

814. **Williams, G., and E. Tumusiime-Mutebile. 1978.** Capitalist and Petty Commodity Production in Nigeria: A Note. *World Development* 6: 1103-1104.

Petty commodity production/ Small or micro-enterprises/ Relation to formal economy/ Nigeria

815. **Williams, M. 1994.** Gender, Productivity and Macro-Economic Policies in the Context of Structural Adjustment and Change. In *The Strategic Silence: Gender and Economic Policy*. Ed. I. Bakker, pp. 71-87. London: Zed Books.

Williams argues that, though still invisible in mainstream economic analyses, women's labor is a central factor in stabilizing productivity growth in the course of economic restructuring. Reconceptualizing productivity highlights a largely overlooked connection between increasing female employment and growth in many of the most productive and innovative industries. In addition, increasing pressures on households caused by new macro-economic adjustment policies have been largely mediated by women who have increased both their household services as well as their participation in formal and informal work. Given this economic subsidy, a framework for analyzing gender and economic policy is proposed to help gain women's rights to greater economic decision-making power.

Economic restructuring/ Gender inequality/ Household division of labor/ Structural adjustment/ Relation to capital/ Unpaid labor/ Double-day/ Household/ Subsidy to capital/ Empowerment

816. **Wilson, F. 1986a.** Labour Struggle and Clandestine Industry: The Story of a Labour Petition in Mexico. *Labour, Capital and Society* 19: 218-237.

Industrial restructuring/ Rural/ Gender ideology/ Labor movements/ Mexico

817. —— **. 1986b.** Urban Craftsmen and Their Struggle Against Capitalism: A Case Study from Peru. *Social Analysis* 20 (December): 69-78.

Wilson provides a case study of urban craftsmen in Peru focusing on the motivating factors behind and the development of organized resistance to capitalist socioeconomic change.

Petty commodity production/ Artisanal production/ Political mobilization/ Class processes/ Peru

818. —— **. 1993.** Workshops as Domestic Domains: Reflections on Small-Scale Industry in Mexico. *World Development* 21: 67-80.

The expansion of informal production in recent decades articulates with ideological constructions that define households as the private family space under the purview of family values and beyond the jurisdiction of the state. With economic deregulation, households increasingly become the site of industrial production, where women form a large share of the labor force and labor relations are governed by domestic ideology. Though oppressive, these developments do not preclude the formation of potentially challenging identities and social exchanges among women based on shared experiences of work and subordination. Examining trends in workshop-based industrialization in Mestizo Latin America, Wilson notes the role of local cultural, social, and religious institutions in shaping gendered labor relations.

Economic restructuring/ Home-based production/ Gender ideology/ Latin America

819. **Wilson, K. L., and A. Portes. 1980.** Immigrant Enclaves: An Analysis of the Labor Market Experience of Cubans in Miami. *American Journal of Sociology* 86: 295-319.

Labor market segmentation/ Migration/ Ethnicity/ Social networks/ U.S.A.

820. **Windebank, J. 1991.** *The Informal Economy in France*. Aldershot, Hants, U.K.: Avebury.

Review/ Pattern or magnitude/ France

821. **Wines, S. W. 1985.** Stages of Microenterprise Growth in the Dominican Informal Sector. *Grassroots Development: Journal of the Inter-American Foundation* 9 (2): 33-41.

Small or micro-enterprises/ Dominican Republic

822. **Winter, M., E. W. Morris, and A. D. Murphy. 1990.** Planning and Implementation in the Informal Sector: Evidence from Oaxaca, Mexico. *City and Society* 4: 131-143.

Gender division of labor/ Small or micro-enterprises/ Project assistance/ Mexico

823. **Witte, A. 1987.** The Nature and Extent of Unrecorded Activity: A Survey Concentrating on Recent US Research. In *The Unofficial Economy: Consequences and Perspectives in Different Economic Systems*. Ed. S. Alessandrini and B. Dallago, pp. 61-81. Aldershot, Hants, U.K.; Brookfield, Vt.: Gower Publishing.

Witte examines unrecorded activities in the United States, taking into account the legal and illegal production of goods and services which are neither officially recorded nor measured. She concludes that unrecorded activity primarily involves relatively disadvantaged people and areas and thus has a stabilizing and equalizing economic effect. She also examines quantitative estimates of unrecorded activities developed by U.S. government agencies.

Pattern or magnitude/ U.S.A.

824. **Wolff, E. 1985.** The Disappearance of Domestic Servants and the Underground Economy. In *The Economics of the Shadow Economy*. Ed. W. Gaertner and A. Wenig, pp. 316-329. Berlin, F.R.G.: Springer-Verlag.

Wolff explores the purported rise in the relative size of the underground economy in the United States. through an examination of employment among domestic servants. He finds that since 1964 there has been a sharp decline in both the relative and the absolute levels of employment of domestic workers. Moreover, on prima facie grounds, household employment seems an obvious candidate for under-reporting since it is difficult to report earned income. Wolff develops a model to relate home-based employment to traditional consumer demand variables and concludes that the decline in the employment of household workers can be explained by these traditional consumer demand variables.

Domestic service/ Pattern or magnitude/ U.S.A.

825. **Wolpe, H. 1972.** Capitalism and Cheap Labour Power in South Africa: From Segregation to Apartheid. *Economy and Society* 1: 424-456.

Wolpe argues that apartheid is not merely a reflection of racial ideology but a mechanism for the maintenance of a cheap labor force in the face of dissolving precapitalist modes of production via the penetration of capitalism.

Racial inequality/ Relation to capital/ South Africa

826. **Wong, P. 1991.** The Formal, Informal and Voluntary Sectors in Development Theory. *Nonprofit and Voluntary Sector Quarterly* 20: 237-243.

Review/ Project assistance/ Volunteer work/ Third World

827. **Yamada, G. 1996.** Urban Informal Employment and Self-Employment in Developing Countries: Theory and Evidence. *Economic Development and Cultural Change* 44 (2): 289-314.

Recognizing that one in five jobs are secured in the urban and self-employed sector, Yamada examines the sector's competitiveness in terms of both incomes and returns to investment. He finds that those involved in informal activities enjoy both voluntary choice in terms of access and earn competitive returns. Using cross-sectional and longitudinal data from Lima, Peru, and drawing on comparative evidence he concludes that the sector must provide access to capital markets at competitive rates to ensure the accumulation of physical and human capital. Coupled with entrepreneurial skills, such investment will boost capitalist development in Third World cities.

Self-employment/ Credit/ Policy prescriptions/ Comparative/ Peru

828. **Ybarra, J. 1989.** Informalization in the Valencian Economy: A Model for Underdevelopment. In *The Informal Economy: Studies in Advanced and Less Developed Countries*. Ed. A. Portes, M. Castells, and L. A. Benton, pp. 216-227. Baltimore, Md.; London: Johns Hopkins Press.

Gender division of labor/ Survival strategies/ Spain

829. **Yeung, Y., R. Keles, and I. Nazrul. 1988.** Livelihoods for the Urban Poor: Case for a Greater Role by Metropolitan Governments. *Regional Development Dialogue* 9 (4): 40-54.

Survival strategies/ State practice/ Policy prescriptions/ Philippines/ South Korea/ Malaysia

830. **Yotopoulos, P. A., and S. L. Floro. 1992.** Income Distribution, Transaction Costs and Market Fragmentation in Informal Credit Markets. *Cambridge Journal of Economics* 16: 303-326.

Credit/ Gender inequality/ Entrepreneurship/ Small or micro-enterprises

831. **Young, K., C. Wolkowitz, and R. McCullagh, eds. 1981.** *Of Marriage and the Market: Woman's Subordination in International Perspective*. London: CSE Press.

Gender division of labor/ Gender ideology/ New international division of labor/ Gender relations/ Class processes/ Unpaid labor/ Household/ Labor processes/ Comparative/ Morocco/ Ghana/ Britain/ Yugoslavia/ Industrialized economies/ Centrally planned economies/ Third World

INDEXES

Subject Index

Country and Region Index